Tourism
and Visitor Attractions:
Leisure, Culture
and Commerce

Edited by

Neil Ravenscroft

Deborah Philips

Marion Bennett

LSA

Publication No. 61

First published in 1998 by
Leisure Studies Association

The collection as a whole © 1998 LSA
The individual contributions © 1998 the respective authors

A catalogue record for this book
is available from the British Library.

ISBN: 0 906337 71 2

Layout design and typesetting by Myrene L. McFee
Reproduction by University of Brighton
Binding by Kensett Ltd., Hove

Contents

Introduction

Neil Ravenscroft, University of Surrey

Deborah Philips, Brunel University College

Marion Bennett, University of Surrey

Tourism offers a model for understanding the construction and representation of 'consuming' and 'consumed' spaces (Shields, 1992; Urry, 1995), in that the product the tourist industry sells is the consumption and representation of particular sites. The tourist attraction offers a paradigm for an understanding of the commodification of leisure; as more and more sites introduce entrance charges and come to rely on retailing outlets to subsidise their funding, so these have increasingly become key elements in the economics of leisure. Sites of national and historical significance, educational activities and 'heritage' sites have all had to learn and to borrow from forms of commercial leisure, to become 'experiences' which offer theming and commodities.

Tourist spaces can be characterised as heterotopias, in Foucault's term. Tourist sites or attractions are not utopian in the strict sense (although they may suggest utopian sensibilities), as they are constructed not as whole worlds, but rather as compensatory spaces. As Foucault puts it, in terms which describe the experience of many tourist attractions: "the heterotopia has the power of juxtaposing in a single real place different spaces and locations that are incompatible with each other" (Foucault, 1986: p.14).

Tourism is one of the ways in which we make sense of the global, in which 'foreign' regions, countries and nationalities are ordered into sets of signifying practices. Such organising principles become increasingly important in the context of globalisation, as Foucault suggests:

> ... from Galileo onwards, ever since the 17th century, localization was replaced by extension.
>
> Nowadays arrangement has taken over from extension, which had once replaced localization. It is defined by relationships of neighbourhood between points and elements, which can be described formally as series, trees and networks. (Foucault, 1986: p.10)

Foucault is here speaking of architectural space, but the networks he speaks of can be understood in terms of the organisation of tourism. His phrase 'relationships of neighbourhood' is thus highly apposite to the subject of the case studies of many of the papers collected here. In representing a tourism of increasing post modernity and consumption, the papers in this volume challenge many of the pre-existing modernist metanarratives, particularly those constructing tourism as a "separated and regulated sphere", in contra-distinction to its polar opposite, work (Urry, 1990: p. 2). These papers arise from work originally aired in a number of themed strands at the 1997 Leisure Studies Association conference (September, Roehampton Institute London). They are presented here, in finalised versions prepared for this volume, in three interrelated sections: work, leisure and culture; identity and commodification; and representation.

Work, Leisure and Culture

In one of the keynote presentations of the conference, JUNG (1998) suggests that, with respect to Central and Eastern Europe, the former functional productionist relationships under modernity have been replaced by a dichotomy, between the consumption strategies of the 'well-to-do', and the survival strategies of the 'underclass'. These, he argues, are mediated by a learned discourse of culture and leisure, practised by the political elite. Another example of this change in the relationship between work and leisure, here applied to Western Europe, is given in John Lennon's paper, in a case study of the role of business development for the leisure and tourism industries of Dublin and Glasgow. In his paper, Lennon makes the point that urban tourism has long been linked to the economic regeneration — and hence post-industrialisation — of cities. However, he suggests that transformations such as Dublin's Temple Bar reflect a new scale of operation, in which the intervention and mediation of the public sector is seen to be critical to the development of culture and leisure industries in the city.

As Lennon observes, not only do the resultant consumption practices of the 'well-to-do' contribute to the diversification of the economic base of urban centres, but this diversification also provides employment (and thus survival) opportunities for the relatively low skilled workers acutely affected by industrial decline. This schism replicates wider trends in the changing structure of employment. This is both through shifts from manufacturing to services and manual to non-manual labour, as well as a recognition that much of the service sector does not involve either 'white collar', or full time, occupations (Roberts, 1995: pp. 7-8).

Analysis of the implications of the changing structure of work is continued in Margaret Graham and Malcolm Foley's paper, which considers the nature and role of volunteers in urban museum services. In differentiating between voluntarism, as altruistic citizenship, and volunteerism, as an opportunistic response to new social imperatives, Graham and Foley's paper uses an historical account of volunteering within museums to position current trends and structures. In so doing, the paper illustrates new forms of synergy in which museum professionals harness the skills and energy of volunteers, in an environment which the latter value as a scarce source of experience and training. It is recognised, however, that this linkage has the potential to create a mis-match between the goals and objectives of the museum and the expectations of volunteer staff.

Identity and commodification

As the structure and signification of work changes to reflect new forms of post-industrialisation, our understanding of the social construction of leisure and tourism — and the resulting significance of their associated practices — must similarly alter. Central to the changing social arena and practice of tourism, argues Urry (1990, 1995), is an engagement with the *processes* of postmodernisation: the 'visualisation' of culture; the transformation of time; and the collapse of stable identities. Traditionally fixed identities, formed through class, work, family and religious affiliations, are thus being replaced by more 'open and fluid' social identities (Urry, 1995: p. 215), characterised by a unidimensional superficiality in which consumption and appearance are dominant.

With its largely market-driven definition and signification, the nature of social identity is thus increasingly at odds with boundaries established through public policy. This is well illustrated in Brian Simpson's paper, on the legal boundaries of tourism. In the paper, he questions how far market-driven definitions of tourism and tourist identities can operate in opposition to public policy. Using the example of Australian government attempts to criminalise child sex tourism, Simpson makes the point that such ideology and resultant legislation fails to challenge market hegemony, concentrating instead on a particular type of tourism which is felt to be 'out of favour'. This is highly redolent of MacCannell's (1991) recognition of tourism's imperialist connections, with Simpson reporting political debates apparently able, on the one hand, to view child sex tourism as "...one of the most vile forms of colonial exploitation", while simultaneously suggesting that it might be tolerated on the basis that "the receiving countries could be ... less ambivalent towards the rights of sex tourists, being glad of the money from tourism...".

The idea of the market as a replacement, or surrogate, for political approbation and legitimacy is similarly explored by Malcolm Foley and Gavin Reid, in their paper on activity tourism in Scotland. Through an examination of the implications of explicit attempts to define and 'capture' particular elements of the 'tourism' market, Foley and Reid analyse not only the changing identity of tourists, but also their changing relationship to host communities. The outcome and implications of this intermixture of identities — both tourist and local — is viewed as highly relevant to the public sector, particularly when services such as local sports provision are redefined and repackaged as potential tourism resources. In addition, questions are raised about the potential impact of tourism promotion, particularly on popular and fragile sites, such as Loch Lomond in Scotland.

The potential negative impacts of tourism development are similarly explored in other papers. Heather Gibson, in her paper on sport tourism (published in the conference edition of *Leisure Studies*, Vol. 17, No. 2, forthcoming) argues that while physical activity is consistently promoted as a positive contribution to people's quality of life, the development and marketing of concepts such as sport tourism often deny this, in favour of a commodification which underpins existing class inequalities. Rather than the unproblematic possibility of new mass markets, therefore, both Gibson and Foley and Reid suggest that public agencies, in particular, need to give careful consideration to the reconciliation of the needs of all potential tourists, as well as the needs of locals.

As Shields has pointed out, sites of consumption (which include the great majority of tourist sites and attractions) are central to an understanding of cultural and leisure practices:

> Both major and minor consumption sites, such as any one of the multitude of sub-regional shopping centres everywhere in the developed world, have emerged as key centres of cultural change. Consumption spaces are host to unique cultural forms by combining economic and leisure forms which demand new practices such as tribalism and the elaboration of personae.... The civic culture of consumption sites and space is a culture of the present, of carnivalesque inversions and alternatives to rational social order. (Shields, 1992: pp. 16-17)

The beach, the museum, the sports centre, the theme park and the countryside can, as a number of the papers in this volume demonstrate, increasingly be understood as such 'consumption sites'. As Shields has also suggested, leisure sites are no less engaged with commerce and consumption than are the practices of everyday life: "even in its most carnivalesque forms, social exchange is marked by economic exchange" (Shields, 1992: p.9).

This theme is examined by Deborah Philips, in her paper on the commodification of the carnivalesque at Disneyland. In exploring the paradox of theme parks, such as Disneyland, which claim to offer an infinite variety of 'fantasies and pleasure' (as in Dann's, 1996, sociolinguistics of tourism) within a highly controlled and surveilled site, Philips makes the point that rather than Bakhtin's (1984) production orientation, the carnivalesque of the theme park is one which is constructed for consumption. Participation, as far as it is encouraged is therefore, in Philips' terms, "predicated on consumption" with the "public... positioned entirely as spectators, invited to gaze but firmly discouraged from any other form of participation".

As a consequence, the carnival of the theme park is less a commodified version of the Bakhtian original, than it is a nostalgic simulacrum, claiming allegiance to a mythical and authentic version of the original which never actually existed. Likewise, as tourist attractions have become key to the selling of particular areas or regions, they have come to embody the commodification of a range of sites once thought to be outside commercial imperatives. Museums, nature trails and heritage sites are no longer in a position to refuse marketing strategies. And as local and regional authorities compete for funding, so they have had to learn to market their assets to tourism. The distinction between theme park, museum, nature trail and shopping mall has become increasingly blurred. The Victorian spirit of Rational Recreation is now displaced by one of consumption, in which the purchase of a souvenir or artefact can become of greater significance than the visit itself.

In a climate in which the Minister for Culture, Sport and Leisure can advise the British Museum that it must expand its retailing, and suggests that entrance charges to museums and galleries may not be unthinkable, no national institution is able to resist exploiting its commercial potential. Museums and galleries have had to develop retail outlets, and local history centres to learn to market themselves as attractions, often with the 'support' of commercial sponsorship.

In their paper, Gayle McPherson, Malcolm Foley and Alastair Durie directly address the question of marketing and the increasing significance of commerce within the museum environment, using examples from museums in Glasgow. Concentrating on retail outlets within museums, they argue that the experience of purchasing commodities on a museum visit has become integral to the experience, and helps to shape the visitor's perception of the museum. The museum shop may thus provide a partial solution to a short term funding problem. However, the authors argue that rather than its former ancillary function, the shop is rapidly assuming part of the 'overall cultural experience'. The shop therefore becomes a commercial representation of the artefacts held in the museum, resulting in the "visitor... consuming the museum through purchases in the shop". Their research, echoing Donald Horne's (1984) work, thus raises the question of whether the postmodern museum has now become a site of consumption rather than one of education and curation.

The commodification debate is continued by Philippa Hunter-Jones and Cheryl Hayward, in their paper on 'leisure consumption and the UK zoo'. In reflecting wider interest within the tourist attraction industry about the implications of information technology (IT), the authors examine the perceived difficulty of transforming zoos into interactive experiences. Traditionally the zoo, like so many other tourist attractions, has offered a passive experience, but technology, and in particular, virtual reality, offers the opportunity for passivity to be converted into interactivity, thereby altering the entire visitor experience. This point is endorsed by McPherson, Foley and Durie, who argue that IT can enable the visitor to become 'a participant in the experience'.

There is no doubt that IT is enabling attractions to offer a more interactive experience and thus to compete more effectively in the wider leisure/tourism attractions market. However, issues are raised concerning authenticity, particularly in the case of heritage attractions, where it is questioned whether IT is assisting the provision of enhanced interpretation, or merely adding new elements of commercialised entertainment. This is a highly contentious issue which is very much at the core of wider commodification debates, particularly in challenging conventional positivist associations between visits to heritage attractions and the voluntary production of increased knowledge through education.

A number of the papers demonstrate, either explicitly or implicitly, the growing salience of interest groups in tourism development. The different interest groups involved in the setting up of a tourist site and the sources of its funding, as David Clark's paper suggests in the particular context of the Jewish museum, have a profound effect on the shaping of the attraction itself, and on its perceived objectives.

Clark's paper charts the recent history of the development of the Jewish museum, and examines its contemporary manifestations. The paper investigates the different forms of alliances that are involved in developing such a museum, and the ways in which the structures of finance and the local range of interest groups shape the kind of experience that the museum offers. A key conclusion of the paper is that while alliances bring undoubted benefits, they also generate their own set of problems, notably in the form of varying (and sometimes competing) agendas. This touches on a much wider issue regarding strategic alliances, which is becoming increasingly pervasive within the tourism industry in general, due to the pressures of competition and globalisation.

Jim Butterfield and Jonathan Long extend a postmodern awareness of the spaces of consumption into an analysis of the consumption of the rural. They take leisure and marketing models of the consumer and apply them to the leisure experience of those visiting the countryside, and suggest that such traditional models as the 'Leisure and the Family Life Cycle' (Rapoport and Rapoport, 1975) need to be reformulated in the postmodern condition, in order to understand the significance of lifestyle choices in consuming and leisure practices. Using a reading of Giddens' (1991) reflexivity, the authors argue that rather than social activity and material relations being a function of life cycle, they are increasingly subject to fundamental and on-going revision, as individuals assimilate new information.

In offering a reading of Wilson's biophilia hypothesis (Wilson and Kellert, 1992), the authors posit that all individuals have an innate capacity to identify with other forms of life, suggesting that, freed from life cycle constraints, individuals may become more environmentally conscious, through experiencing and enjoying nature in their outdoor recreational activities. In condemning the life cycle thesis to its historical specificity, therefore, Butterfield and Long suggest that the future for outdoor recreation is defined by the dichotomy between the increasing consumption orientation of 'postmodern' hedonists and the emerging production orientation of responsible reflexive citizens. Their conclusions thus have important resonances for an ecological understanding, in pointing to the conflicting interests between conservation and consumption in the rural context.

John Jenkins similarly considers outdoor recreation, but in Australia rather than the UK. In providing an interesting alternative to the rights debates more redolent of the UK (Ravenscroft, 1995), Jenkins describes a situation more akin to North America, in which access to private land has to be negotiated on an individual basis. Rather than rights of access, therefore, what Jenkins describes are rights of exclusion, with land-owners in two case study areas of New South Wales exhibiting a distrust and dislike of potential recreationists every bit as strong as their British counterparts.

Representation

As David Chaney (1994: p. 69) suggests, strategies of representation — "the use of signs or symbols to convey meaning" — are increasingly inherent in the 'management of everyday interaction'. An example of this is Daniel O'Hare's paper on the production and consumption of cultural landscapes for coastal tourism in Australia. Using a case study of Noosa, in Queensland, O'Hare illustrates the similarities between the vacation decisions of tourists and the process of 'comparative' shopping, in which consumers use a multitude of information and signs to make comparisons of goods and services prior to purchase. The result, argues O'Hare, is that destination resorts increasingly combine distinctive physical forms with associated product narratives which suggest both similarity with, and distinction from, competing destinations. In consciously adopting references, within both official plans and tourist guides, to 'The Noosa Style', it is argued that staged forms of semiotic identity are created which, in reflecting the simulacrum, represent copies of originals that never existed. This is typified by official descriptions of one end of the main street as 'The Paris end of Hastings Street', simultaneously comparing Noosa to a fashionable area of Melbourne, while also inferring European style and sophistication.

Such forms of commodification have led to new constructions of the representation of tourist activity. The marketing of such spaces can often involve a form of narrativisation; the attaching of a familiar story to an unfamiliar space in order to render it less alien. Countryside walking is marketed as a 'nature experience' in 'Beatrix Potter country', parts of the British Isles become 'Catherine Cookson' or 'Last of the Summer Wine' Country; Bath, as Judith Brown's paper demonstrates, is now marketed less for its architecture, than for the 'Jane Austen experience'.

Brown investigates representations of Bath in a selection of novels and guide books in order to trace the promotion of Bath's resources in three distinct historical periods, from the late eighteenth and early nineteenth centuries to the present. She demonstrates that the championing of the medical efficacy of its waters, the celebration of its architecture and its appeal to social snobbery are balanced differently in each of the periods she investigates. She points out the ways in which the perceived and recommended benefits of a visit to Bath have changed in emphasis, and will continue to do so.

The marketing of a site is also significant in Jenny Iles' paper on the Beamish Open Air Museum, in which she argues that, in its sanitised representation of 'heritage', the museum denies any context for the identities of local people and their communities. This is characterised by tensions between the educational, as well as social and political, significance of 'authentic' and 'artificial' representation. Thus, Iles constructs the Beamish Open Air Museum as, concurrently, a repository for an 'outstanding' collection of historical artefacts, and a misrepresentation of the social, cultural and political histories of local people, packaged in 'an entertaining day out for all the family'. In common with Philips' analysis of the carnivalesque at Disneyland, Iles constructs the Beamish Open Air Museum as a 'nostalgic simulacrum' of an original which certainly did not exist in this form, if it existed within the same cultural paradigm at all.

Conversely, Nick Couldry, in his examination of the Coronation Street set as tourist attraction (published in the conference edition of *Leisure Studies*, Vol. 17, No. 2, forthcoming), challenges an understanding of such locations as examples of Baudrillard's (1981) hyperreality, in which 'model' and 'reality' are, reportedly, endlessly confused. In confronting what he sees as a reductionist shortcoming of postmodernism, Couldry argues that visitors to such sites are well able to distinguish fiction from 'reality', instead being more concerned with experiencing the 'actual place' where filming has occurred. As such, Couldry posits the Granada Studios Tour as a 'ritual space' (Lash and Urry, 1994), "part theme park, part museum and part pilgrimage site", in which power relations are produced and reproduced. He therefore argues that an analysis of visitor experiences offers a means of understanding not only an audience's relationship with a particular programme, but also with the power relations of television itself.

Conclusion

Our understanding of the terms *culture* and *commerce* are clearly evolving, with a shift from positivist constructions of objectivity to new socially-constructed and specific identities and meanings (Whannel, 1997). The papers collected in this volume indicate that this fragmentation is very much the trajectory of tourism and tourist practice. In particular, they demonstrate the gradual decoupling from an overwhelmingly market-driven neo-classical orthodoxy, towards new understandings of the socially-constructed and reconstructed relationship between tourism and its wider physical, economic, political and social environment.

References

Bahktin, M.1984 *Rabelais and his world* (trans. H. Iswolsky). Bloomington: Indiana University Press.

Baudrillard, J. (1981) *For a critique of the political economy of the sign*. St. Louis, MO: Telos Press.

Chaney, D. (1994) *The cultural turn.* London: Routledge.

Couldry, N. (1998) 'The view from inside the simulacrum: Visitors' tales from the set of Coronation Street', *Leisure Studies* Vol. 17, No. 2. (forthcoming).

Dann, G. (1996) *The language of tourism.* Wallingford, Oxon: CAB International.

Foucault, M. (1986) 'Other spaces: The principles of heterotopia', *Lotus International: Quarterly Architectural Review* 48/49: pp. 9-17.

Gibson, H (1998) ' Sport tourism for all?', *Leisure Studies* Vol. 17, No. 2. (forthcoming).

Giddens, A. (1991) *Modernity and self identity.* Cambridge: Polity Press.

Horne, D. (1984) *The great museum.* London: Pluto Press.

Jung, B. (1998) 'Leisure, consumption and the state', *Leisure Studies* Vol. 17, No. 2. (forthcoming).

Lash, S. and Urry, J. (1994) *Economies of signs and space.* London: Sage.

MacCannell, D. (1991) *Empty meeting places: The tourism papers.* London: Routledge.

Rapoport, R. and Rapoport, R.N. (1975) *Leisure and the family life cycle.* London: Routledge and Kegan Paul.

Ravenscroft, N. (1995) 'Recreational access to the countryside of England and Wales: popular leisure as the legitimation of private property'. *Journal of Property Research* No. 12: pp. 63-74.

Roberts, K. (1995) 'Great Britain: Socioeconomic polarisation and the implications for leisure', in Critcher, C., Bramham, P. and Tomlinson, A. (eds) *Sociology of leisure: A reader.* London: Spon, pp. 6-19.

Shields, R. (1992) 'Spaces for the subject of consumption', in Shields, R. (ed) *Lifestyle shopping: The subject of consumption.* London: Routledge, pp. 1-21.

Urry, J. (1990) *The tourist gaze. Leisure and travel in contemporary societies.* London: Sage.

——— (1995) *Consuming spaces.* London: Routledge.

Whannel, G. (1997) 'What's the colour of money?' *Leisure Studies Association Newsletter No. 45*: pp. 32-33.

Wilson, E.O. and Kellert, S. (1992) *The biophilia hypothesis.* Washington DC: Island Press.

I

WORK, LEISURE AND CULTURE

Contrasting Roles in Business Development for the Tourism and Leisure Industries: the case of Dublin and Glasgow

J John Lennon

Glasgow Caledonian University

Introduction

This paper has its origins in a Glasgow Development Agency (GDA) funded analysis of Dublin Tourism success over the period of 1986–1996. The general objective of the project was to consider the two urban regions of Dublin and Glasgow and to ascertain what conditions, tourism development strategies and policies were necessary to maximise the economic impact of leisure behaviour and expenditure of tourists on a host city. To this end the dynamics of tourism development policy and the main implementation mechanisms were examined for both cities.

The emphasis and direction of the research was to attempt to understand the reasons for and the extent of the success of Dublin's development and this cities' ability to attract significant numbers of tourists. Thus for the purposes of this paper presentation emphasis will be placed primarily on explanation and evaluation of Dublin development agencies and funding sources.

In development terms the report will highlight:

- the role of the various agencies and authorities involved in tourism/ leisure business development;
- the role of EU and other development funding sources involved in developing, shaping and exploiting tourism and leisure activities;
- the extent of development funding available.

3

Urban tourism — the panacea for post industrial cities

After periods of continuous expansion following the industrial revolution many of the major cities in the industrialised countries of Europe were faced with problems related to de-population and collapse in traditional sources of employment for host populations (Berg *et al.*, 1995) . Traditional economic activities were in decline and urban populations were relocating to suburbs, smaller towns and peripheral locations. In a number of cases the urban centres were abandoned, most particularly by higher income earning residents and larger industrial employers. This caused the foundation of many cities in Europe to be substantially eroded; this was the case in large parts of both Glasgow and Dublin.

Local governments under severe financial pressure reduced spending allocations for aspects of city infrastructure, transport and other municipal facilities. In addition urban centres became the focus of unemployment, crime and decay. Further problems of congestion and pollution became significant issues.

In the 1980s, following general world-wide economic recovery, many of the major cities of Western Europe began to be the subject of regeneration programmes aimed at arresting the problems of decline. In the emergent areas of urban management, city marketing and urban regeneration programmes, tourism has become an increasingly significant industry. Its importance in the generation of jobs and wealth is well documented and the phenomena of urban tourism is now recognised in tourism literature (Page, 1995).

The positive period of growth for many urban tourist locations up to the early 1990s was followed by a period of significant economic recession and the Gulf War. However, given the level of commitment made to cities over the previous decade, the city tourism product has proved resilient and lasting. Destination analysis conducted for this paper has identified in excess of 160 European cities offering vacations based in urban environments. The emergence of the Central and Eastern European countries in tourism terms since 1990 has served to increase the number and range of destinations significantly (Lennon, 1996).

In their analysis and comparison of European destinations Berg *et al.* identified:

> 'Classic' or 'best selling' tourist cities... In total there are nineteen classic destinations: Amsterdam, Athens, Barcelona, Berlin, Budapest, Dublin, Florence, Istanbul, London, Lisbon, Madrid, Moscow, Paris, Prague, Rome, St. Petersburg, Stockholm, Venice and Vienna. (1995: p. 9)

Glasgow — industrial decline and service sector expansion

Glasgow, although not perceived by Berg *et al.* (1995) as a 'classic' destination, certainly exhibited many of the major characteristics of urban decay and regeneration around service industries and particularly tourism (Sneddon, 1995). Problems of decline in traditional industries, a reduction in prosperity and spiralling unemployment caused the city to focus efforts on revitalisation of the urban economy. Tourism and its recognition as a significant industry was at the core of the regeneration strategy for the city (Sneddon, 1995).

Key agencies in the reorientation of the city's economy have been Glasgow City Council and Glasgow Development Agency (and previously the Scottish Development Agency). The council strategy for tourism focused on:

(1) developing significant and new tourist attractions
(2) attracting and establishing major events
(3) marketing the city as a destination through the city Tourist Board and Convention Bureau
(4) investing in a range of environmental projects
(5) developing Glasgow as a major destination for cultural tourism
(6) supporting and developing cultural industries

A particular focus has been the importance of business tourism and specifically the attraction of large conferences, conventions and the staging of significant events over this period, commencing with the staging of the Garden Festival (1988) and the City of Culture in 1990. These two land mark events helped to position a strategy that recognised the significance of critical events and business tourism. The synergistic relationship between the two have been demonstrated again almost a decade later with the successful hosting of Rotary International (1997) and the American Society of Travel Agents (1997) which will be followed in 1999 by the city assuming the mantle of the International City of Architecture and Design. The market exposure that such events provide for the city is obviously beneficial and enables the City to develop related sales strategies in:

• conferences, meetings and conventions;

• cultural tourism specifically focused around short breaks (the recent focus on the design and design related industries through the 1996 Year of Design is a good example).

Image was central to council strategy in the 1980s and the famous 'Glasgow's Miles Better' campaign was a council-inspired attempt to replicate the 'I Love New York' campaign. The 'Glasgow's Miles Better' campaign has never been equalled and has undergone a revival in 1995 that continues in generic city promotional materials. Indeed the centrality of image and perception of the city in a leisure and cultural context is also reflected in the city's Public Realm Strategy, which constitutes a programme of works targeted at improving the appearance and amenity of the city centre and further enhancing the City's reputation as a destination for tourists and inward investment. In total, a programme of expenditure of some £23,840,000 is planned over the period 1997–2002 (Glasgow Development Agency, 1997a). The programme will receive financial support from the City of Glasgow Council, Strathclyde European Partnership (via ERDF) and support is also being sought from the Millennium Commission. The 'Public Realm' is defined as:

> ...the spaces outside — the streets, spaces and lanes which make up the cohesive, pleasant, safe, attractive and at all times exciting matrix of a great city, which provides the setting for grand buildings, the thoroughfares of commerce and the spaces for activity, street theatres, contemplation and promenading; for living and working. (Glasgow Development Agency, 1997a: p. 3)

Taking their strategy from inward investment indicators and research conducted on competitor sites, Glasgow Development Agency has led an approach aimed at improving the quality of the urban environment for both visitors and residents. Indeed in the case of one area, the Merchant City, a separate and independent strategy has been provided to develop this cultural, residential and retail space.

Glasgow Development Agency, as the primary economic and development agency, are also responsible for the main-stays of the tourism development strategy (Glasgow Development Agency, 1997b). This is the primary agent for assistance to attractions and tourism businesses within the city and it delivers policy and direct assistance around six broad themes:

- Attraction upgrade and development
- Accommodation upgrade and development
- Customer care and quality of service
- Marketing and Public Relations
- Events
- Conference Industry Development

The budget for investment in 1997 was in the region of £3.7 million per annum from Glasgow Development Agency (1997b,c) with further contributions coming from Strathclyde European Partnership (SEP) for major infrastructure development activities. SEP administrates European Funds, of which approximately £22.5 million has been designated for tourism related projects for the years 1997-2000. Glasgow receives this funding since it is classified along with all of Strathclyde as an Objective 2 region. Such a classification occurs for regions which have experienced economic problems following structural shifts in employment and the collapse of traditional industries.

Local government funding via the City of Glasgow Council is currently extremely limited. Contributions are restricted to training assistance, some joint environmental works and partnership in major projects such as the development of the new extension to the Scottish Exhibition and Conference Centre. Thus total annual funding for tourism for 1997 appears as shown in **Table 1 below**.

The success of Glasgow in tourism terms is well illustrated by its ability to unseat Edinburgh as the primary destination for UK domestic tourism in 1996. While achieving greater numbers of domestic tourists, Glasgow still fails to generate the expenditure of domestic tourists to Scotland's capital (see **Table 2** below).

Table 1:   Annual funding for tourism in Glasgow 1997

Funding Source	Amount
Strathclyde European Partnership	£7.5 m
Glasgow Development Agency	£3.7m*
City of Glasgow Council	£2.2m
TOTAL	£13.4m**

*   This does not include the public realm strategy funding element which will contribute some £23.84m in city centre upgrade over the years 1997-2002.
** Invariably such a calculation will always exclude large elements of infra-structure projects which may well indirectly influence tourism perception and improve services.
(Sources: Strathclyde European Partnership, 1997; City of Glasgow Council *et al.*, 1995; Glasgow Development Agency, 1997a, d).

Table 2:   British Tourism to Glasgow and Edinburgh 1996

Location	Trips	Nights	Expenditure
Glasgow	1.2m	3.6m	£ 132m
Edinburgh	1.1m	3.4m	£ 161m

Source: Scottish Tourist Board (1997)

Furthermore, Edinburgh still maintains its appeal to overseas tourists in all categories of measurement (see **Table 3** below).

Table 3:   International Tourism flows — Glasgow and Edinburgh 1996

Location	Trips	Nights	Expenditure
Glasgow	0.49m	3.5m	£155m
Edinburgh	0.92m	6.1m	£256m

Source: Scottish Tourist Board (1997)

Despite the efforts of both marketing agents and development bodies, the growth of Glasgow's tourism industry remains in the shadow of both Edinburgh and Dublin in the all-important arena of international tourism.

Irish tourism development: the role of development funds

Ireland and the UK are so different in population, size, economic structure and politics that it may seem unlikely that there are any lessons to come out of a comparison of the urban tourist locations of Glasgow and Dublin. Yet despite the obvious differences there are important elements of the Dublin product that merit further analysis.

Dublin (population 1,024,400), as the capital of Ireland, accounts for approximately 29% of the nation's population. It is nearly twice as large as the combined total of the next four largest cities in Ireland and constitutes the economic, political and industrial heart of the country. It is also the major tourist attraction in Ireland with a buoyant arts, theatre and music scene. Like Glasgow it is the home of three universities and, like Glasgow, it has seen a shift in employment from manufacturing to services, with tourism becoming an increasingly important element of the city's economy (MacLaren, 1996).

Tourism revenues to Ireland have grown at an unprecedented rate of 9% per annum over the years 1988-1993, while the performance of Irish tourism in the latter part of that decade has been quite phenomenal by comparison with the record of the previous 20 years. Furthermore, the belief that tourism has a focal position in economic development and in attempts to increase employment levels gained credence during the 1980s, a view reinforced by the application of the EU Structural Funds to this sector. The numbers of tourist arrivals to Ireland totalled 70 million in 1960 and rose to 285 million by 1980. The total number of overseas visitors to Ireland increased by 119 per cent over the period 1981–1994, from 1.68 million to 3.67 million (see **Table 4**).

Table 4:   Annual average percentage change in overseas visitor numbers to Ireland by source, 1981-1994

	1981-85	1985-90	1990-94
UK	-1.1	10.1	3.4
Europe	4.6	17.5	7.3
USA	17.6	1.4	2.8
Other Areas	14.0	8.6	6.4
Total	3.5	9.9	4.4

Source: Central Statistical Office (1995); Borde Failte Eireann (1994)

While various causes have been advanced for the growth in tourism from mainland Europe — such as cheaper air fares and more charter air services — the growth of urban, as opposed to coastal, resorts and the environmental appeal of the location suggest that Ireland was suddenly 'discovered' by many European tourists over the period 1985–1990 (Deegan and Dineen, 1997). Comparisons with a number of popular European country destinations (Greece, Portugal, Italy, Spain, UK) indicates that Ireland had more rapid growth in foreign visitor numbers since 1985 and particularly since 1988. Europe has overtaken Britain as the most significant source of tourists. Seven markets account for 85% of tourists to Ireland: UK, France, Germany, Italy, Netherlands, USA, and Australia. The outstanding performance of tourism over this period is often contrasted with the reduction in marketing expenditure by Bord Failte over the same period. A number of possible causes can be advanced for this growth pattern:

- changing trends in the intentional tourism market place with a shift towards alternative tourism and a movement away from traditional sun based holidays;
- the liberalisation of air fares particularly on the Irish — UK routes;
- the convergence of a number of government policies which have influenced the image and perception of Ireland and particularly Dublin;
- investment support for tourism by the Government with the aid of the EU's Structural Funds.

In respect of this last element, it should be noted that over the period of growth in incoming tourists there was a significant improvement in the tourism product, principally due to the EU Structural Funds and the significant increase in investment in Irish tourism under the Operational Programme for Tourism, 1989–1993, and its successor, the 1994–1999 Operational Programme.

Ireland was also classified as a single Objective 1 region for the purposes of Structural Fund transfers via the European Regional Development Fund (ERDF). Objective 1 regions were defined generally as having higher that average employment rates and GDP per capita below 75 per cent of the EU average. Indeed, since joining the EU, Ireland has been a net recipient of funds. Initially the immediate benefits were to agricultural, infrastructure, education and social policy. More recently tourism has received substantial funding through the designated Operational Programme(s) for Tourism. However even prior to this, significant investment had been made in tourism (see **Table 5** below).

**Table 5:   Distribution of ERDF assistance
            by types of tourism project**

Type of Project	EC (%)	Ireland (%)
Infrastructure	32.4	18.9
Accommodation	6.4	—
Leisure complexes	10.6	—
Port facilities	9.2	22.3
Winter sports facilities	2.5	—
Other sports facilities	4.2	—
Thermal resorts	3.1	—
Museums/ historic centres/ restoration	11.7	24.0
Cultural and visitor centres	5.8	34.8
Conference centres	9.0	—
Other	5.1	—
Total 1975 — 1988	100.00	100.00

(Source: Pearce, 1992)

It is interesting to note the amount of expenditure Ireland devoted to projects with a cultural/historic theme, demonstrating clearly an early indication of the emphasis being placed on 'culture' as an integral element of Irish tourism.

The first Operational Programme for Tourism provided what many regarded as the most serious commitment to the industry that bore significant fruit in terms of visitor numbers. It is discussed more fully below.

The Operational Programme for tourism 1989—1993

The main aim of the Operational Programme was to improve the competitiveness of the Irish Tourism industry via concentration on improvements in the quality of the product. Investment in the physical product was also being matched by investment in the quality of service and marketing. Such investment was proposed as the primary foundation for a sustainable tourism industry for the future.

It is estimated that some IR £450 million (about 557 million ECU) was invested in tourist facilities, training and marketing in Ireland during the period 1989–1993. **Table 6** details the initial investment targets for EU co-funded expenditure.

Table 6:   Total co-funded investment achieved by the tourism Operational Programme, 1989 — 1993 (IR £million)

	Programme Targets	Forecast /outcome
Product development	263.4	278.7
Marketing	23.0	48.3
Training	49.2	52.1
Technical Assistance	0.3	0.7
Total	335.9	379.8

(Source: Stationery Office, 1994)

In total the breakdown of the IR £380m investment was as follows: 53% EU, 30% private sector and 17% by the Irish government. During the period 1989–1993, total ERDF project grants to Ireland were IR £1387.3 million, of which tourism grants accounted for 11%, or IR £157.6 million.

Dublin achieved a regional allocation of 23.7% of total expenditure (approximately IR £ 2,420 million) for all development projects. This, considering the population was not that significant and in terms of a per capita expenditure analysis, was the most cost effective in the country (see **Table 7** below).

Table 7:   Regional allocation of spending under the 1989-93 Structural Funds (IR £ million)

Region	Total expenditure	Per capita expenditure	EU contribution	EU % contribution
West	1,157	3,455	400	12.8%
North West	1,077	3,455	383	12.3%
Mid-West	1,122	2,860	356	11.4%
South	1,248	2,657	422	13.5%
South East	984	2,567	320	10.2%
Midlands East	1,423	2,378	501	16.1%
Dublin	2,420	2,362	740	23.7%
TOTAL	9,431	2,677	3,122	100.0

(Source: Stationery Office, 1994)

The Operational Programme for tourism 1994-99

The total product investment available for key sectors under the Operational Programme in the period 1994–1999 could total in excess of £1000 million compared with the £850 million invested in the previous Operational Programme 1989–1993. In addition a further expenditure of £500 million is anticipated for transport infrastructure development. The current investment in tourism related aspects thus breaks down as shown in **Table 8** for the period 1994–1999.

Dublin: tourism and urban development

Thus Ireland and its capital has at its disposal a comprehensive level of funds that are available for investment in key aspects of the product. However it is not accurate to consider this as merely grant-aided intervention. In the case of accommodation (which is the tourism industry's largest investment category) some £400 million worth of non-assisted projects are scheduled to occur over the time frame 1994-99. The concentration will be notably on the capital, Dublin. Indeed, in Dublin the growth in hotels alone would appear to be based primarily on market demand, with no grants or incentives available for development (although some tax incentives are possible under the Business Expansion Scheme). Yet an estimated increase in bedroom capacity of 114% is forecast for the period 1995–1998. In terms of numbers of operations the growth has been significant (see **Table 9**).

Table 8:   Current investment in Irish tourism-related programmes 1994–1999

Investment	£M
Tourism Operational Programme	412
Agritourism	34
Local, Urban and Rural Development	40
LEADER	50
INTERREG	30
International Fund for Ireland	45
Other Schemes	4
Non-assisted investment	400
Infrastructure and services	500
TOTAL	1,515

(Source: Stationery Office, 1994)

Table 9:   Hotel development in Dublin 1984-1997

Year	No of Hotels	Increase year on year (%)
1984	65	
1992	76	+ 16.9%
1996	87	+ 14.4%
1997	104	+ 19.5%
1998	143*	+ 37.5%

(Source: Ryan 1996; Dublin Tourism 1997)

*   Forecast based upon Dublin Tourism accommodation supply data (1997)

Indeed Dublin's growth has been much faster than other European cities, with a growth in tourism revenues from £242.6m in 1991 to £475m in 1997 (Flynn, 1997a) and with an average tourist stay of 6.5 days against a typical European average of 2.5 days for an urban location.

The infrastructure upgrades and area regeneration in Dublin undertaken with the assistance of European structural funds have also provided a foundation upon which to build urban tourism and encourage inward investment. The planned regeneration of the Collins Barracks area and the Smithfield district to the north of the city centre (as part of Dublin Corporation's Historical Area Rejuvenation Plan, HARP) and the proposed Dublin Docklands redevelopment to the east of the city are current projects aimed at further developing and sustaining the city. Clearly the success of the cultural quarter known as Temple Bar has demonstrated the viability and importance of mixed urban regeneration projects. Temple Bar has won international recognition as a strategically planned approach to developing a sustainable cultural quarter which was not led by commercial property development interests (Montgomery, 1995). In this mixed-use development, culturally-led regeneration has been used to develop a dynamic and innovative environment. Indeed by 1996, within this 218 acre site there are six hotels, 200+ retail outlets, 40 restaurants; 14 cultural centres and a residential population in excess of 2000 persons. Furthermore it is estimated that this formerly derelict inner city area now employs more that 2000 persons (Montgomery, 1995). Once again the growth and development of this aspect of Dublin's tourism product cannot be attributed solely to structural assistance. There is a widely held misconception that Temple Bar Properties (the development company for Temple Bar) had grant-aided and controlled the areas re-development via large subventions from European funds. Essentially it has received IR £ 40.6m in the form of EU grants and has the option to access up to IR £ 60m in revolving loans. Private investment in the area currently stands at more than IR £ 100 (Flynn, 1997b). Total outstanding debt has never exceeded IR £15m and properties have been redeveloped and sold, reducing debt substantially. The anticipated completion of the project has been scheduled for the year 2000. As the Managing Director of Temple Bar Properties commented:

> Temple Bar Properties has developed directly about one third of the property in the area and our own commercial/social financial breakdown has been 70:30. By and large we were able to bring about the kind of commercial, cultural and social mix we wanted. The private sector has developed the balancing two thirds. All development in the area is subject to planning permission by Dublin Corporation, and tax incentives given by Temple Bar Renewal (the policy-making body that administers tax incentives for Temple Bar). Almost without exception, the private sector has developed with regard to the bottom line only and has been restricted only by the parameters set by the planning permission and tax incentive mechanism. (Magahy, 1997: p. 7)

This type of vision is informing the 1,300 acre docklands redevelopment scheme. This is being undertaken with a clear vision of creating a better environment, taking account of the existing residential population of 16 700, stimulating employment and capitalising on natural assets. The River Liffey will be targetted specifically to enhance amenity value of the project (McDonald, 1997b). This approach clearly offers much more than a purely commercially-led redevelopment proposal and builds on the lessons of the Temple Bar Development. Similar thinking has informed the planning for the HARP initiative in the 260 acre Smithfield site in the north of the city. Here a major new civic space is planned which will become a centre for the existing and developing urban community (Dublin Corporation, 1997; McDonald, 1997a).

Dublin then represents a major success story in tourism terms. Arrivals to the city have been steadily increasing, ensuring record levels of visitor numbers. Dublin is now Western Europe's fastest growing tourism destination (Collins, 1997). It is also interesting to note that despite this dramatic rise in incoming tourists, crime has not risen significantly and evidence suggests a decline in real terms (Tourist Victim Support Service, 1997). The Tourist Victim Support service (TVSS) which was modelled on the Amsterdam Tourist Assistance Service, provides a service not yet available in Glasgow, that offers practical and counselling based support for visitors who have been victims of crime. It offers such individuals meals, travel tickets and assistance in Embassy liaison, credit card cancellation and passport/ID replacement (World Tourism Organisation, 1996). All problems are handled centrally by the service and it offers both emotional support and practical help despite the fact that serious tourist crime is not yet a problem (see **Table 10**).

Table 10:   Tourist Crime in Dublin 1994-9

	1994	1995	1996
No of Crimes Reported	267	375	408

(Source: Tourism Victim Support Service, 1997)

If one takes into account the increases in visitor numbers over the above period then there is a potential decrease per capita in tourist crime levels. Yet the potential for negative tourist feedback following incidents of crime has catalysed the tourism and business sector to fund this service with the aim of ensuring that crime victims feel cared for and part of a local quality tourism experience (World Tourism Organisation, 1996). This is an interesting example of how the private sector has recognised the significance of tourism perceptions and image of the city and funded a support service accordingly.

Comparisons and indications for future development

Clearly tourism is now established as a prime industry that catalyses economic and employment activity and diversifies the economic base of urban destinations such as Glasgow and Dublin. Most particularly tourism generates employment for relatively low skilled labour, a segment of the labour market acutely effected by the downturn in traditional manufacturing industry and who can be problematic in terms of assistance via job creation. Urban tourism further benefits the host location in terms of its ability to significantly influence the level of infrastructure and support services.

Dublin, then, possesses a range of clear advantages as the national capital, with an international history of literature and culture further enhanced by the government's decision to reduce taxation on artists, musicians and the arts. Such a policy reinforces the reputation of the city as a contemporary as well as historic cultural centre. However also significant is the demographic profile of the country (predominantly youthful) and the problems of youth unemployment. The centrality of Dublin for employment acts as a magnet for Irish youth and this results in a capital with a predominantly youthful profile that reinforces its fashionability and vibrancy in areas such as music and style. Image and reputation are an intangible element of any city product and, though extremely popular in marketing strategies and plans, they are rarely founded on detailed effect analysis. The international growth in Irish pubs has undoubtedly acted as a very effective 'soft sell' for the whole country as have the catalogue of films located for production in Ireland because of tax incentives offered. Indeed the influence of such films (e.g. *My Left Foot, The Commitments, Far and Away, The Field, The Dead, Michael Collins, Hear My Song*) has undoubtedly affected tourist demand. A similar effect has been recognised in Scotland with the release of the so-called 'kilt movies' (e.g. *Braveheart, Rob Roy*) and the impact on tourism has been the subject of some preliminary analysis by the Scottish Tourist Board (1997).

Other factors influencing tourist demand such as the 'peace dividend' and the growth of cheaper air access to the capital is complicated by other causation factors which makes the influence of development assistance harder to isolate. Dublin has clearly benefited from tourism but it would appear that lessons have been learned and developments adapted and future policies shaped by the success and failures to date. A continually voiced concern has been the situation facing the tourist industry post 1999 when the structural funds disappear and the level of intervention and assistance becomes closer to the levels of the mid 1980s. Yet it is clear that sustainable practice has been developed in a scenario that, whilst not excluding commercial interests, guards against its worst excesses and is predicated on a learning scenario. The structural funds have not been the sole or central catalyst to the success of Dublin and the Dublin model is not without problems. Unemployment levels remain considerable, with some inner city areas recording male unemployment levels of close to 70% (MacLaren, 1996).

In addition, the escalation of property values in the city centre and the bias in ownership away from families towards young professional groups has significantly impacted upon host communities in the inner cities (Centre for Urban and Regional Studies, 1995). The lack of an international conference and exhibition arena clearly reduces the appeal of the capital for larger elements of the business tourism market. Furthermore the development of some of the larger scale tourist attractions in the city (utilising EU structural assistance) and their problematic relationship to tourist demand for the urban location merits further examination. In initial analysis it would appear that such developments are simply not a causation factor for deciding to visit the city. Indeed a minority are experiencing problems of low visitor numbers and low satisfaction rates, making their operation marginal.

In comparison Glasgow has simply not benefited from the learning experience that such fast track tourism development offered to Dublin. Without structural assistance so deliberately targeted at tourism and perhaps more importantly, with a government whose attitude to the industry could at best be described as indifferent, Glasgow was unable to develop the foundations for growth in the 1980s that offered a base for a more sophisticated second stage of more sustainable development into the 1990s and beyond. In such a context the performance of Glasgow may flounder. Tourism development must be predicated on learning from the examples of others in the context of both culture and leisure.

Note

The author wishes to acknowledge the assistance of Glasgow Development Agency (GDA) in the assistance offered to this project. This paper deals with extracted elements from a larger analysis of urban tourism performance in Glasgow and Dublin undertaken for GDA in 1996-97

References

Berg, L., Borg, J. and Meer, J. (1995) *Urban tourism performance and strategies in eight European cities.* Aldershot: Avebury.

Bord Failte Eireann (1994) *Developing sustainable tourism, Tourism Development Plan 1994-1999.*

Central Statistical Office (1995) *Tourism and travel facts.* London: HMSO.

Centre for Urban and Regional Studies (1995) *Residential development in Central Dublin: A survey of current occupiers.* Trinity College, Dublin: CURS.

City of Glasgow Council, Glasgow Development Agency, Greater Glasgow and Clyde Valley Tourist Board (1995) *Glasgow Tourism Strategy and Action Plan (1995-1999).* Glasgow: Glasgow City Council.

Collins, G. (1997) 'Dublin leads Euro tourism league as take tops £475m', *The Irish Independent* 5 August 1997: p. 1.

Deegan, J. and Dineen, D. (1997) *Tourism policy and performance — The Irish experience.* London: International Thompson Press.

Dublin Corporation (1997) *Historic Area Rejuvenation Plan.* Dublin: Dublin Corporation.

Dublin Tourism (1997) *Accommodation supply data* (internal document). Dublin: Dublin Tourism.

Flynn, G. (1997a) 'Capital gains: how business is booming for a city's tourism', *The Irish Independent* 10 April 1997: p. 6.

—— (1997b) '£80m boost for second phase of Temple Bar development', *The Irish Independent* 10 April 1997: p. 6.

Glasgow Development Agency (1997a) *Glasgow city centre public realm* (management paper for approval). Glasgow: GDA.

—— (1997b) *Tourism business partnership: Progress and development* (management paper for approval). Glasgow: GDA.

—— (1997c) *Tourism Development Strategy Part Two — action plan* (internal strategy paper). Glasgow: GDA.

—— (1997d) *Business plan 1997.* Glasgow: GDA.

Lennon, J. (1996) 'Marketing Eastern European tourism destinations', in Seaton, A. and Bennett, M. (eds) (1996) *Marketing tourism products.* London: International Thompson Press.

MacLaren, A. (1996) 'Dublin: the creation of a regional problem', *Forum — Assembly of European Regions, Scientific Committee of the Assembly of the European Regions,* Vol VII, No 3: pp. 165-169.

Magahy, L. (1997) 'Working to a plan — Opera house would be an ideal project', *The Irish Times Property Supplement* 20 March 1997: p. 10.

McDonald, F. (1997a) 'Dublin Corporation announces competition for redesign of Smithfield as new civic area', *The Irish Times* 10 April 1997: p. 4.

—— (1997b) 'Development plan must take on board lessons of the last decade', *The Irish Times Property Supplement* 20 March 1997: p. 9.

Montgomery, J. (1995) 'The Story of Temple Bar: Creating Dublin's cultural quarter', *Planning Practice and Research* Vol. 10, No. 2: pp. 135-172.

Page, S. (1995) *Urban tourism.* London: Routledge.

Pearce, D. (1992) 'Tourism and the European Regional Development Fund: the first fourteen years', *Journal of Travel Research* Vol. 30, No. 3 (Winter): pp. 44-51.

Ryan, J. (1996) 'Number of Dublin hotel rooms to double by 1998', *Irish Times* 4 December 1996: p. 3.

Scottish Tourist Board (1997) *Tourism in Scotland 1996*. Edinburgh: Scottish Tourist Board

Sneddon, G. (1996) Glasgow — *Developing tourism in an urban context*. Internal mimeo. Glasgow City Council.

Stationery Office (1989) *National Development Plan 1989-1993*. Dublin: Stationery Office.

Stationery Office (1994) *Operational Programme for Tourism 1994-99*. Dublin: Stationery Office.

Strathclyde European Partnership (1996) *Operating Plan 1996-1999*. Glasgow.

Tourist Victim Support Service (1997) *Third Annual General Meeting of the Tourist Victim Support Service*, 24 February 1997. Dublin: Tourist Victim Support Service.

World Tourism Organisation (1996) *Tourist safety and security — Practical measures for destinations*. Madrid: WTO.

Volunteering in an Urban Museums Service: A Definitional Reassessment

Margaret Graham and Malcolm Foley

Glasgow Caledonian University

Methods

This paper draws from a wider study of volunteers working in museums in Glasgow. Seven museum sites were selected in the city: 2 independent; 1 university; and 4 local authority. The rationale of the research is to clarify understanding of change currently underway in museum volunteering in the city. The primary aim is to help volunteer managers maximise the utility of their volunteers, while helping achieve both museums' organisational objectives and the personal objectives of volunteers themselves.

Research methods take the form of a historical analysis and an ethnographic study, employing a range of different types of data collection, such as observational, interview and questionnaire techniques (Hammersley, 1992).

Analytical approach

Analytical procedures include an historical study, using secondary sources, to monitor background developments, as both museums and voluntarism are culturally and ethically embedded in ideological traditions. This accommodates the hypothesis that museums and volunteering nurture values that are consistent with traditional industrial societies. For this reason, contemporary urban museum volunteering will be considered within the context of a post-industrial framework, by applying the more appropriate post-Fordism imperative. Bell (1974) identified a broad view of service sector prominence and development, alongside the decline of traditional, manual, factory based manufacturing industry. He visualised the gradual emergence of a more affluent, knowledgeable, leisure society, dependent on access to information networks and professional expertise, to realise potential in terms of socio-economic status. Post-Fordist theory suggests the end of both consumer rationality and the mass consumption of standard products. Adding weight to this theoretical perspective, Atkinson and Gregory's (1986) dual labour force thesis argues that employers maximise the utility of human capital to suit the needs of fickle unpredictable markets, exploiting opportunities brought about by an environment of chronic unemployment and weakened worker unionisation. Here the labour-force is structured into core and periphery categories, allowing employers to deal with the unpredictable nature of market forces. Differentiation, flexibility, adaptability and choice will be key concepts used to explain contemporary volunteering and its contribution to the delivery of museum cultural products in Glasgow.

Conceptual development

In a definitional sense, volunteering can be conceptualised as 'voluntarism' or 'volunteerism'. The term 'voluntarism' will be used when considering traditional museum philanthropy, and its association with acts of unprescribed citizenship of an altruistic nature (Kendall and Knapp, 1995). 'Volunteerism', on the other hand, is more suited to contemporary volunteering and is not burdened by the images, labels and myths that have become attached to voluntarism, with the passage of time (Kendall and Knapp, 1995; Sheard, 1995). Volunteerism accommodates a more professional and definitional variety of volunteering types (Tedrick, *et al.*, 1984). The term volunteerism, therefore, will be used to define contemporary urban museum volunteering, as it contains a significant element of prescription and instrumental purpose.

Museums in their charitable context, have always been, and continue to be, one of the country's great causes. Prosler (1996) argues that the earliest 15th and 16th century museums in Europe were utilised like 'encyclopaedias' of global discovery. Through physical and intellectual exploration and collection, the drive towards creating superior civilised societies was channelled through an insatiable appetite for knowledge. From then, European museums emerged as national status symbols, with a sharp rise in the growth of international museums being realised by 1870 (Prosler, 1996). Britain led the way with the establishment of the British Museum, one of the first state-run national collections (Hudson, 1976). In this way, museum purpose became globally politicised, where one country's collection competes with another's to flaunt its material, military and economic achievement. However, cultural aspects of museum interpretation have broadened considerably since then, with their potential, in a commercial sense, challenging long established ideals.

Educationally and culturally, museums provide interpretations of artifacts that add to the written historical record of societies, their development and their environments. Museum ethics and policy continue to adhere and prioritise values that reflect ideals more suited to Victorian philanthropy than to commercial businesses. Both of these perspectives have tended to legitimise museums' relative non-participation in the leisure economy and to sustain their dependency on various forms of public subsidy. Regardless of this, a critical eye is now being cast on the lack of both entrepreneurial spirit and managerial efficiency present in the museum sector, at a time when opportunities to follow new directions are ripe. Cameron (1995) argues that it is time for museums to reconsider their purpose by redirecting their resources towards new priorities. Indeed, museum volunteers are being considered more confidently, as being potential agents to ease the passage of change. However, in public perceptions, museum volunteers tend to elicit images of unskilled elderly middle-class females. Attached to this volunteer stereotype are concepts of unreliability and the inability to discipline and control. On the other hand, museum voluntary work carries a status that separates these volunteers from many other voluntary roles. The following background will help explain this and other images associated with museum traditionalism.

Background

> We cannot create the new because we know too little of the old. I suggest that research into the deep origins of this strange and pervasive creature of human societies — the museum — is the most critical museum research today. (Cameron, 1995: p. 48).

Cameron argues that too little is known about the origins of museum tradition to make confident decisions about the future course museums should follow. Taking Cameron's advice, a brief account of museum history will be considered both to follow the path of change and to provide an understanding of the identity crisis museums and their volunteers have faced since the late 1980s.

Tracing the historical legacy of museum volunteering and attempting to find the origins of its poor image is problematic, as very little information is recorded regarding early accounts of museum philanthropy. However, extensive investigation unearths a long-established link between museum founders, visitors, and paid staff and unpaid work.

An important consideration arising from the 18th and 19th centuries, is the role of individuals, their duty as citizens and their obligation to the nation (Prosler, 1996). At this time museum philanthropy was demonstrated both through the giving of donations and gifts and through active participation (Hudson, 1976). Museums consisted of personal collections, often displayed in the homes of their owners, usually an elite group of male aristocratic individuals, defined as museum specific both in their intellectual interests and professional expertise. It can be argued that, at this time, volunteers were the owners of museums themselves, and their friends and acquaintances were encouraged to support the museum in some way. The ultimate voluntary acts were the bequest of collections to the community, leading to the development of public sector museums.

By the turn of the 19th century, the voluntary sector in British urban society was vast, due to the social upheaval caused by industrial advance. Although no Glasgow examples have been uncovered, museum voluntarism had a general role to play in helping to improve the educational and moral fibre of the poor (Hudson, 1976). In an institutional sense, voluntarism in Glasgow has particular significance, due to the strong association between the voluntary sector, religion and local politics, and their joint effort to prevent the continued reproduction of moral decay amongst the poorest citizens. Between 1811 and 1836 the city doubled its population (Harvey, 1976), mainly through Irish migration. Like other major cities in Britain, Glasgow hosted a plethora of philanthropic societies whose main role was to help civilise the city's immoral and uncultured masses. It is worth considering that most recorded philanthropy in Glasgow has strong connections with Evangelism, as did local politicians of influence. Social control was not the only motive behind voluntary work. Glasgow's Jewish, Catholic and Quaker societies also played a considerable role. Religious motives were significant and for individual volunteers there were strong elements of altruism involved in their voluntary commitments. Segregated, defined spaces allocated to the urban poor were fraught with threats to health and safety. Furthermore, voluntary activity was considered a respectable and altruistic pursuit of the upper and middling classes and tended to be categorically gendered. Trustees and management boards were dominated by men, who controlled resource allocation and policy. Philanthropic societies marginalised women, apparently in tune with contemporary patriarchal values (Hall, 1990; Gordon, 1990). Prior to 1914, women provided supportive, not leadership, roles as members of various charitable societies and auxiliaries, and they were often more involved in passive, practical help tasks, such as collecting donations for various causes, as well as feeding, nursing and teaching basic educational and domestic skills to the cities poorest (Checkland, 1980; Hillis, 1987; Byrne, 1990; Gordon, 1990). In this way, voluntarism had an important role in transferring home-centred middle-class values to the working classes (Pahl, 1984). Indeed, the female philanthropic stereotype, like very many other images of women, became ideologically cultivated in Scotland, mimicking the gendered ideals of contemporary Victorian England (Gordon, 1990).

During this period, museums can be viewed as educational status institutions. It is important at this point to make the link between the reproduction of museum voluntarism and select museum visitors. Elite educational elements attached to museums set them apart from other organisations utilising volunteers. Students of science, art and literature were the most encouraged category of visitor, and it was they who made the most gains from museum collections. Indeed, there is a long tradition of student and graduate volunteering pre-empting museum paid work (Hall, 1995). However, the earliest student volunteers were male scholars, defying the traditional museum volunteer stereotype. In fact, institutional patriarchy all but eliminated women from university participation in Scotland until 1892 (Gordon, 1990) and, therefore, higher education students tended to be male.

The Universities (Scotland) Act of 1889 led the way to women following graduate careers that challenged the norms of Victorian femininity. Although more opportunities emerged for women in scientific and technical fields, horizontal and, in particular, vertical segregation continued to marginalise women from positions of power.

Voluntarism had an increasing role to play as more people became involved in unpaid museum tasks, alongside the rise of free access for all. Hudson argues that early museums required visitors to have considerable literacy skills, specialist knowledge and powers of imagination to draw maximum benefit from their visit. Although most of their visitors were members of the gentry, many of these visited museums to confirm their social status in the community, rather than for any intellectual stimulation. In practice, popular access was difficult to sustain, with dress, language, levels of literacy and behaviour being the main barriers to social cohesion between class extremes. More importantly, museum interpretation had little in common with the material aspects of the lives of ordinary people. The values and manners of aristocrats prevented them from describing the social problems that the lowest orders brought into their museums. However, for some, admission charges and categorising the poor as either deserving or undeserving, helped to eliminate those whose behaviour could least be tolerated. In 1777, one independent museum owner in London 'tired out with the insolence of the common people', published a notice in the London press informing 'the publick' that entry to the museum would be by ticket only, to be provided on the recommendation of one of his 'lady or gentlemen friends' (Hudson, 1976). This ticket would entitle the visitor to bring up to eleven guests for a visit before noon, provided no lady or gentlemen were visiting the museum at the time. However, prior to the visit, the recipient of the ticket would be given instructions on how the visit should be conducted. The role of invitees would be similar to that of an attendant, with responsibility for supervising the conduct of the party (Hudson, 1976).

The Great Exhibition of 1851 was to change attitudes towards unrestrained free access to museums. The working class, unexpectedly, received the exhibition in an organised and controllable manner. From this time, policy allowing free access to museums was advanced more confidently. It is this long-established ideology that continues to hold presence in the psyche of contemporary museum professionals in both the private and public sectors (Moore, 1994). Museum voluntary activity at this time becomes more evident in the literature, indicating that the museum, institutionally, became associated as a charitable cause as well as a site of conservation, education and status. Institutional discrimination against what were widely seen as the undeserving, pagan elements that posed a threat to 'decent' society, was exercised in other improving institutions, like the church at the time. Children and employed manual labour were deemed more deserving of improvement. Exhibitions were created for use in schools (Prosler, 1996). Even the lower working classes were accommodated, with a rise in agricultural and industrial exhibitions. Working men's societies were particularly involved in the social and educational cultivation of male labour, partially through museum education. In 1883 the Secretary of the Working-Men's Lord's Day Rest Association in London reported the findings of a survey monitoring the impact of the introduction of evening opening at several museums in the city. Visitor numbers had increased considerably, indicating the presence of more working class visitors (Hudson, 1976). Weekend voluntary work also played an important role in allowing visits by people who were not able to attend during the working week. This comprised working class men at one end of the social strata, and elite professionals such as barristers and politicians at the other. Hudson (1976) identified the continuation of the two tier system mentioned earlier, whereby Saturday visits tended to be set up for working men through various working men's societies. These were conducted voluntarily by the academic volunteers mentioned earlier. Sir William Flowers, Director of a London National Museum, conducted Saturday museum tours unpaid for working men, and on Sundays he led visits for dignitaries, providing a tour of the exhibits, followed by refreshments and the opportunity for his eminent guests to mingle and socialise. This latter voluntary gesture can be assumed to be connected with anticipation of future support, such as soliciting donations towards the museum's collection.

Pahl tries to explain patterns of differential levels of change, linked to development, when he argues:

> We can avoid the constraints of a benign or malign historicism by adopting the kaleidoscope theory of social life. The coloured pieces can form a variety of patterns: the pieces are the same but the pattern can change dramatically, depending on the severity of the knock. Alternatively, the kaleidoscope can shift imperceptibly, so that we do not notice that the pieces are shifting, until the new pattern jumps into view. (Pahl, 1984: p. 2)

Into the 20th century, museum core goals and standards of performance tended to rest on collecting and protecting unique objects in order to further museum growth. Although education was documented as a primary function, generally visitor contact went no further than an awareness of being scrutinised under the watchful eye of uniformed, military style, security staff. The aura of high art continued to persist in museums, eliminating the interest of a significant number of ordinary people, who felt threatened in such an environment. Key staff became increasingly specialised in fairly narrow technical, scientific and art fields, with more evidence of women participating. Generally, female science graduates were channelled towards lower paid careers, leading to some museum professions becoming dominated by women, although led by male directorates.

During this time, Britain also witnessed significant economic and social upheavals, not least the effects of two world wars and the development, followed more recently by the decline, of the welfare state. This may also account for the origins of the predominant female museum volunteer stereotype, as the state intervened in social welfare and the need for voluntary assistance, shifted elsewhere. However, as welfare dependence loses its credibility, welfare services, including public sector museums, are being edged towards self generated sources of income. Another relevant development, partially due to the success of the feminist movement, concerns the equal opportunities legislation of the 1970s which dramatically changed employment prospects, expectations and values of women, particularly the young. Although most fabric conservationists continue to be female and most curators male (Prince 1994) with no female directors of national museums and galleries in Britain, the glass ceiling is cracking, as women directors become more visible at regional and district level, particularly in Scotland. For example, the Scottish Museums Council, Dundee City Council's Art Galleries and Museums Service and North Lanarkshire Council's Museums and Heritage Section, are all led by women. In addition, unemployment patterns no longer respect class status and affect all ages and academic abilities (Allen, *et al.*, 1986; Baine, *et al.*, 1992). Glasgow has one of the highest incidences of poverty in the UK, due to long term unemployment (Baine, *et al.*, 1992). Unemployed school leavers, new graduates, the early retired and the redundant are becoming increasingly involved in the 'reserve' army. Appropriate knowledge, skill and experience are important credentials in the search for paid work at all levels. Alongside this, museum professionals have been forced to review their operations. In terms of accountability, museum conservation, interpretation and education policy are being encouraged to comply to new standards of excellence, maximising the utility of resources while targeting new, in some cases unconventional, markets. In the process, museum meaning and purpose has diversified considerably in an attempt to meet a whole raft of new objectives. This has broadened the scope of museum professionalism, as traditional museum administration makes way for a new proactive managerial approach and as museum functions become more sensitive to competition and market forces. All of these issues have immense implications for the future development of volunteers.

Museum volunteerism — the contemporary perspective

Most museum visitors come from social class A, B and C1 households; this can also confidently be applied to the profile of most contemporary museum volunteers. Attitudes towards volunteers continue to be of dependent distrust. Museums depend on volunteers to carry out routine tasks usually connected with areas of low priority, such as administration, but they are distrusted with any responsibilities to do with more specialised museum work. Contemporary commentators have tended to take a Janus-faced approach to volunteers. On the negative side, in terms of human resource management, the stress is only moving marginally away from the amateur profile of the volunteer, with more emphasis being placed on issues of discipline, reliability and control (Friedman, 1994). The myth of the altruistic, selfless volunteer has persisted, and has afforded voluntarism respect and status that has protected volunteers from being treated in the same way as paid staff. This has reduced the potential utility of non-remunerated resources from being realised. In order for museums to help achieve their goals and meet their objectives, as well as those of their volunteers, a relationship of mutual understanding needs to be developed between the museum and their unpaid staff. Unchecked, the paths that highly motivated volunteers may wish to follow may be contrary to the mission of the museum, while for the same reason, the museum may lose potentially good volunteers, whose aspirations have not been met by their hosts.

Patterns of differentiation

The stereotypical image of museum volunteers was tested for change, hypothesising that gender, age and class were dependent variables, transforming the profile of volunteering in this post-industrial era.

Up until the late 1980s, museums in Glasgow had to take all the volunteers they could, because of such a short supply. Volunteer types were typical of volunteering at that time: they were predominantly female and were involved in routine tasks not normally associated with a museum specialism. Numerically, museum volunteering has broadened considerably since then and museums can afford to be more selective. From questionnaire responses involving 58 volunteers in Glasgow, **Figure 1** shows that, although volunteering is dominated by women, (64%) more than a third of volunteer respondents (36%) are male. According to recent European trends, women have increased their participation in the public arena of paid work despite remaining less economically active than men (Baine, *et al.*, 1992). The Glasgow result would, therefore, reflect this trend, as more women become involved in paid work, less are involved in charitable activities. One volunteer organiser, representing the independent Glasgow Art Gallery and Museums Association (GAGMA) commented that gender is becoming less of an issue. However, the Association wished to attract much younger volunteers to meet demand for sites that anticipate attracting a much younger market, such as the city's new Gallery of Modern Art (GOMA). Following an advertisement for more museum volunteers, an overwhelming response was received, but failed to bring as many younger volunteers as they had hoped.

Figure 2 shows that women predominate in most age groups. However, of particular interest, are volunteers within the '65 and over category', where men outnumber women, and within the '35 to 44' category, where there were no women at all. In the first category all were retired, while the latter contained both unemployed and employed males. The youngest categories, comprised mostly short-term teenage and student volunteering on placement or work experience had low male representation. This was confirmed during interviews with museum professionals. During interviews and participant observation, it was noted that long term unemployment and early retirement and redundancy accounted for an increased number of volunteers.

Figure 1: Volunteers in Glasgow Museums by Gender

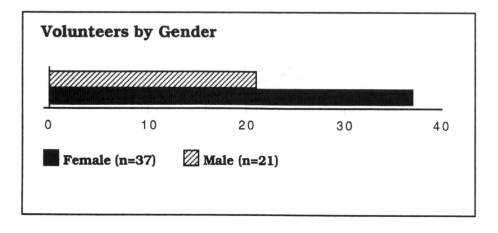

Figure 2: Volunteers in Glasgow Museums by Age and Gender

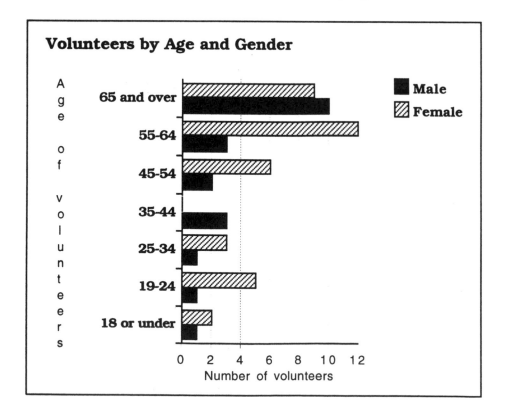

Figure 3:   Female Volunteers in Glasgow Museums by Age and class

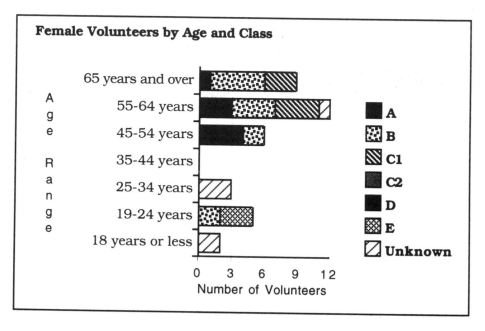

Figure 4:   Male Volunteers in Glasgow Museums by Age and Class

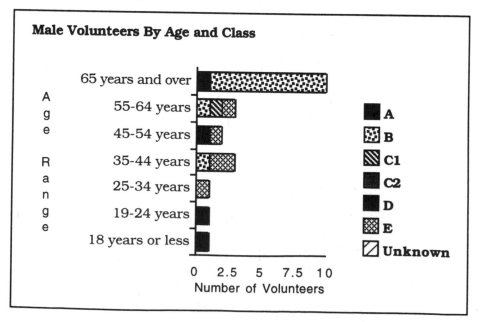

However, the largest group of volunteers consisted of 57 people, both men and women, working on a temporary exhibition for the local authority's open museum. This site was set up to reflect the cultural diversity of the city and to allow an outlet for a variety of historical interpretations of the lives of 'ordinary' Glasgow citizens, which otherwise would go unrecorded. This particular group of volunteers had only just been established and did not participate in the questionnaire survey. Most of the volunteers came from two inner city job centres, as part of a Museum Information Technology Initiative, (MITech is a Government sponsored employment training initiative for the structurally unemployed), involving a large group of the long term unemployed, ranging from 20 to 50 years of age. Qualitative data was gathered from this group through interviews with their supervisor, a member of the museum's curatorial staff, and as participant observer, during informal discussions with them.

All female volunteers aged above 45 years were concentrated in 'white collar' households, represented in **Figure 3** by class categories A, B and C1.

All male volunteers (**Figure 4**) aged over 65 years are retired (one early retirement reported) and come from A or B households. Male volunteers between age categories '55 and 64 years' were equally distributed between class B, C1 and E. All male volunteers within age categories '18 years or less' and '19 to 24' were either students or school pupils from group A households. Volunteers from E households were spread between age '25 to 64'. They included unemployed graduates and those unemployed due to redundancy.

Most of the open site museum volunteers, not represented in Figure 4, come from socio-economic households of C2, D and E.

Volunteering professionalism — adaptability

The skills of contemporary volunteers are wide ranging, and, in this context it is in the area of professionalism that a new perspective has been developed. Tedrick, *et al.* (1984) used the term volunteerism in their theory to identify a continuing upsurge in volunteering opportunities in leisure, accompanied by the development of a more cosmopolitan, professional and powerful label being attached to the image of volunteers.

Volunteer adaptability to the museum environment can be problematical, regardless of the museums' prerogative of choice during the volunteer selection process. Personal and organisational values may not be compatible. Some volunteers can be 'worth their weight in gold' while others can be 'volunteers from hell' was the response one museum professional gave when asked about volunteer professionalism. Dealing with 'bad volunteers' was seen as 'awkward'. There was a general consensus among volunteer supervisors that the problem was not one of retention, but one of assimilation. One volunteer organiser, being a volunteer herself, commented that "bad volunteers do not stay, they simply do not fit in with the rest of us". One museum professional draws on volunteers with specific skills to help with conservation work. "Although some women would prefer to chat than work, with time you learn who to ask and who to avoid". Two volunteer supervisors, both museum professionals from different museum types, specifically mentioned problems they had with some retired male professionals. Both had experienced situations where volunteers expected their voluntary work would give them the levels of control over other people that they had had in paid work. In the public sector, some tasks would not be offered to some retired men from particular professions. It seems that museum priorities may differ from theirs and, as one museum professional commentated, "we run the risk that they would want to take over". Another museum professional argued that one retired, highly specialised volunteer owned a particularly rare collection. He had a lifetime's knowledge in the field not matched by any paid museum expert in the department. However, he exerted considerable control over one young female paid member of specialist staff, demeaning her authority, asking her to run errands and making sexist remarks about her appearance. Although she became extremely upset by this, she was encouraged by her superior to tolerate the volunteer's behaviour because of the unique nature of his skills and their use in museum conservation and interpretation. More importantly, the museum anticipated that one day the volunteer's collection would be bequeathed to the museum.

All museums had volunteers with rare skills who provided considerable support to remunerated functions. Both male and female volunteers provide these skills, ranging from expertise in antique silverware and textiles through skills associated with art and design and mechanical maintenance.

However, volunteers involved in routine tasks are particularly important for all sites. This allows museum professionals to concentrate on other, more demanding, tasks. In particular, women, even those with little obvious skill, were viewed as being extremely important due, in many cases, to skills adaptability. Some women have skills that are no longer easily accessible, many being adapted from domestic use to suit conservation, such as basic sewing skills. A female volunteer in one site has a highly skilled specialism in fabrics that supports paid conservation functions. She continues to update her skills by attending classes at her own expense.

Volunteer development

The process of achieving assimilation into the museum environment, for most volunteer types, has been eased through skills development. Training and work experience, involving museum professionals and volunteers working together, has helped achieve a high level of consensus between the values of volunteers and their supervisors. In the process, organisational instrumentalities and volunteering instrumentalities have de-differentiated work and leisure. In other words, the issue of volunteering is that it is, at curatorial level, viewed as a human resource management issue, rather than a personal development issue. Quite often volunteers are perceived for what they can contribute to the work of the museum and seldom in the context of what volunteers expect to achieve from their voluntary work. However, there are some marked exceptions to this, where agencies will think of their personal, in some cases personal professional, development. Although training has been a significant new development for volunteers, financial restrictions have prevented its widespread utility. Glasgow museums have been involved with other agencies in the area of volunteer development. For example, Scottish Enterprise, in conjunction with a Dunbartonshire Training Project, involve museum volunteers from most local authority sites in a tourism training package. It is important to mention at this point that the values attached to tourism have met considerable resistance, not only from museums in Glasgow but from museums elsewhere in the country and indeed from some of their supporting agencies. Yet the Volunteer Guide Service that has emerged from this package has become an important part of service delivery at local authority sites. From the volunteers' point of view, training has helped intensify their interest in the museum's subject matter and channelled their enthusiasm in a positive way, entertaining and educating museum visitors at all levels. Those involved in this training initiative form the largest part of the long term volunteer pool at local authority sites. Initially, an elite group of volunteers are trained in guiding skills of interpretation and visitor care. In turn, they train new volunteer recruits. Performance standards are monitored and training is updated from time to time. The volunteers involved are both men and women, mainly from A, B and C1 households. In this way the process of assimilation takes a new dimension as volunteers are involved in an independent role set firmly apart from those of museum professionals, while at the same time the concept of tourism is introduced into the museum environment.

There are a variety of innovative approaches to volunteer development that may appear to be primarily aimed at the personal development of the volunteer. Training, skills development and confidence building are the most important personal development outcomes intended for the open site volunteers. Seminars include training in interview technique and the operation of audio visual equipment. Volunteers are then sent to record the histories of 2000 older Glasgow citizens, who in turn volunteered (through advertising in the media) to participate in this oral history project. It is anticipated that the recorded urban experiences will provide the museum with an exhibition and an unique archive collection.

Motivation

Historical analysis revealed that a significant element of museum inspiration and voluntarism was centred around nationalism, patriotism and civic pride. Cameron (1995) argues that museums should reassess their moral purpose and move from damaging radical ideals towards values that promote a sense of international realism and global cultural understanding, thus contributing towards world peace. He used, as an example, the role of museums and the spread of political propaganda in the Third Reich and in the Soviet Union under Stalin.

Discussions with volunteers and comments made in questionnaires revealed an element of national and civic altruism being attached to the interest in museum volunteering, both passive and active. Volunteers welcomed the expansion of museum interpretation and, although there were a few radical views of museum practice expressed, these appeared to be fairly low among motivational priorities. However, observational analysis revealed a small, but more active, group of volunteer types. During a volunteer meeting, one volunteer expressed concerns about an exhibit that was not kept under the correct conditions. All of this group expressed anger towards recent job losses by established museum staff through restructuring, a problem being faced by an increasing number of museums in the UK due to chronic financial constraints. Their resistance was kept under control by a museum professional attending the meeting, to whom they demonstrated their support.

Most volunteers had a plurality of volunteering motivations, some altruistic others more instrumental. However, there tended to be one predominant motivation: for example, the long-term unemployed and students reported that volunteering was primarily instigated as a prerequisite to paid work; most retired volunteers viewed their voluntary work as they would a hobby.

Hierarchy of volunteering and levels of commitment

This research reveals that volunteerism in Glasgow Museums has diversified considerably. However, in terms of supporting paid functions, some museum volunteers are involved in core volunteering roles while others are on the periphery and beyond. This is best demonstrated utilising the principles of Atkinson and Gregory's (1986) flexible labour market theory. Volunteers with a range of skills can be involved in various roles, being deployed as required. For example, at a meeting of trained volunteer guides, a member of museum staff asked for volunteers to assist with preparation for the winter closure of one site. This involved making fabric bags to store textile exhibits and the packaging of more fragile objects. One museum professional commented, "Volunteers can be involved one day in fairly routine tasks while the next they can be asked to support work that demands considerable skill". She added that they search for talents and use them if they can, regardless of the sex and age of the volunteer. However, another museum respondent from the public sector said:

> We used to have volunteers in the workshop, about ten, but this type of conservation is up in the air at the moment because recent restructuring has reduced the number of paid staff suitable to supervise them. Staff are beginning to look at volunteers differently now. Volunteers being used more in the technical side, say in conservation is now being viewed as a threat to paid work. Our main direction is definitely the volunteer guide service. New recruits come under the

wing of GAGMA and they make sure they know what to do. Guides can deal with special interest tours, adapting to what pre-booked visitors want to see. However, some volunteers are unreliable and simply do not turn up while with others it is difficult to know when they will be there.

This suggests that issues of volunteer supervision need to be addressed.

Supervision

Although there is a plethora of dormant volunteers, museums can only recruit new volunteers when there are sufficient paid staff to organise projects and provide supervision. One museum professional commented that this must have a detrimental effect on volunteer satisfaction. According to the questionnaire, volunteers generally assumed their work was appreciated, while discussions with some volunteers revealed a greater element of uncertainty. One volunteer guide organiser said "We are involved in much more than the volunteer guide service. However, you do not know what the paid staff think of you. Some make us feel appreciated while others do not." Volunteerism is generally assumed to be part of cost reduction, by drawing upon a cheap source of human capital. One local authority supervisor estimated that the volunteer guide service alone was worth tens of thousands of pounds in financial terms. A former local authority museum keeper added weight to this argument by saying that placements, only briefly mentioned in this paper, were a major category of museum volunteer that has now replaced paid graduate trainees, disbanded because there was no guarantee of future work. She suggested that the amount of money saved since this change, combined with the value of placement work, is immense. A volunteer organiser pointed out that volunteerism does not only include practical work. GAGMA membership is compulsory for local authority volunteers, with the organisation having 2,200 members in October 1996. However, only a small minority volunteer their time, with most members joining only to enjoy GAGMA's subsidised social events, such as outings and international trips. Regardless of this, membership fees provide funding for various museum projects in Glasgow throughout the year.

The main costs of supervising volunteers concern the time lost by paid museum professionals, which can be as much as 35 per cent of the work time of the volunteer, although this would vary according to the amount of supervision the volunteer requires. Regardless, taking account of the value of museum professionals' time, this can be considered to be a significant cost where volunteers require a high degree of supervision. Students were reported to be the greatest supervision problem, mainly because placements and work experience tend to be for a short term, from a duration of one to eight weeks among domestic students, and six months to one year in the case of international students. Due to recent budget cuts and increasing shortages of established museum professionals, some museums in Glasgow are unable to host as many volunteers as they would wish, even although there is work for them. University and local authority museums reported a considerable reduction in the number of volunteers they were able to supervise, particularly from categories of placement or work experience and among the unemployed, involved in Government run initiatives.

Conclusion

When applying the post-Fordist thesis of the flexible firm (Pollert 1989; Sloan 1989; Pinch, *et al.* 1991) to the volunteer museum relationship, it is clear that volunteering in Glasgow Museums accommodates considerable numeric and functional flexibility. Indeed, flexible work practices are wide ranging and, on the surface, may appear to involve managerial motivations that view volunteering as a partial solution to problems associated with current funding constraints. This perspective of organisational instrumentality perceives volunteers as masking chronic shortages of paid staff, by contributing towards the number of museum task completions. Moreover, it can be expanded to commercial considerations, such as introducing volunteers to new roles and approaches geared towards heightening visitor satisfaction and broadening market scope, in line with other types of visitor attractions.

Looking at consumption from a different perspective, the personal instrumentality of volunteers themselves can be satisfied by a limited, but varied, supply of museum volunteering experiences. For example, volunteers as repeat visitors allow for a more active participative association with the museum than the conventional visitor. This may provide the opportunity for a volunteer's interest in the museum's subject matter to be developed, or museum volunteering may be a new leisure interest or hobby. Indeed, voluntary participation can be viewed as an affirmation of citizenship. Looking at this in terms of conservation and conservatism, volunteers can be viewed as both actively preserving local heritage, while lobbying to maintain the status quo. Alternatively, the museum may provide a free source of training or an opportunity to retrain, not necessarily as a pre-requisite for paid work. For example, the third age volunteers involved in retraining as volunteer guides are being coached in new voluntary roles involving visitor contact, interpretation and education.

Volunteers appear to be viewed more favourably, with more value being attached to their skills and their potential. For example, the European Social Fund provided almost half of the funding towards a National Vocational Qualification (NVQ) training programme for structurally unemployed people of all ages, involved in voluntary work in a museum in Milton Keynes. The museum's training supervisor commented that she would prefer to employ a volunteer who had achieved an NVQ level three or four qualification, rather than someone with a Masters degree who did not have the "same hands-on experience" (Reynolds, 1997: p. 9).

References

Allen, S., *et al.* (1986) *The experience of unemployment.* London: Macmillan.

Atkinson, J., and Gregory, D. (1986) 'A flexible future', *Marxism Today*, April, pp. 12-17.

Baine, S., Benington, J. and Russell, J. (1992) *Changing Europe.* London: NCVO Publications.

Bell, D. (1974) *The coming of post industrial society: A venture in social forecasting.* London: Heinmann Education Books.

Byrne, T. (1990) *Social services.* Oxford: Heinemann Professional Publishing Ltd.

Cameron, D. F. (1995) 'The pilgrim and the shrine: The icon and the oracle', *Museum Management and Curatorship*, Vol. 14, No. 1: pp. 47-55.

Checkland, O. (1980) *Philanthropy in Victorian Scotland.* Edinburgh: J. Donald.

Friedman, R. (1994) 'The special problems of personnel management in museums and historical agencies', in K. Moore (ed) *Museum management.* London: Routledge, pp. 120-127.

Gershuny, J. I. (1977) 'Post industrial society: The myth of the service economy', *Futures*, April: pp. 103-113.

Gordon, E. (1995) 'Women's spheres', in Fraser W. H., and Morris R. J. (eds) *People and Society in Scotland.* Vol. II. Edinburgh: John Donald Publishers Ltd., pp. 206-235.

Hall, L. (1995) 'All for the love', *Museums Journal*, October: pp. 25-28.

Hammersley, M. (1992) 'Introducing ethnography', *Sociology Review*, Vol. 2, No. 2: pp. 18-23.

Harvey, C. (1976) *Midnight scenes and social photographs: Streets, wynds and dens of Glasgow.* Milngavie: Heatherbank Press.

Hillis, P. L. M. (1987) 'Education and evangelisation, Presbyterian Missions in nineteenth century Glasgow', *Scottish Historical Review* LXVI (181): pp. 46-62.

Hudson, K. (1976) *A social history of museums.* London: Macmillan Press Ltd.

Kendall, J. and Knapp, M. (1995) 'A loose and baggy monster: Boundaries, definitions and topologies', in Smith, Rochester and Hedley (eds) *An introduction to the voluntary sector.* London: Routledge, pp. 66-95.

Moore, K. (1994) 'Introduction', in K. Moore (ed) *Museum management.* London: Routledge, pp. 1-14.

Pahl, R. E. (1984) *Divisions of labour.* Oxford: Basil Blackwell Ltd.

Pinch, S., Mason, C. and Witt, S. (1991) 'Flexible employment strategies in British Industry', *Regional Studies* Vol. 25: pp. 207-218.

Pollert, A. (1989) 'The flexible firm: Fixation or fact', *Work, Employment and Society*, Vol. 2: pp. 281-316.

Prince, Dr. R. (1994) 'Women in museums', in G. Kavenagh (ed) *Museum provision and professionalism*. London: Routledge, pp. 212-226.

Prosler, M. (1996) 'Museums and globalisation', in Macdonald, S. and Fyfe, G (eds). *Theorizing museums*. Oxford: Blackwell, pp. 21-44.

Reynolds, P. (1997) 'Museum skills way forward for unemployed volunteers', *Museums Journal*, March: pp. 9.

Sheard, J. (1995) 'From lady bountiful to active citizen', in J. D. Smith, C. Rochester and R. Hedley (eds) *An introduction to the voluntary sector*. London: Routledge.

Sloan, P. J. (1989) 'Flexible manpower resourcing', *Journal of Management Studies*, Vol. 26: pp. 129-150.

Tedrick, T., Davis, W. W., and Coutant, G. J. (1984) 'The effective management of a volunteer corps', *Journal of Parks and Recreation* Vol. 19, No. 2: pp. 55-59.

II

IDENTITY AND COMMODIFICATION

The Legal Boundaries of Tourism: The State versus the Marketplace in Defining the Tourist

Brian Simpson

The Flinders University of South Australia

The raising of the question of how 'tourism' and 'tourist' are to be defined may seem to be overly legalistic in style and approach. But this matter of definition does appear to be important for tourism and leisure studies. Most standard texts on tourism begin with a definition of the terms. Even in popular discourse we are aware that many tourists prefer to be known as 'travellers', suggesting that there is something less than wholesome about being categorised as tourists (see Lengkeek, 1995: p. 33). The fact that such a distinction is drawn suggests that certain values inform the discussion of how tourism is to be defined, even if they are not always well articulated. A question to be examined is what role the law should play in shaping that definition and stating the values upon which it is based.

This paper thus addresses the values which define tourism. What might be called a 'traditional approach' has been to posit the tourism experience in terms of what people do and where they go, without reference to the social, economic or political implications of defining the experience as value free. This has much to do with the role of the marketplace in defining the tourism experience. Clearly, commercial gains will be limited by attempts to constrain what may properly be described as tourism. The market tends towards an 'unregulated' environment rather than one which places limits on how one can behave.

Such an approach to defining tourism is now under serious challenge as many commentators are beginning to question the morals and ethics of certain forms of tourism. The law has been instrumental in this process. For example, legislation exists which delimits the boundaries of acceptable tourism, particularly in the case of 'sex tourism'.

Nevertheless, there is an ongoing struggle between the state and the marketplace in defining these boundaries. This struggle is complex because on the one hand the state must defend the marketplace, given current social structures, while it also has the role of curbing its excesses. In this sense the struggle is not just between the state and the marketplace but also within the state. Thus there is still much confusion about the legal boundaries of tourism and indeed what should be defined as tourism due to the opportunities to exploit certain areas for profit within the marketplace. Some of this confusion might be extinguished if the state can reassert itself as defender of the 'public interest', defined not just in terms of the needs of the market and business, but also in terms of the weak and powerless. In other words, the state needs to articulate the public interest in the area of tourism as being about the protection of those who are often exploited by tourists and the tourism industry.

The role of the law is critical in this process, as a statement of fundamental values and as a benchmark against which behaviour can be judged as 'tourism' or not. But as debates on the legislation which addressed 'child sex tourism' indicate, the process of defining the legal boundaries of tourism reflects the dilemmas which exist in defining tourism generally. Indeed, the fact that the law recognises forms of 'sex tourism' as tourism in itself directs and constrains thinking abut this issue.

Defining the tourist in neutral terms

In 1978 a Committee of the Australian House of Representatives reported on tourism. This report begins with a definition of 'tourist' which seems innocuous. The Report defines tourists as:

> ...persons who travel more than 40 kilometres from their normal place of residence for any reason other than to commute to a normal place of work. (Australia, 1978: para.19)

The notable aspect of this definition is that it does not include any notion of purpose within its terms. The New South Wales Department of Tourism had argued before the Committee for the inclusion of a purpose dimension. Their submission identified three categories of tourists: persons who are travelling away from home for more than 24 hours for recreation, holiday, sport, health, hobby or certain kinds of study; persons who are travelling away from home for more than 24 hours for business, education, family, friends, missions or meetings; and day trippers travelling away from home for less than 24 hours "for discretionary reasons" (Australia, 1978: para.16). The breadth of these categories might suggest that there is little point to limiting the definition of a tourist by reference to purpose. In one sense there would be few people, based on these categories, who would not fall within the definition of a tourist when travelling.

The problem is that under these definitions the serial killer who travels more than 40 kilometres to murder his or her next victim is also a tourist. So too is the person who travels overseas to sexually abuse children. And people who travel to places knowing that the services they will consume are provided by workers who are underpaid also will be labelled as tourists. Even the notion that tourism is about "attempts to escape everyday life and to seek new worlds" (Lengkeek, 1995: p. 23) raises the problem of whether one is properly called a 'tourist' if one is seeking a new world which involves exploitation and abuse.

The fact that the definition of a tourist can be expressed in such apparently neutral terms and lead to applications of the label 'tourist' in such cases gives rise to a number of moral and ethical issues. The fundamental question is whether persons who travel for these purposes should be classified as tourists at all. Indeed, is it that the label acts as some kind of shield which justifies or legitimates the activities of the person so labelled? And if the term should be defined more carefully, how do we reach agreement as a community on this definition?

This is not mere semantics. The manner in which we define the travel experience has much contemporary importance, especially for those who market it. The image which is sold to tourists is as much a part of the tourist experience as the tour itself:

> Taking a tour makes me a tourist — right? 'No. Tourists go to Benidorm on package deals,' the agent answered. 'You're a traveller.' The brochures were anxious to reassure me on this point. What happens between making the booking and reaching for the sun cream? The brochures fall over each other feeding on their collective hype to make me an 'adventurer', 'imaginative traveller', 'world traveller', 'globe-trotter', 'expeditionist', 'journeyman' and even 'individual'. Anything but 'tourist'. At last the penny drops. OK, so it's about what we like to tell ourselves that we are rather than what we actually do. (Rughani, 1993: p. 7)

Although the label 'tourist' may carry some stigma it might also be that the name disguises the activity more than explains it. But one thing seems apparent. This ambiguity which surrounds the definition of 'tourist' — or whatever other label is given to those who travel — provides greater flexibility to those who market travel experiences. The result is that persons can be sold 'tours' and acquire the status of 'tourist' in order to justify their participation in behaviour which might otherwise be classified as immoral, unethical or even illegal.

Thus it is argued here that the consequence of a vague and poorly thought out definition of tourism is that the values of the marketplace will determine its meaning. The effect is that the behaviour which will fall within its terms will have more to do with the economic and political power of those who market and purchase travel, than it has to do with community-wide concerns about human rights and the protection of vulnerable people from exploitation. This is not to assert a naive belief that activities which are currently practised under the guise of 'tourism' will necessarily disappear because they are taken outside the notion of what constitutes tourism. What is asserted is a belief that a definition of tourism which is grounded in an inclusive and broad view of the public interest enforced by the state will act as some constraint on behaviour which is exploitative and oppressive.

The role of the market in defining the tourist

There is clearly much money to be made out of tourism. As Ennew comments:

> Tourism has emerged out of an exploitative system in which national
> images are manipulated by profit-seeking companies for sale to
> pleasure-seeking customers. Many of the host nations exploit this
> and see tourism as a vital component of national growth. The mes-
> sage of the Thai Tourist Authority for instance is that Thailand, Asia's
> most exotic destination offers the visitor many unique and unforget-
> table experiences'. It is also recognized that some of these experiences
> will be sexual. (Ennew, 1986: p. 98 citing O'Grady, 1980: p. 13)

The increasing economic importance of tourism for national economies is well
documented. But a less often stated aspect of the value of tourism is the
extent to which the economic gain arises from activities which might be
described as being on the 'dark side' of tourism. This is an aspect of tourism
in all countries:

> In contemporary accounts of tourism and prostitution, attention has
> tended to focus on the growth of prostitution in less developed
> countries and in particular tourist destinations in south-east Asia.
> However, a similar relationship exists in western tourist destinations.
>   Just as Miami has become synonymous with vice, the combi-
> nation of sun, sea, sand and sex has become associated with tourism
> resorts in general. Tourist promotion may play on the more licentious
> attributes of the tourist and highlight the unseemly characteristics
> of the tourist destination....
>   The 'red light' districts of many cities, such as Sydney's Kings
> Cross, are often seen as tourist attractions which attract the sen-
> sation-seeking tourist as participant observer. When conditions
> become too threatening or dangerous the visitor can be driven off, but
> where a degree of control over illegal activities is maintained, then
> certain classes of tourists may be attracted. (Hall, 1995: p. 241,
> references omitted)

Such approaches to the promotion of tourism find constant expression. While
it is true that civic leaders often embark on efforts to 'clean up the seedier
side of town' the resilience of such locations is often used to assert the
continuing demand for such places. It is then a short step to the argument
that it is better to regulate and profit from the activities which take place there
rather than to pretend that they can ever be eliminated. Such arguments play
a part in discussions on urban revitalisation as one recent newspaper report
in Adelaide stated:

> Hindley Street should become Adelaide's street of sleaze, says a city
> adult bookshop owner.
>   Mr John Nash said Hindley Street should mirror Sydney's
> Kings Cross or St Kilda in Melbourne. And if prostitution was

decriminalised in [South Australia], the street could become Adelaide's premier 'red light district'.

Locals and tourists could come to Hindley Street and say this is Adelaide's naughty street', said Mr Nash, who has run *The Pleasure Shop* in the street for 15 years.

It's taken 50 years to get this dirty reputation. Now people want to tidy it up'.

His plan follows the release of three consultants' reports aimed at cleaning up and revitalising the street. Out would go sex shops, tattoo and pinball parlors, and motorcycle shops, as the Adelaide City Council prepares to take a broom to the precinct.

But Mr Nash said the council should 'make a dollar' on the seedy image.

Hindley Street is never going to become the family entertainment strip council wants it to be'. he said. Mr Nash said council should zone the area 'red light' in preparation for the decriminalisation of prostitution.

But Adelaide Deputy Lord Mayor, Mr Bob Angove, said Mr Nash was at odds with other businesses.

They want an image of Hindley Street as a good, clean, family-oriented street'. Mr Angove said. 'This is Adelaide, not Sydney or Melbourne. And quite frankly we could well do without that kind of tourism'. ('Make Hindley naughty street', *Sunday Mail*, 20 July 1997, p. 11)

The point here is that the promotion of such activities is regarded by many as a legitimate part of the tourist experience. In this sense the activity helps to define the very notion of what it means to be a tourist. Thus it might be said that the expression 'sensation-seeking tourist' is (at least for some tourists) a tautology. Of course, such attempts to incorporate this form of tourism into the 'mainstream' also gives rise to the counter argument that it is not proper or appropriate tourism. It is then a struggle to define 'tourism'.

If one accepts that the economic imperatives of the marketplace are powerful forces in shaping the meaning of tourism, then it must also be accepted that shifts in the marketplace can also cause a decrease in the importance of exploitative or 'sleazy' activities in defining tourism. For example, it has been argued that the increase in the number of Japanese women tourists has facilitated Thai government attempts to control the Thai sex industry which has had a substantial dependence on Japanese male tourists for financial and cultural support (Leheny, 1995). As Leheny explains:

Japanese tourists currently rank second (behind Thailand's neighbor, Malaysia) among incoming visitors to this country, making up about 11% of arrivals. Because Japanese are currently the biggest spenders in the industry, however, they are of greater economic significance for Thailand than even their impressive share of the inbound market might indicate. Additionally, although Japanese men do not constitute the sole source of demand for Thai sex tourism, Japanese foreign investment policies — specifically for tourism projects — make them doubly important for developing countries, because they are designed to reflect and encourage Japanese outbound tourism. The case of Japanese tourists in Thailand thus highlights not only the financial links that support the sex tourism industry, but also the ways in which sociocultural conditions in one state can be transmitted, through market means, to another. (Leheny, 1995: p. 368, references omitted)

But the number of Japanese women tourists is increasing and their affluence and spending patterns means that they are a lucrative market to tap. Leheny continues:

Japanese men do not represent the most potentially profitable demand group; Japanese *women* do. Consequently, the rapidly increasing number of Japanese women traveling abroad may pressure the government to change Thailand's sex market image...The symbolic and perhaps only partial effort to eradicate Thailand's image as a sex market, therefore, may appeal to Japanese women travelers, who represent the wave of the future to a developing country hoping to increase foreign finance and direct foreign currency injections. (Leheny, 1995: p. 380)

Leheny discounts the importance of domestic pressure — from Japanese Christians, feminist organizations and labor unions — in changing the culture against sex tours (Leheny, 1995: p. 378). For him, the economic pressures which result in Japanese women taking their money to shopping destinations is more significant as an influence on Thailand to shift its image away from sex tourism and towards the type of tourism which will attract the female tourist.

It must be accepted that the marketplace exercises such influence in determining the prevailing image of the tourist. But the failing of this analysis is that it ignores other powerful factors which also affect the imagery and reality of tourism. Even Leheny concedes that the change in imagery as a result of market forces may be cosmetic. Thus it must be considered whether other forces might result in real change in the patterns of behaviour by tourists. In other words, Leheny might be criticised for assuming that the marketplace is the sole arbiter of the practice of tourism.

The role of the state in defining tourism

The state has an obvious interest in tourism given the amount of income that the industry generates:

In 1995 tourism generated $A13.1 billion in export earnings for
Australia which is 12.6% of all export earnings for the country.
(Australian Tourism Commission, 1997)

The tourism sector also has immense consequences for employment in a
country, including the flow-on effects of tourism in creating jobs in other
areas of the economy (see French *et al.*, 1995: p. 264). A vibrant tourist
industry thus has far-reaching implications for the standard of living enjoyed
by a community. It might then be expected that a responsible government
would have a deep concern with the direction of tourist development for the
welfare of its citizens as well as the political advantages for the government
of the day in encouraging economic growth through tourism.

But the role of the state in regulating and defining tourism is complex
and potentially contradictory. On the one hand it might be expected to
facilitate the free rein of the market in determining the direction of tourist
development on the basis that unfettered demand and supply will generate
maximum earnings. But at the same time the state must also act as guardian
of the public interest and protect the community from the negative impacts
of tourism which might include low paid jobs and poor working conditions
(French *et al.*, 1995: p. 271); an increase in gambling, begging, prostitution
and crime, (French *et al.*, 1995: p. 272; Beke and Edwards, 1995); the com-
mercialising and trivialising of local culture (French *et al.*, 1995: pp. 280-81);
and negative effects on the environment, including pollution (French *et al.*,
1995: p. 287).

There is clearly some expectation that the state will act to both police
and limit these impacts of tourism on a community. For example, the
Statutes of the World Tourism Organization state the fundamental aim of that
organization as being:

> The promotion and development of tourism with a view to contri-
> buting to economic development, international understanding, peace,
> prosperity, and universal respect for, and observance of, human
> rights and fundamental freedoms for all without distinction as to race,
> sex, language or religion. (Australian Treaty Series 1979, article 3 [1])

> In addition the interests of developing countries are to be given
> particular attention. (Article 3 [2])

Thus the context within which tourism development is to take place extends
far beyond the simple mechanism of the marketplace.

A concern with the negative impacts of tourism, including drug abuse,
sex tours, child exploitation, crime and environmental degradation, led to an
international meeting convened by the World Tourism Organization and the
Philippines Government in May 1997. The meeting gave rise to the Manila
Declaration on the Social Impacts of Tourism which "urges governments and
the private sector to maximise the positive impacts of tourism, such as job
creation, while at the same time eradicating negative impacts" (World Tourism

Organization, 1997a). At the meeting the Philippines President called for the tourism sector to be "more equitable and socially responsible":

> The growth in global tourism has brought its share of problems and complications, some of which are serious enough to threaten the social cohesion and ecological equilibrium of communities.
>
> *Our idea of tourism* cannot simply be that of setting up a world-class resort for affluent tourists with thousands of unemployed and hungry people milling outside the gates. Rather we must engage the skills and energies of the many, especially those of the surrounding community, knowing that they can be among our strongest attractions. (World Tourism Organization, 1997a, my emphasis)

Such statements underline the manner in which the idea of tourism is being contested by a state concerned with the social equity of unregulated tourism development. Within this framework, to be a tourist means to be engaged in the delivery of social justice. In a similar vein another outcome of the Manila meeting was an agreement to work towards the formulation and adoption of a Global Code of Ethics for Tourism (World Tourism Organization, 1997a).

State versus marketplace: the example of child sex tourism

Perhaps the best known example in recent times of an attempt by the state to redefine the content of tourism is that of 'child sex tourism'. Although a world-wide phenomenon, much of the attention in this area has focused on Asia where the number of children working in the sex trade has been put at one million (World Tourism Organization, 1997b). A House of Representatives Committee in Australia quoted a study which put the figure at between 20,000 and 800,000, causing them to say that "even the smallest 'guesstimate' is appallingly and unacceptably large" (Australia, 1994: p. 8). The context within which much of this sex trade takes place is that of affluent people from developed countries visiting poorer countries which need the foreign exchange brought in by the visitors. The result can be an acceptance that the sexual exploitation of women and children is a necessary part of tourism:

> The flow of sex tourists is mainly from the economically developed world (Western Europe, Scandinavian countries, North America, Australasia, the Gulf States) to poorer countries of South-East Asia, Africa, Latin America and the Caribbean. However, some wealthy individuals from less economically developed countries such as Mexico, Argentina and India, are also known to practise sex tourism and there are a small number of sex tourist destinations (for example Amsterdam, New Orleans, Las Vegas) in affluent countries. Some countries in Eastern Europe are also now beginning to attract sex tourists and export child prostitution to other countries. There is

enormous variation between the receiving countries in terms of the degree of national level involvement in organising sex tourism. Many receiving countries are under economic and political pressures to promote tourism as a means of generating foreign exchange revenue. In some cases, there is what amounts to official acceptance of the fact that *tourism means sex tourism*, some government officials have spoken of 'sacrificing a generation of women' in pursuit of economic development. (World Congress Against Commercial Sexual Exploitation of Children, 1996, my emphasis)

For poorer countries, economic development and growth has been linked to tourism. The result is that:

[F]or some of these countries sex tourism (including child sex) is seen as an unfortunate but necessary part of tourism development. There is a frequently quoted statement by a former Deputy Prime Minister of a government in Asia when his country was developing its tourism industry. Speaking to Provincial Governors in October 1980 he said that they should contribute to the national tourism effort by developing scenic spots while at the same time encouraging "certain entertainments which some of you may find disgusting and embarrassing because they are related to sexual pleasures". The Deputy Police General responded to the challenge to promote tourism "by lengthening service hours on entertainment places...to welcome tourists". The link between tourism and prostitution is a mind-set in may places. (World Congress Against Commercial Sexual Exploitation of Children, 1996)

But this is not the only question. It must also be asked whether the mind set of 'tourism means sex tourism' is not just an unhappy downside of allowing other more appropriate forms of tourism to be promoted but is the essence of tourism generally. Thus:

[B]y treating the child as a commodity which can be purchased, hired, sold or thrown away the issue is no longer just a question of poverty but rather one of values — and in particular the values of consumerism.

This is a subtle distinction but of considerable importance for the way in which tourism is marketed. When tourism advertising promotes the values of consumerism and hedonism as the central goal of the tourism experience it is affirming the same values which make the prostitution of children possible. Tourism promotion must always recognise the need to 'protect children against all forms of exploitation and sexual violence attributable to the activities of tourists'. (World Congress Against Commercial Sexual Exploitation of Children, 1996)

To a great extent the values of the marketplace are about the exploitation of people and profiting from their toil. If the marketplace governs the tourist experience then we must accept that exploitation for profit without necessary regard for the consequences to people or places will be an inevitable outcome. There is thus an obligation on the state to protect the public interest in such matters and challenge the values of the marketplace. The difficulty for the state in doing so is that while it must protect the public interest generally, it must also promote the marketplace as the linchpin of the economy. The result might therefore be a failure to tackle fully the broader issues of tourism and exploitation. Where laws are passed this might mean legislation which is difficult to enforce and a lack of commitment to resourcing the implementation of the law.

Australian legislation on child sex tourism

In 1994 the Australian Parliament passed the Crimes (Child Sex Tourism) Amendment Act. This legislation amended the Commonwealth Crimes Act and created offences in relation to the sexual abuse of children by Australian residents overseas and the organisation and promotion of child sex tours. The legislation was passed against the background of concern about the exploitation of children primarily in South East Asia by Australian 'sex tourists' and was also based upon a view that a failure to do so would constitute a breach of Australia's international legal obligations under the United Nations Convention on the Rights of the Child.

But in spite of the title of the Act and this context it can also be said that the Act actually has very little to do with the question of the manner in which tourism is connected with exploitation. As the Opposition spokesperson (and now Attorney-General) said in the debates on the Bill:

> It is not inappropriate to suggest that the title of the bill is unnecessarily emotive.
>
> The term 'child sex tourism' used in the current title is colloquial but, in my submission, it is also inappropriate and even misleading because the subject matter of the bill is not, as the title suggests, limited to exploitation of children by tourists. The view of the coalition is that the bill could be more appropriately titled the Crimes (Overseas Exploitation of Children) Bill 1994. (Weekly Hansard, 1994a: p. 82)

This may indeed be a more accurate description of the legislation, but it also begs the question: why should 'child sex tourism' be designated as 'tourism' at all? As the above passage suggests, is there perhaps a line which, once crossed, ceases to define people as tourists but as exploiters? If so, what are the implications for the tourism industry?

It is clear that these questions are difficult for any government to confront as they go to the heart of the values of the free market which at present most political parties hold dear. But that did not prevent some members of Parliament from identifying the issues:

> It is quite clear that there is no single cause for child prostitution and, as a consequence, there is no simple solution. There are a variety of

reasons for child prostitution, as I have already mentioned, such as terrible poverty, lack of job opportunities and the problems of debt. As a consequence of indebtedness on the part of the children's parents or guardians or the children themselves, they are forced into bondage—almost a form of child slavery—prostitution and brothels. We know that at times parents, guardians or families are forced or tricked into selling their children into sexual slavery. We also know that, in the predominant areas of this activity, tourism is of great importance to the host countries. Because of debt or the desire to earn greater foreign income, tourism tends to take on importance over the welfare of those particular youngsters who are involved in these disgusting activities.

The desire to encourage tourism on the part of the countries that are the principal areas of this activity often leads to officials turning a blind eye to the activities. In some instances they are actually encouraging the trade or being involved in the trade, as some evidence has shown to be the case, particularly in Thailand. Cheap sex and a small likelihood of punishment are not insignificant inducements or incentives for those looking for that type of activity to visit those countries and gratify their peculiar sexual desires on the local population, including the local children. (Weekly Hansard, 1994b: p. 84)

Although this member identified the connection between international debt, poverty and the need to develop a form of tourism which exploits the weak, he proceeded to turn the debate against those who participated in the sex tours:

One of the sources of the problem is the people who are looking to participate in these offences: the tourists themselves— the paedophiles who are going overseas, either individually or in groups, and participating in some of this behaviour. (Weekly Hansard, 1994c: p. 85)

While such persons must bear responsibility for their acts, such an approach ignores the broader social responsibility for the creation of the conditions under which such forms of tourism develop. It thus avoids the opportunity to reconsider what the tourism experience should entail and how tourists are to be defined. Thus much of the debate tends to focus on the phenomenon as the 'ugly' face of tourism — but tourism nevertheless. A Labor MP commented:

This legislation should become the law of Australia. This parliament should say to Australians that our public norms apply to them no matter where they go. We have a duty to maintain our international reputation. I am fully confident that we are doing the right thing in passing this legislation. It may not always be able to be used but its existence will add a note of fear into the degenerate Australians who molest children in Asia. This fear is a good thing. I am pleased to vote for this bill, and in doing so give some hope and encouragement to those in Asia fighting the good fight on behalf of Asian children. (Weekly Hansard, 1994d: p. 147)

Another member said:

These people partake in acts that, if they were perpetrated in Australia, would lead to prosecution and gaol here. I think these acts on child prostitutes overseas are despicable. They are condemned by something in excess of 99 per cent of the people who live in this country and contribute to harming these children overseas, both mentally and physically...The Australians who do this damage our reputation overseas, and the term 'ugly Australian' which grew out of the 1950s is now taking on a new and more sinister meaning. (Weekly Hansard, 1994e: p. 153)

He continued later in the debate:

I want to speak briefly about the perpetrators of these crimes. They tend to be although I stress not always — the worst of society's specimens. They range in age from the relatively young to the quite elderly. A disproportionately high percentage of them are deviants and obnoxious characters who have difficulty fitting in socially in this country. (Weekly Hansard, 1994e: p. 155)

The difficulty with this 'demonisation' of the 'sex tourist' is that it ignores the possibility that many people participate in activities while visiting other countries which they would not engage in at home. Viewed in this way it is not so much a matter of targeting the 'deviant minority' but rather to prevent such exploitation by educating all tourists about how their behaviour might harm and exploit. The possibility of using this legislation to create standards within tourism was not completely ignored. A Liberal MP stated:

Closer scrutiny now will result in better legislation to enforce the law against these ugly Australians who abuse children in other countries. We need to ensure that when this legislation becomes law it will impose a standard of behaviour on Australians visiting other countries in relation to sexual contact involving children. (Weekly Hansard, 1994f: p. 147)

This latter comment does suggest that one role of the law is to set down the limits of appropriate tourist behaviour. But it still falls far short of a fuller analysis of the nature of tourism. This is to be contrasted with the analysis of the reasons for the existence of sex tourism in the first place, which acknowledged the 'realities' of the tourism industry:

Very few Australian males who have travelled widely in Asia have not been propositioned. Very few Australians that I know who have travelled to Bangkok, for example, have not visited Soi Cowboy or

Patpong. Most Australians, male and female, who have visited Thailand are well aware of the tourist nature of the sex industry in Bangkok. It is one of the big selling points of Bangkok. It is no different elsewhere. (Weekly Hansard, 1994g: p.151)

This member discussed the size of the sex industry in Thailand and its connection with the international drug market and hence the availability of money for corruption. There seemed to be a certain degree of inevitability that the 'industry' would endure, according to this politician:

I do not think that, until there is a will in the countries concerned to take their own actions to regulate their industries and to impose their own controls upon them, this legislation will reduce the sex industry or the availability of young boys and girls for western tourists in these countries. (Weekly Hansard, 1994g: p. 152)

But as another MP stated with an air of resignation:

While there is a market and the police are part of the pay-off, there will be no great change. Everything becomes a commodity, even the human beings. (Weekly Hansard, 1994h: p. 166)

Yet while the sex industry achieved some form of legitimacy — even if grudgingly — by virtue of its clout in the marketplace, the legislation was characterised as a 'brave' attempt to control the behaviour of tourists elsewhere:

All in all, this bill has my support. I think it is indeed a very brave act by this parliament to pass legislation affecting behaviour in a country other than Australia, and I think we should recognise that that is in fact what we are doing. (Weekly Hansard, 1994g: p. 153)

On the one hand child sex tourism, although condemned, is portrayed as an 'industry' earning foreign income for poor nations while the legal response, although supported, is characterised as being novel and problematic.

Social responsibility and the meaning of tourism

Many members of Parliament were deeply concerned about the manner in which the sex tourism industry made the nation confront issues of abuse and exploitation, but few were able to express this concern in terms of the nature of tourism. One MP came close, in saying:

Child sex tourism is an emerging industry which must be stopped right now. Possibly due to our physical isolation as a nation, Australians are naive in regard to the responsibility we have as tourists and the power we have through our financial capacities. The sexual abuse of children in developing countries, particularly by people from wealthier nations, is the most powerful and awful abuse of human rights. This abuse of human rights can also reflect the disparity of wealth within a nation.

> Legislators have a responsibility to show what is right and what
> is wrong. (Weekly Hansard, 1994i: p. 158)

This member then embarked on an analysis of the responsibilities of tourists
in this area which drew heavily on the biblical principles:

> The implications for children and their communities of the child sex
> tourism industry and child prostitution are devastating. When a
> visiting Australian male participates to any extent in the child sex
> tourism industry, he is supporting and condoning the kidnapping of
> children from their families, violence and the suffering from many
> sexually transmitted diseases including, in many cases, AIDS. In
> Australia the same men who participate in child prostitution in these
> foreign countries would not tolerate the same terrible implications if
> it were to relate to their own families. This is hypocrisy at the most
> horrendous level.
>
> The commandment and golden rule 'Do unto others as you would
> have them do unto you' has been a part of the Australian ethos from
> time immemorial. Australians are now living in an age where travel
> to overseas countries has redefined who our neighbours are. It is
> essential, therefore, that the philosophy behind this commandment
> is brought into a modern day context when dealing with children in
> these foreign countries. A mutual respect for other people, whether
> at home or abroad, underpins the very nature and substance of
> Australian society. (Weekly Hansard, 1994i: p. 58)

Such expressions of concern and distaste might be the foundation for
reconceptualising the nature of tourism. But for the most part the legislators
struggled with the imperatives of business and what is essentially the
exploitation of the poor:

> It is alarming to note that some corporations now use sex, just like
> alcohol, to service clients and socialise with their colleagues. (Weekly
> Hansard, 1994i: 158)
>
> According to another recent report about sex tours, men ques-
> tioned about involvement believe that they are contributing to the
> country's economy by visiting and exploiting young girls in that
> particular country. With that kind of attitude, obviously today's
> legislation is more than timely.
>
> That report, which I read also, stated that sex tours now have
> become part of accepted and entrenched business practices...Young
> impoverished girls come from vast squatter areas offering sex services
> to business and other foreign tourists. It is critical and crucial that
> countries like Australia — I understand that Germany is also intro-
> ducing similar legislation — persist in stamping out these abhorrent
> practices of exploiting young children. If we are blasé and continue
> to be complacent, then any action or publicity about the subject will
> just dissipate. (Weekly Hansard, 1994j: pp. 159-60)

Again one can observe the near resignation that unless condemnation continues the industry will inevitably continue to thrive. This is an important point because it shows how difficult it is to recast the responsibilities of tourism when the values of the marketplace have dominated the definition of tourism for so long. It explains why even its harshest critics continue to speak of sex tourism as a business or industry, even if they do so in disparaging terms:

> Essentially this bill is looking to provide a deterrent to two categories of people who feed off the 'sick' industry of sexually abusing children form overseas countries: firstly, the perpetrators of these insidious acts and, secondly, those people or organisations who promote, organise and profit form this vile form of tourism — the child sex trade. What we are essentially talking about is one of the most vile forms of colonial exploitation. (Weekly Hansard, 1994k: p. 162)

The same member, later in her speech, spoke of the connection between child sex tourism and the nature of tourism:

> As Ron O'Grady mentions in his material on child sex tourism:
> Tourism is the selling of dreams. It gives ordinary middle class people from Western nations the chance to live like royalty. In their own country the tourist income and savings may appear modest and they may have a somewhat boring and servile occupation, but once they enter a poor country they have the instant capacity to live as if they were rulers.
> This is nowhere seen more clearly than in child prostitution. Thomas, an American paedophile, is a carpenter. He travels as a tourist to Thailand and the Philippines as often as he can afford to do so. In Bangkok, he says:
> "They have a warehouse full of young boys and you can do whatever you want with them."
> The meaning is clear. The tourist is purchasing a slave for his own use. For a few hours the slave can be required to do whatever the tourist master desires and the child ceases to have any rights in the relationship. This form of modern slavery naturally opens the door to all forms of sadism. I think this is one of the worst forms of exploitation of foreign children in that because of ignorance and racism it allows an absolute abuse of power, which these people know is not tolerated in their own country. (Weekly Hansard, 1994k: p. 164)

Such a view of tourism goes well beyond the sexual exploitation of children and could also be applied to the use of cheap labour in the hospitality industry, transport and all the other industries which support tourism.

In the Senate similar points were made to those in the lower House, but a Greens Senator cast the debate in broader terms. She said that it was important "to look more deeply than simply legislative responses" (Weekly Hansard, 1994: p. 2493). She referred to the legal consequences in the

Philippines of a foreigner being found guilty of sexual exploitation, and continued:

> But no systematic attempt has been made to address the causes. Law alone will not suffice. The legislation must be enforced to be effective and the problems in enforcing it, and enforcing it consistently, are obvious. The receiving countries could be, on the one hand, less ambivalent towards the rights of sex tourists, being glad of the money from tourism, but, on the other hand, not pleased with the aspect of sexual exploitation.
>
> Protective measures — for example, prostituted children's refuges or safe houses to which the police could make appropriate referrals — need to be given far more support and investigation than has been the case so far. Reform of the police — ensuring that they are paid adequately, trained and educated and enjoy reasonable working conditions — would reduce the corruption that can inevitably result when they are not reasonably paid. We could follow the Sri Lankan initiative of creating a specialist child protection police unit with a special mandate to investigate child prostitution, pornography and paedophile rings. (Weekly Hansard, 1994l: p. 2494)

But it was to the causes of the problem that she made her strongest comments:

> Education campaigns need to be conducted. Responsible tourism requires public education to dispel the myths that child prostitution in South-East Asia is legal and culturally relevant; to increase awareness of the social unacceptability of child sex tourism; and to let the tourist know what is acceptable and illegal behaviour in a country and the penalties at home if apprehended. Tourism and airline industries should restrain their members from organising or promoting sex tourism. *Maybe we need a responsible tourist code of ethics* . (Weekly Hansard, 1994l: pp. 2494-95, my emphasis)

In effect this is a call for a reconceptualising of what it means to be a tourist.

The Act came into force on 5 July 1994. To date there have been only a handful of prosecutions under this legislation. In July 1997 it was reported that the Australian Federal Police had downgraded the priority they give to investigating breaches of the child sex tourism laws because of Government funding cuts, although a spokesperson couched the shift in terms of economic rationalism:

> Monitoring the movements of paedophiles or suspected paedophiles in and out of Australia is an operational priority for the AFP. There has never been any suggestion that this function would be scaled down or ceased but rather that we look at the most efficient way possible to maintain it. (Anon, 1997: p. 4)

As the values of the marketplace invade the mechanisms of the state one might question the ability of the state to redefine the legal boundaries of tourism. But perhaps more than ever this is exactly what the state must be called on to do.

From laissez-faire tourism to responsible tourism

Sex tourism can be regarded as the 'ugly side' of tourism with a simple solution — the shutting down of the sex tourism industry. The danger in enacting laws in this area is that it isolates one aspect of a broader problem and falsely suggests that it alone is the problem. While some politicians debating the Crimes (Child Sex Tourism) Amendment Act were able to make connections between child sex tourism and the more general problems associated with the nature of tourism in a market economy, few seemed capable of identifying the solution in terms of a recasting of the essence of tourism.

There is little doubt that it is easy to be horrified by the sexual exploitation of children and support any move which is perceived to address that concern. But it is not so easy to construct the debate in terms of the nature of tourism when most countries are coming to rely more heavily on that industry for the generation of wealth. Simply, how could the legislators say that child sexual exploitation was one of the natural consequences of an exploitative industry — tourism — when the same industry is being relied on in their own country to create work and money? At one level the Crimes (Child Sex Tourism) Amendment Act puts the problem 'over there' in another country — yet can it be seriously argued that the sexual exploitation of children by tourists does not occur in Australia too?

But the larger issue is the extent to which the question of the definition of tourism should be raised only in relation to sex tourism. The environmental impact of tourism, the forced resettlement of people to make way for tourist development, the creation of low skilled and seasonal jobs in the tourism industry and the exploitation of child labour in the tourism industry are also an aspect of this discussion (see e.g. *New Internationalist*, No. 245, July 1993: p. 19). Tourists who travel to countries who engage in these practices can also be seen as supporting these forms of exploitation.

Debates about the nature of tourism and the extent to which it infringes human rights or can be reformed for the betterment of all have taken place for many years (see e.g. Crick, 1989: p. 320). But it seems timely to consider the extent to which the values of the marketplace have begun to distort the definition of tourism when the state appears to be stepping back from its traditional role of articulating the public interest. A definition of tourism which promotes social responsibility will only occur if the state challenges the values of the marketplace.

References

Anon (1997) 'Police scale down war on sex tours', *The Sunday Age*, 20 July: p. 4.

Australia (1978) *Parliament of the Commonwealth of Australia Final Report of the House of Representatives Select Committee on Tourism.* Canberra: Australian Government Publishing Service.

———— House of Representatives Standing Committee on Legal and Constitutional Affairs Advisory Report Crimes (Child Sex Tourism) Amendment Bill 1994 (Parliament of the Commonwealth of Australia).

Australian Tourism Commission (1997) *Facts and figures.* http://tourism.gov.au/factsfig.html, 8 January, 1997.

Australian Treaty Series (1979) *World Tourism Organization Statutes*, No. 15. Canberra: Australian Government Publishing Service.

Beke, B. and Edwards, B. (1995) 'Managing deviant tourist behaviour' in G. J. Ashworth & A. G. J. Dietvorst (eds) *Tourism and spatial transformations: Implications for policy and planning.* Oxford, CAB International.

Crick, M. (1989) 'Representations of international tourism in the social sciences: Sun, sex, sights, savings and servility', *Vol. 18 Annual Review of Anthropology* Vol. 18: pp. 307-344.

Ennew, J. (1986) *The sexual exploitation of children.* New York: St Martin's Press.

French, C. N., Craig-Smith, S. J. and Collier, A. (1995) *Principles of tourism.* Melbourne: Longman.

Hall, C.M. (1995) *Introduction to tourism in Australia: Impacts, planning and development* (2nd edn.). Melbourne: Longman.

Lengkeek, J. (1995) 'Materializing the imagined: On the dynamics and assessment of tourist recreational transformation processes', in G. J. Ashworth & A. G. J. Dietvorst (eds) *Tourism and spatial transformations: Implications for policy and planning.* Oxford: CAB International, pp. 17-36.

Leheny, D. (1995) 'A political economy of Asian sex tourism', *Annals of Tourism Research* Vol. 22: pp. 367-384.

O'Grady, R. (ed) (1980) *Third World Tourism:* Report of a workshop on tourism held in Manila, September 12-25, 1980. Singapore: Christian Conference of Asia.

Rughani, P. (1993) 'Tourism: The final brochure', *New Internationalist*, No. 245: pp. 7-12

Weekly Hansard (1994a) Parliamentary Debates, House of Representatives, 3 May 1994, (Mr Williams) pp. 79-83.

—— (1994b) Parliamentary Debates, House of Representatives, 3 May 1994, (Mr Filing) pp. 84-87.

—— (1994c) Parliamentary Debates, House of Representatives, 3 May 1994, (Mr Filing) pp. 84-87.

—— (1994d) Parliamentary Debates, House of Representatives, 4 May 1994, (Mrs. Easson) pp. 145-147.

—— (1994e) Parliamentary Debates, House of Representatives, 4 May 1994, (Mr Cobb) pp. 153-156.

—— (1994f) Parliamentary Debates, House of Representatives, 4 May 1994, (Ms Worth) pp. 147-150.

—— (1994g) Parliamentary Debates, House of Representatives, 4 May 1994, (Mr Cleeland) pp. 150-153.

—— (1994h) Parliamentary Debates, House of Representatives, 4 May 1994, (Mr Adams) pp. 165-166.

—— (1994i) Parliamentary Debates, House of Representatives, 4 May 1994, (Mr Quick) pp. 156-159.

—— (1994j) Parliamentary Debates, House of Representatives, 4 May 1994, (Mrs. Crosio) pp. 159-162.

—— (1994k) Parliamentary Debates, House of Representatives, 4 May 1994, (Ms Henzell) pp. 162-165.

—— (1994l) Parliamentary Debates, Senate, 30 June 1994, (Senator Chamarette) pp. 2492-2495.

World Congress Against Commercial Sexual Exploitation of Children (1996) 'Tourism and children in prostitution', http://www.usis.usemb.se/children/csec/216a.htm

World Tourism Organization (1997a) Press Release 'Tourism sector unites over social problems' (Manila, 23 May), http://www.world-tourism.org/pressrel/manila.htm.

—— (1997b) WTO News 'Campaign Launched Against Child Sex Tourism' (May), http//www.world-tourism.org/newslett/may97/childpro.htm.

Activities, Holidays and Activity Holidays in Scotland

Malcolm Foley and Gavin Reid

Glasgow Caledonian University

Background

Activity holidays represent one increasingly important aspect of what has come to be termed, in its broadest sense, 'sports tourism'. Those writing in the field (Law, 1993) have outlined the close relationship that now exists between sport and tourism in the modern world, where the needs of tourists are increasingly met by the international provision of sporting facilities and experiences. At the national level, for instance, Scotland is a popular choice as a sports tourism destination owing to its status as the 'home of golf' and its renowned ski resorts and sporting estates. It also has one of the most famous arenas in the rugby 'Five Nations' championship where home matches contribute much to the local economy. In relation to the subject of this paper, the increasing significance of activity holidays has been high-lighted by a recent study (Scottish Tourist Board, 1994) which stated that, on average, 1.5 million activity holiday trips were undertaken annually between 1990-93, with expenditure during these amounting to £255 million. It is, thus, increasingly obvious that activity holidays represent a sector of growing significance for those practitioners and their institutions interested in tourism and in sport.

The increasing demand for active holidays, in contrast to the sun, sea and sand beach holiday traditionally offered by Mediterranean resorts, for example, is a function of a number of different factors. These range from: the greater awareness within society in general of health and fitness matters; government 'Sport for All' policies encouraging the take-up of a range of sports; expanding incomes and free time for those fortunate to be in secure, well-paid employment or for those taking early retirement; and developments in advertising and technology (Law, 1993). The latter has been crucial in facilitating mass social mobility and a resulting international sporting playground for the athletic tourist (Pearce, 1990).

61

In addition, the increasing propensity to take short breaks rather than be away from work for too long, and for second holidays in the UK, are other developments that have contributed to the development of sports tourism (Haverson, 1997). Such a duration is apparently perfect for the 'one-off' sporting event, or the two/three day ski or cycle in the outdoors. Major cities have sought to use sports such as football, for which they are internationally known, to assist tourism by offering sport weekend breaks involving hotel accommodation, pre and post match entertainment and, of course, the game itself (Haverson, 1997). This linkage between sport and economic impact (Getz, 1991) forms part of a wider development in public policy for leisure which, since the 1980s, has seen the adoption of a more market-orientated approach as leisure increasingly becomes part of the drive for an enterprise culture (Henry, 1993). The nature of the Scottish landscape and the culture of outdoor activities evident in Scotland suggest that activity holidays may be made attractive to a mass audience, thus further enhancing this shift.

Activity holidays have been defined as "any themed or activity holiday or short break which is bought as a package commonly including accommodation, tuition and organised activities" (KPMG Peat Marwick and the Tourism Company, 1994). Crucially, this definition does not take into account day-trip tourism which is being seen as increasingly significant by local authorities keen to use leisure as an aspect of economic regeneration. For instance, it is apparent that some publicly-owned recreation facilities have applied to become classified/graded under the Scottish Tourist Board's quality initiative as venues for day trip and overnight tourism. Staff within some sporting venues have received 'Welcome Host' training, which is an STB initiative designed to enable organisations to: understand the value of tourism; be aware of local knowledge; improve communication skills; and improve customer service. It does appear that the tourism segment is becoming more important in ensuring the viability of sport and recreation management contracts.

Activity holiday operators falling within the above definition are predominantly encountered in Tayside (19% of the total), North Highlands (18%), Argyll and Islands (15%) and Moray, Badenoch and Strathspey (11%) ((KPMG Peat Marwick and the Tourism Company, 1994). Packages are generally made up of outdoor activities such as skiing, walking, fishing, riding, watersports, mountain biking and golf, with the popularity of certain activities related to geographical area (e.g. golf in lowland Scotland and walking in the Highlands). Operators within the activity holiday sector, who are said to number as many as 900 (KPMG, 1994), are generally small-scale they thus face many of the issues associated with small businesses such as marketing and business development problems. These difficulties are exacerbated by the 'outdoor' background of many operators which, according to organisations charged with disseminating business advice, such as Scottish Enterprise (SE) and Scottish Activity Holidays Association (SAHA), can lead them to prioritise their chosen activity over 'business' considerations. This being said, there are a number of operators who take an entirely different approach, carving out a specialised market niche for themselves by joining forces with local hotels and transport sectors to improve the quality of their overall package. Some operators have come from an agricultural background and, as that sector has declined, have used spare land not generating income to diversify into activities — such as quad-biking or four wheel drive circuits — for a corporate market, normally based locally.

Not only are there differences in the type of operators inhabiting the activity holiday sector, there are also differences in the types of activities offered. Operators can offer either single or multi activity breaks. The former are usually associated with committed sports persons keen to extend their interest in a chosen activity. In contrast, multi-activity holidays offer the sports tourist a range of activities with which to engage. It is this latter component of activity holidays that is deemed to be the most popular with individuals under the age of 55 years (KPMG, 1994). It would appear that both types of activity holiday have the potential to impact on the policies of a range of organisations whose remit covers sports development and sports participation. These include the Scottish Sports Council and the governing bodies of the sports mentioned above. Issues likely to be of concern are those also identified as interesting to activity holiday takers themselves, such as quality of tuition and safety standards The extent to which they had recognised the implications of the activity holiday sector and what their policy response (if any) was, formed one part of this research. Another important aspect was a consideration of the implications for sport and recreation planners, policy-makers and managers of attempting to capture a 'tourism' market. Previous research (KPMG, 1994) had highlighted the need for greater linkages between operators and those offering local accommodation and transport services. The possibility of greater linkages between operators and (say) governing bodies of sport keen to enhance their sports development practice appears to have been underplayed.

Policy context

The combination of an increasing demand for activity holidays, a perceived lack of a strategic vision driving the area forward, and increasing competition from countries with similar products (e.g. Ireland) led to an apparent 'meeting of minds' between the strategic bodies responsible for sport and tourism in Scotland. As befits a sector that operates mainly in rural areas, requiring access to the countryside for its initial and continued survival, the organisations involved were diverse, including Scottish Enterprise, Scottish Tourist Board, Forest Enterprise, Scottish Natural Heritage, the Scottish Sports Council and the Scottish Landowners Federation. The catalyst for the whole approach was a study into activity holidays conducted by KPMG and the Tourism Company at the behest of Scottish Enterprise, in association with the Scottish Tourist Board, Highlands & Islands Enterprise and two Local Enterprise Companies (KPMG, 1994). This proposed a series of recommendations, including the need for greater strategic direction by the public sector in terms of business and marketing and the need, at the local level, for Area Tourist Boards and Local Enterprise Companies to offer a 'onestopshop' for operators providing general business advice. What then followed was the creation of a National Steering Group, made up of a range of organisations, which could enable the creation of a strategic framework for the sector. The extent to which this framework supplied a sustainable direction with which to lead the area forward will now be explored via recourse to empirical work.

Judging by the comments made by their representatives on their key motivation for getting involved in the sector, a number of the above organisations had, individually, recognised the significance of activity holidays . Normally these comments reinforced the particular remit of the organisation represented. For instance, the representative from Scottish Enterprise identified activity holidays as "an ideal potential growth sector". This was particularly in relation to individual sports such as skiing, walking and mountaineering, rather than Scotland's traditional team sports of rugby and football, which were perceived as unable to generate the levels of income possible in the former activities. Such a description befits an organisation with an economic development rationale. Their remit thus prioritised business development issues by examining the constraints facing the sector, such as European Union legislation, safety and accreditation, access and marketing.

The desire of Scottish Enterprise to accentuate the commercial potential of activity holidays extended to financial assistance for the sector's trade association (Scottish Activity Holidays Association) and to organisations such as the Scottish Association of Country Sports (SACS) for the training and development of gamekeepers and the general promotion of sporting estates. Another aspect of the work of Scottish Enterprise in the area was to obtain greater co-ordination of Local Enterprise Companies (LECs). These organisations were deemed to have much input into the continued growth of activity holidays via capital development grants for resources such as archery ranges and/or money for the completion of governing body of sport awards. It was recognised, however, that each Local Enterprise Company has differing priorities according to their financial and geographical situation, with certain areas such as Grampian giving activity holidays a high priority while predominantly urban areas such as Edinburgh and Glasgow show little interest.

This paper has already touched on the existence of single activity and multi activity packages and, in terms of the future connections between Scottish Enterprise and sport, it is perhaps significant that the single activity package was described as "not our market ... ours is to get tourists into the market and spending money which the serious sports person won't do to the same extent as the multi activity family group". This raises issues for the holiday industry (a private enterprise activity) interrelating with a range of public and voluntary institutions pursuing potentially conflicting remits. For instance, the desire of governing bodies of sports such as cycling to promote their activity in the outdoors via the creation of new cycling routes may have a supporter in the Scottish Tourist Board, with its desire to promote activity holidays, but may come up against the conservation remit of Scottish Natural Heritage.

Another organisation with a keen interest in the activity holiday sector is the Scottish Activity Holidays Association (SAHA). Interestingly, the SAHA representative saw two definitions of activity holidays, one coinciding with KPMG (1994) and the other a much wider definition that includes cultural pursuits such as art and crafts courses. The Development Officer, whose post is currently being funded by Scottish Enterprise and Highlands and Islands Enterprise, outlined that these activities while "not traditionally seen as activity holidays, were used to develop the Association's membership nationally. Only traditionalists can define activity holidays as committed sports people". The officer saw SAHA as part of a wider strategy with a remit predominantly geared towards developing memberships and with the aim of being self-financing within three years. This had been done by developing a package of benefits, including the giving of information on marketing, how to package activities to tour operators and invitations to trade shows at reduced rates. A database of operators had also been constructed which was used to disseminate promotional material (e.g. the 'Active' publication) with the aim of giving the organisation's name and promotional functions a higher profile. The main motivation for the officer's involvement was the perception that "the Association felt there was a need for what I do...it is a good idea for a growing industry to have a strong trade voice which can communicate members' interests to the National Steering Group".

Not surprisingly, given SAHA's funding arrangements and the Development Officer's role in offering business advice to its members, the officer had greatest contact with the tourism team at Scottish Enterprise and the Information Section at the Scottish Tourist Board. These two agencies were described as the sector's "strongest players" due to their extended remit. The latter provided advice on American markets which was then passed on to the Association's members. Connections with Local Enterprise Companies was more erratic, although most had been met by the officer on a formal basis. At the request of Local Enterprise Companies in Thurso and Skye, audits of activity holiday operators in these areas were being undertaken by SAHA which would be used to construct a designated activity tourism brochure with a view to maximising their potential.

In relation to operators, the SAHA officer argued that the main obstacle limiting the continued growth in Association membership was operators' lifestyles. Their attachment to their chosen activity made it increasingly difficult, particularly if the weather was good, to reach them by phone and/ or to respond to their promotional material in the manner of 'normal' businesses. This is an obvious concern for an organisation such as SAHA preoccupied with business development and achieving a greater degree of trade ownership of the organisation. While some operators were said by the officer to "just want enough money to survive", there were others who took a far more commercially-orientated approach. One, in particular, was reported to have recognised the importance of good quality accommodation in attracting the corporate market. This was achieved, according to the officer, by the operator "packaging with other hotels and other activity companies such as off-road driving to offer more than canoeing, climbing and orienteering. He also does kids' birthday parties, corporate groups and conferences, basically anything and thus, while in the minority at the moment, that's good business development as we see it".

An organisation that was perceived as likely to be driven by objectives within which commerce was only one facet of their interest in activity holidays was the Scottish Sports Council (SSC). A recent publication by the Scottish Tourist Board stated that:

> ... given that 25 per cent of expenditure on tourism in Scotland is by Scots themselves, the marketing of activity holidays can have an impact on sports participation and increase skill levels. (Scottish Tourist board, 1996: p. 14)

It has been argued, therefore, that the SSC and the STB share a common interest in promoting major sporting events and that this needs extended co-operation. The Scottish Sports Council has advisory services and works with other agencies on safety concerns and appropriate qualifications for outdoor providers and activity holiday operators. It is also concerned with the existence of links to sports development given the existence of a captive market of sports participants while on activity holidays. The SSC in its recent policy document 'Sport 21', identified that sport is of value to the country as it "encourages inward investment, promotes tourism and attracts major events" (Scottish Tourist Board, 1996: p. 4). Similarly, there has been a recognition by the Council that the increasing demands being placed on achieving value for money from public spending was increasing the need for inter-agency co-operation. This has led to the creation of communities of sport which are deemed to "present a unique opportunity to create sustainable development: (Scottish Sports Council 1996: p. 3).

The representative from the SSC stated that the agency was involved in activity holidays via its input into the National Steering Group. Its main motivation was to ensure standards and safety within the industry, a motivation that had pre-occupied its predecessor, the Scottish Council for Physical Recreation. According to the officer, "When the SSC was formed in 1972 it took on the role of working with the STB to make sure that tuition was appropriate so that the public could go (say) sailing, and if the SSC logo was put alongside a particular operation in the STB brochure then the customer would know that the standards of tuition and equipment were up to scratch and procedures were well-managed". Another key motivation was that the SSC sees activity holidays as a means of introducing the general public, and families in particular, to a lifelong commitment to sport. The link with sports development was thus acknowledged with the officer arguing that the link was fulfilled owing to the existence on the National Steering Group of the Scottish Sports Association representing all the governing bodies of sport.

The officer pointed out that the SSC did not have a formal definition for activity holidays. His thoughts were that "it was more physical activity as opposed to recreation, requiring physical skill and co-ordination, progression of tuition and performance and proficiency". While he argued that the Council had invested resources into the sector, via the coaching courses offered at its three national sports centres as "a sort of activity holiday", it was recognised that the organisation would be likely to reduce its financial commitment in the area because of its strategy of prioritising youth sport and performance and excellence. As he argued, "limited resources of money, staff and time will see to this".

Despite their commercialism, the SSC representative had no pressing concern with multi activity operators. Rather, he felt that "the idea is good for beginners new to the outdoors to select from a wide sample which they can then return to later in their holiday for more experience". The only problem was deemed to be those operators offering both wet and dry facilities and securing staff suitably qualified across these activities. As the officer argued, "If the centre is specialising in watersports then, generally, instructors are likely to be qualified in all aspects e.g. sailing, windsurfing and canoeing. However, when you get a mixture of wet and dry then problems can arise". This was particularly acute in relation to seasonal staff who, even among some well-respected operators employ staff who lack the requisite qualifications.

Concerns had been expressed in the past over the demise of local authority outdoor centres offering activities to schools, and the resultant gap in the market for possible 'cowboy' activity holiday operators. This particular concern, along with the standards of part-time workers in activity centres, was deemed to be of decreasing importance due to the introduction of a licensing scheme and the recognition by operators themselves that increasingly discerning customers will no longer accept such an approach. The licensing issue was contentious for the representative of the SSC. The recent tragedy at Lyme Bay influenced the introduction, approximately eighteen months previously, of a statutory licensing scheme for commercial operators providing activities for those under 18. The scheme also applied to those offering any one or more of six designated activities. It was thus described by the SSC representative as "a statutory scheme for a limited range of activities and limited age groups ... it is too limited and should be widened to include all ages and activities". The Steering Group believes that by setting up a non-statutory scheme this will bring into the fold organisations such as the Scouts, Guides and Duke of Edinburgh Awards, while also extending the perception of standards beyond tuition to include accommodation and general quality of service. The officer believed that this voluntary 'kite mark' could provide a selling point for activity holiday operators, while also widening the net to catch those, possibly less discerning operators, who have circumvented the statutory licensing scheme by moving away from the provision of certain activities to under-18s.

There was a recognition that an expanding activity holiday market could put pressure on conservation which was why, as the officer remarked, the role of the National Steering Group was important in reconciling such potential conflicts by way of continued dialogue. One measure currently being considered by the SSC was based on schemes introduced in inner city areas of Birmingham, Manchester and Liverpool, where canoeing has been offered on local canals, along with the increased provision of climbing walls and artificial ski slopes. Such provision is seen as having the potential to facilitate what were previously seen as rural activities in urban settings.

As befits an organisation with a desire to promote communities of sport, the SSC had a number of connections with other agencies concerned with activity holidays. In addition to their input on the National Steering Group which meets four times a year, there were also a number of sub groups relating to access and safety and accreditation which meet more frequently. The perception of Scotland as being 'a very small place' was said to make the job of co-ordination easier. Contacts also existed between the SSC, the STB and Area Tourist Boards which brought practical results such as the launch of 'Golf Breaks in Scotland' publication. To consolidate the potential link between activity holidays and sports development, it was argued by the officer that governing bodies encourage operators to provide beginners with information on the sport's governing body, a list of local clubs in their area and advice on coaching courses.

To assess the extent to which governing bodies recognised the link between activity holidays and their own sport development policies, a representative from the Scottish Cycling Union was interviewed. Unlike the above organisations, the Scottish Cycling Union (SCU) had no policy position on activity holidays because they had no direct involvement in the area. The situation was attributed to holidays being perceived as being "about recreational cycling, whereas we are an organisation specifically concerned with competitive cycling". This view that there is apparently clear water between the two was contradicted slightly by the officer's perception that the sector could have positive implications for sport development in terms of introducing people to cycling. For instance, multi activity holidays were seen as "offering valuable taster sessions for participants ... introducing them to the foundation and participation levels of the sports development continuum". In a similar vein, the representative of the SCU saw a positive relationship developing between activity holidays and the attraction of international events, with one reinforcing the other.

The SCU officer stated that his organisation had invested "minimal resources" in the activity holiday sector, but that they would "probably" invest more in the future. The only role recognised to-date came about because of being inundated with requests to create an "educational process" for mountain biking. The officer argued that they thus "acted responsibly" by introducing a mountain leader's qualification "to make sure leaders are introducing appropriate standards, as defined by the governing bodies' code of practice". This being said, SCU had little contact with those organisations involved in activity holidays, although it is a member of the Scottish Cycling Forum, which includes Scottish Enterprise.

The issue of responsible use was one much in evidence in discussions with a representative from one of Scotland's local enterprise companies (LECs). The area covered by this LEC included Loch Lomond, which faces many conflicts between different groups seeking to use the water for recreational purposes. Much of this conflict has been due to the improvements in technology which have rendered jet skis more accessible to the general public.

The organisation appeared to be caught in a dilemma, in that they wanted to attract more people (activity tourists) to the area, and indeed had invested money in order to increase their chances of doing so, but were unsure if they wanted more people on the Loch itself. The lack of speed restrictions on the Loch raised the need for what was termed "responsible" activities and activity holidays. The representative argued that they wanted activity holiday makers who were "packaged", rather than the "maverick" who arrived with his jet ski caused havoc and then left. The preference for a longer-stay activity tourist sits relatively comfortably with the LEC's economic rationale. The aim of trying to package activities may become more difficult in relation to more "populist" pursuits such as snowboarding and jet skiing, as improvements in both technology and competition make equipment cheaper and more accessible.

In contrast to the above, the Scottish Tourism Co-ordinating Group have recognised the link between sport and tourism, stating that "many see their holiday as a time for pursuing existing interests or exploring new activities. This is an area of considerable opportunity for Scotland and one where we must expand on our traditional strengths". They make reference to Scotland's "strong reputation for golf, fishing, walking and sailing" while emphasising that "there are still plenty of opportunities to develop holidays based around a wide range of other activities e.g. cycling in Galloway, skiing at Aonach Mor" (Scottish Tourism Co-ordinating Group, 1994: p. 24). While emphasising the need for more long-term planning over such items as countryside routes, staff development, monitoring and marketing, they also highlight the possible need to re-package of the activity holiday product to cater for those looking for a range of activities, tuition standard and accommodation.

While it has been established that the definition of activity holidays within this paper applies generally to a rural setting, local authorities are increasingly viewing the tourist segment as an attractive one for their local sports facilities. One example is North Lanarkshire Council, which has facilities (Aquatec, Strathclyde Regional Park, Time Capsule) perceived as attractive to day-trip tourists. An officer remarked that the Council had identified a limited number of sporting attractions within the area that formed part of its overall tourism product. This enabled marketing to be concentrated where it was most likely to generate returns. The market was increasingly being seen as visitors from both Edinburgh and Glasgow, befitting the Council's geographical location between these two major Scottish cities. What had inspired the Council to link sport and tourism was earlier, heavy investment in expensive sports facilities which, in turn, led to analysis of how such money could be recouped while also generating more income for the local economy.

To this predominantly urban local authority, the definition of activity holiday was one which saw the market as 'incidental tourists' on a day trip or, preferably from an economic point of view, an overnight visit. Rather than the structured package offered in areas such as Perthshire, the sports tourism product meant the attraction of day and overnight tourists to specialist leisure facilities and the hosting of national and international sporting events. Events such as the World Rowing Championships had the double benefit of generating income for the Council while also offering good public relations.

Like the Scottish Cycling Union, the council had little formal links with other organisations involved in activity holidays. While the officer saw the potential for greater links with this sector, the geography of the local authority was felt to render more worthwhile connections with local sports organisations who were bidding for national and international sporting events. Few resources were said to have been devoted to the sports tourism link, a situation which was attributed to the recent reorganisation of local government and the increasing pressure being placed on departmental budgets. A dilemma facing local authority policy-makers and planners, however, concerning the attraction of tourists to their recreational facilities at prices subsidised by local residents. The officer interviewed did not foresee such a problem, arguing that, "unlike Edinburgh and Glasgow our facilities are not over-used and thus congestion is not a problem. To us our residents will always come first". There was, however, an appreciation that a 'balance' would have to be struck when closing particular facilities for events thereby curtailing opportunities for the 'prioritised' local public.

Interestingly, the officer did not think that local sports centre managers were consciously seeking to attract tourists. Rather, they were trying to obtain the prestige of hosting events that befitted their sporting background. This compared with her view of the process from, as she put it, 'an economic angle due to my tourism background'. The implications of these differing backgrounds on the continued development of sports tourism links is an area worthy of further investigation.

Conclusions

The study has identified a range of potentially significant analytical categories within the generic activity holiday product. At one extreme is the organised package, pre-booked by individuals committed to their chosen activity. At the other there are individuals whose participation in sport is incidental to the main reason for their holiday. As shown above, it is not entirely clear which analytical category policy is aimed at, and this may give rise to future difficulties in terms of policy implementation. It is perceived here that each of the categories raise issues which should be of concern to governmental agencies. For instance, if policy is aimed at the organised/commodified end of the product, then it is more likely to reach those activities which attract a high-spending family market (e.g. pony trekking), rather than pursuits such as climbing which, we suggest, do not lend themselves to the commodified experience. Similarly, in the name of achieving greater efficiency within a commercial product, it is more likely that the commodified sporting holiday will be aimed at existing participants via the granting of opportunities to engage in their sport in a more glamorous or challenging setting. The product and the influence of the policy community may thus be influenced by the nature of the participants and the activity, as well as the relationship between the two.

The concept of the lifestyle business alluded to by the SAHA representative highlights the problems facing strategic agencies seeking to commercialise particular operators. While operations providing certain outdoor activities (e.g. mountaineering and canoeing) may see the business side of the operation as purely supportive of their preferred lifestyle, this is less likely to be the case with operators attached to sports such as golf, which has a recognisable retail element. The existence of strategically connected activity holiday businesses involving local hoteliers and transport networks highlights that this is an area central to the commerce/culture debate.

The study also raises an issue concerning the rationale underpinning the development of activity holidays. The desire of planners to attract a family market for purposes of economic development raises serious environmental concerns, particularly in 'honey pot' landscapes such as Loch Lomond. Such potentially conflicting objectives may lead practitioners to target the apparently responsible end of the market, or, drastically scale down the marketing of the site to limit participation to those who already know of its existence.

Before the study was carried out it was felt that activity holidays would be an area of potential significance to governing bodies of sport. Theoretically their role involves issues of safety and accreditation, but it was noticeable that, in our review of literature, none actively endorsed an activity holiday. The nearest approximation was the endorsement by the British Surfing Association of a number of 'fiercely competitive' surf schools that are competing for business in Newquay, Cornwall, an area which has become synonymous with the activity (Harverson, 1997). The overall lack of governing body interest was surprising given that, in many instances, their sport is being used as a commodity in other people's businesses. It may not be long before organisations such as the Scottish Cycling Union or Scottish Canoe Association are asked to endorse particular holidays. While this may yet happen, it could be argued that the lack of a more proactive stance over activity holidays represents a missed opportunity for governing bodies of sport.

In addition to issues raised from the existence of commodified activity holidays, there are also those that arise as a result of the activities of the incidental sporting tourist. Increasingly, more and more sport and recreation facilities in Scotland depend upon income from day trip tourists. That facilities such as the Time Capsule in North Lanarkshire advertise throughout the central belt of Scotland highlights its role as extending beyond being a facility for local citizens only. It thus appears that those planning such facilities had as much of an economic development agenda as one relating to citizenship. What we are witnessing, therefore, is the use of flagship, branded facilities to (in part) bring activities and holidays together.

While the bulk of the paper has concentrated on rural pursuits, the subject also has a strong urban orientation via the association of sporting activities with holidays (Law, 1993). For instance, the staging of events such as the recent Badminton World Championships in Glasgow, attracts a large number of players and support teams providing a boost to the local economy. The attraction of mass spectator events (e.g. Euro 96) provides an even greater boost to economic development. The urban product does, however, raise interesting issues requiring further consideration. For instance, the motivation of governing bodies of sport organising particular events may, because of over-riding concern with sporting competition, lead to tension between them and the local authority supporting the event, owing to the latter's economic development interest. There is some mileage in examining the relationships between agencies working to promote activity holidays, but who do so from the basis of apparently conflicting objectives (e.g. the economic development rationale of Scottish Enterprise versus the conservation rationale of Scottish Natural Heritage).

The implications for local sports development will differ depending on which analytical category is being considered. As mentioned, the incidental activity tourist is likely to frequent a local authority indoor or outdoor facility on a day trip (e.g. Time Capsule), whereas the committed tourist is more likely to swell the population of a particular area (e.g. Speyside). What needs to be established are the implications of such participation for those seeking to develop activities and for the sport itself. For instance, is the continued local existence of some sports solely attributable to the tourism influx? If, as has been suggested above, activity holidays represent a growth area of Scottish tourism, what role should governing bodies of sport have in sustaining an individual's interest upon their return home? Similarly, how should governing bodies ensure appropriate standards of coaching within the commodities packaged by local hotels? There would thus seem to be a number of important issues for sports practitioners which should form the basis of future research into this expanding area.

References

Getz, D. (1991) *Festivals, special events and tourism.* New York: Van Norstrand Reinhold.

Harverson, P. (1997) 'Sporting holidays: A new industry', *The Financial Times*, 24-25th May.

Henry, I. (1993) *The politics of leisure policy.* London: Macmillan.

KPMG Peat Marwick & The Tourism Company (1994) *A study of activity holidays in Scotland.* London: KPMG Peat Marwick.

Law, C. (1993) *Urban tourism.* London: Mansell Publishing Ltd.

Pearce, D. (1990) *Tourism today: A geographical analysis.* New York: Longman Scientific and Technical.

Scottish Sports Council (1996) *New horizons: Directions for Scottish sport.* Edinburgh: Scottish Sports Council.

—— (1997) *Sport 21: Final draft.* Edinburgh: Scottish Sports Council.

Scottish Tourist Board (1994) *UK tourism survey.* Edinburgh: Scottish Tourist Board.

—— (1996) *Strategic plan: Progress report.* Edinburgh: Scottish Tourist Board

Scottish Tourism Co-ordinating Group (1994) *Scottish tourism — Strategic plan.* Edinburgh: Scottish Tourist Board.

Carnival and Control: The Commodification of the Carnivalesque at Disneyland

Deborah Philips

Brunel University

The theme park, and Disneyland in particular, is frequently cited as an example of a postmodern leisure culture. The theme park could be understood as a contemporary form of privatised and bounded carnival, but to what extent can it be classed as 'carnivalesque' in the sense that Bakhtin defines it in *Rabelais and His World*? In Bakhtin's terms:

> ... carnival celebrates temporary liberation from the prevailing truth of the established order; it marks the suspension of all hierarchical rank, privileges, norms and prohibitions. (1984: p. 109)

The theme park offers a zoned space for pleasure, contingent on and convenient to the city, yet apart from it. Sharon Zukin has charted the transition in the urban landscape from a multiple street culture into privatised development. She speaks of:

> The material landscape created by the joint efforts of speculative developers, elected officials, financial institutions and architectural designers respond to these conditions by merging public places and private markets, often under the management of a quasi-public urban development corporation. Significant public life moves inside from the streets. (1991: p. 54)

And as public life moves from the streets into the shopping mall, theme park or leisure centre, so the elements of carnival which must move with it can be that much more contained. These bounded worlds (usually requiring an entrance fee) can be policed and controlled much more easily than the carnivalesque can be in a public market place, street or common. As Shurmer Smith and Hannam have pointed out:

Our pleasure-driven modern Utopias have often quickly disintegrated into the harshest of dystopian confinements. Even such an over-whelmingly fun place as Disneyland is a site of control, surveillance and normalization. (1994: p. 179)

The theme park is not, however, utopian in Thomas More's sense of the term, in that it does not suggest itself as a complete alternative world. Rather, it is a heterotopia, a compensatory fantasy world, a site of leisure contingent on, and structured in, its difference from the world of work.

Heterotopia is Foucault's term; in *Discipline and Punish* Foucault (1979) refers to the disciplining of bodies of people in the army, school, workshops and hospitals — sites of work. The disciplining of the body that he refers to is however equally applicable to sites of play, and the techniques that he describes are similarly employed in the heterotopia. The leisure site demands discipline without any visible punishment — the only punishment exacted at the leisure site (and that punishment is threatened rather than visible) is the removal of an uncooperative body — an unseen expulsion from the Garden of Eden.

Foucault describes the subtle processes by which the control of a large group of people operates, in his discussion of what he calls 'docile bodies', and he identifies new forms of 'constraints, prohibitions or obligations' emerging in the eighteenth century, the moment too of the beginnings of mass pleasure industries. According to Foucault:

... it was a question not of treating the body, en masse, 'wholesale'; as if it were an indissociable unity, but of working it 'retail', indivi-dually; of exercising upon it a subtle coercion, of obtaining holds upon it at the level of the mechanism itself — movements, gestures, attitudes, rapidity: an infinitesimal power over the active body. (1979: p. 137)

Disney is extraordinarily skilled at 'working' the body 'retail', and employs just such an 'infinitesimal power' over its visitors. Compare Foucault's description of the 'subtle coercion' of the active body with Eco's account of a Disneyland ride in *Travels in Hyperreality*, in which he describes the incessant manipulations of the participant's body:

Access to each attraction is regulated by a maze of metal railing which discourages any individual initiative...the officials of the dream, properly dressed in the uniforms suited to each specific attraction not only admit the visitor to the threshold of the chosen sector, but in successive phase, regulate his [sic] every move. (Eco, 1987: p. 48)

The same mechanisms of 'customer control' now operate at most European theme parks; all have similarly trained and controlling "officials of the dream". Foucault speaks of power operating through "... a policy of coercions that act upon the body, a calculated manipulation of its elements, its gestures, its behaviour" (1979: p. 138).

The architecture of the theme park itself acts upon the body of visitors, and every move that each visitor makes is strictly controlled by the cast members of Disneyland. But the policing is not immediately apparent — it is both invisible and visible. In the theme park, the law is perpetually visible. At Disneyland, the custodians of the Magic Kingdom may be dressed like Middle European fairy tale police, but their function is no less to police. At Thorpe Park in England, the custodians are known as Rangers; the furry and colourful creatures who welcome children so warmly are also there to police them. Mickey Mouse himself may be an attraction, but he is also a very visible signifier of the corporation. For Jeremy Bentham (in Foucault's words): "power should be visible and unverifiable" (1979: p. 201). The police at Disneyland are cartoon characters, they are perpetually visible, but unverifiable unless one transgresses. Disney does not need to foreground its surveillance techniques. Instead it works through what Foucault describes as the 'micro-physics' of power: "Small acts of cunning endowed with a great power of diffusion, subtle arrangements, apparently innocent..." (1979: p. 139).

Discipline for Foucault also requires enclosure. The theme park is an enclosed and bounded site, although, like its policing, its boundaries are disguised. In Foucault's terms, it conforms to: "...the specification of a place heterogeneous to all others and closed in upon itself". Theme parks are also, as Foucault says they need to be in order to impose discipline, partitioned. Disneyland — which is now the paradigm for all commercial theme parks — was the first to organise its sites into different lands, generically themed: Adventureland, Fantasyland, Tomorrowland, Frontierland and Main Street, USA. Each of these spaces is screened from the others, and is defined through its theming and also through the appeal of each to different designated gender and age groups. The effect of this partitioning is to separate potentially conflicting groups. Fantasyland is the one site in the Disneyland park that is clearly signed as 'feminine', and is also the space which most clearly welcomes young children, in a geographical and symbolic alliance of the feminine with children. Fantasyland is firmly partitioned away from Discoveryland, which is the site of the park's relatively few white knuckle rides (the most spectacular ride, Space Mountain, is situated there) — and therefore attractive to teenagers and to groups of young men. For Foucault, partitioning effects the splitting of any collective body that the controlling organisation requires. The rules of partition are that the site should, as Foucault puts it:

> Avoid distributions in groups; break up collective dispositions; analyse confused, massive or transient pluralities.... One must eliminate the effects of imprecise distributions, the uncontrolled disappearance of individuals, their diffuse circulation, their unusable and dangerous coagulation. (1979: p. 143)

Disneyland appears to be a site of communality, in which crowds of people mingle together. Theme park rides appear to present a collectivity of people, united in their screaming — but participation in the ride reveals that participants are effectively fragmented, seats are arranged in pairs, or at the most, a nuclear family of four, as they are in restaurant and cafes on the site. The normalising effect is that the convention is not to speak to strangers, the visitor can participate in the carnival to some extent, but, generally, will not speak to anyone other than the group that they came with. And organising mechanisms for the uncontrolled disappearance of individuals are very visible, in the arrangements for lost children, and the siting of meeting points. Circulation around attractions is clearly marked out, through maps, sign posting and the organisation of queues.

Certainly, elements of the carnivalesque are present at Disneyland and at theme parks, they offer a Bakhtinian banquet, an encouragement towards excess, an inversion of many of the normative values. There are clowns and grotesque bodies to be gazed at — but — what are presented as buskers and hustlers are all employed by the site; agents of the privatised space. In Disney's language, these are 'cast members', who are themselves subject to rigorous controls and who are themselves controlling of the crowds. Apparently spontaneous clowns are employed to pacify restless queues at the rides, buskers are sent around the theme park to rally crowds to enjoy themselves, stalls are wheeled around the site to offer souvenirs and beverages branded with the name of the theme park, or with the names of what Disney calls their 'family of sponsors'. There are apparent transient pluralities at the theme park site, clowns, stall holders mimic the effects of a fairground heterogeneity — but although these 'cast members' may be costumed differently, they will all be licensed and controlled from a central base, and sent to specified parts of the park by mobile phones. As the manager of Thorpe park describes (in language that clearly owes much to Disney management speak): "I'm constantly monitoring rides and adjusting cast-levels to control queue lineage and foot-flow" (Randell, 1997: p. 3).

Timetabling, according to Foucault, is another form of regulation, which functions to: "establish rhythms, impose particular occupations, regulate the cycles of repetition" (1979: p. 149). The leisure activities of Disneyland are as strictly timetabled as any form of work, in the timetabling of performances and events. The Main Street Parade show times operate to regulate the flow of visitors to particular sites at particular times. The final nightly parade draws spectators to the central area of Main Street. Visitors are advised that the best vantage point for the final spectacle of a fireworks display is from in front of the fairy tale castle — the nearest point to the exit, and the point from which a crowd can be most easily dispersed.

All these forms of 'subtle arrangement' must be organised from a central agency of control, which Foucault describes as a Panopticon:

> It is a type of location of bodies in space, of distribution of individuals
> in relation to one another, of hierarchical organisation, of disposition
> of centres and channels of power, of definition of the instruments and
> modes of intervention of power, which can be implemented in hospi-
> tals, workshops, schools, prisons. Whenever one is dealing with a

multiplicity of individuals on whom a task or a particular form of behaviour must be imposed, the panoptic schema may be used. (1979: p. 204)

The panoptic schema need no longer be architectural but can become electronic, in the form of the surveillance camera, as Foucault explains:

> The perfect disciplinary apparatus would make it possible for a single gaze to see everything constantly...: a perfect eye that nothing would escape and a centre towards which all gazes would be turned. (1979: p. 173)

If visitors are not in fact under the perpetual surveillance of a single gaze at Disneyland, they can be made to feel as if they were. For Foucault:

> ... the major effect of the Panopticon: is to induce in the inmate a state of conscious and permanent visibility that assures the automatic functioning of its power. So to arrange things that the surveillance is permanent in its effect, even if it is discontinuous in its action; that the perfection of power should tend to render its actual exercise unnecessary; that this architectural apparatus should be a machine for creating and sustaining a power relation independent of the person who exercises it. (1979: p. 201)

The unofficial Disney site on the Web is dominated by tales of the placing of surveillance cameras at the Disney sites — these are, as with most Web material, unverifiable, but they do testify to a generalised belief that Disneyland operates through constant surveillance. A range of cameras across the site can illuminate everything, and converge in an invisible central control booth. Alan Randell, manager of Thorpe Park describes: "... having a radio, so everything that happens in the park comes over and I know about it immediately, whether its inside No Way Out ... over the Flying Fish by Pot Bellies or on Miss Hippo's Fungle Safari" (Randell, 1997: p. 3). As Foucault puts it: "Inspection functions ceaselessly. The gaze is alert everywhere" (1979: p. 195).

For Foucault, the panopticon works through the paradox of surveillance being perpetually present, while never making itself visible: "The Panopticon is a machine for dissociating the see/being seen dyad: in the peripheric ring, one is totally seen, without ever seeing; in the central tower, one sees everything without ever being seen" (1979: p. 202)

One of the features of Disneyland is the invisibility of the mechanics of the site. Even from the top of the Swiss Robinson tree house, the highest point, which apparently gives a panoramic view over the park, it is not possible to see the offices, bins, dressing rooms for the 'cast members' and all the paraphernalia required for an operation of that size. These are all buried underground. Disney does not need to be seen to exercise its power:

> A real subjection is born mechanically from a fictitious relation. So it is not necessary to use force to constrain the convict to good

behaviour, the madman to calm, the worker to work, the schoolboy
to application, the patient to the observation of the regulations. (1979:
p. 202)

Or, it could be added, the theme park customer. Nor is it necessary to use
force to ensure that a 'good time' is contained within the parameters of
normative behaviour. The panopticon also allows for the surveillance not only
of visitors (or inmates) but also of employees:

In this central tower, the director may spy on all the employees he
has under his orders: nurses, doctors, foremen, teachers, warders;
he will be able to judge them continuously, alter their behaviour,
impose upon them the methods he thinks best .... (1979: p. 204)

Disneyland's control over its 'cast-members' is notorious — the corporation's
clothes code (which extends to weight) for its employees, as Linda MacDowell
points out, works to effect: "...the establishment of corporate norms to which
the employees must conform.... The gaze of both the employer and of the
clients and customers ... ensure this 'normalisation'" (McDowell, 1995: pp.
77-78).

The Thorpe Park manager, Alan Randell, describes one of the first tasks
of the day as checking on his cast: "At 9.00am all cast members (staff) (have)
signed in and been surveyed for their costume, hair length and entertainment
presence" (Randell, 1998: p. 3).

For Foucault the panopticon extends beyond the direct requirements of
Discipline and Punishment to become a part of everyday life: "The Panopticon
... must be understood as a generalizable model of functioning; a way of
defining power relations in terms of the everyday life of men". This generalizable model is familiar to consumers from the shopping mall, the leisure
centre and entertainment complex. As Foucault puts it: "The panoptic
arrangement ... programmes, at the level of an elementary and easily trans-
ferable mechanism, the basic functioning of a society penetrated through and
through with disciplinary mechanisms" (1995: p. 209).

The theme park deals with a multiplicity of individuals on a daily basis,
and requires of them that they conform to a particular form of behaviour.
Though a site of leisure, it is no less one of those 'establishments' of which
Bentham speaks: "a site: ... in which, within a space not too large to be
covered or commanded by buildings, a number of persons are meant to be
kept under inspection" (Foucault, 1979: p. 206).

Pleasure itself and sites in which large numbers of people congregate for
the purposes of leisure are potentially subversive and dangerous; crowds
must be disciplined and controlled and the potential for transgressive
behaviour curtailed. The drinking of alcohol is actively discouraged at
Disneyland sites, it was not permitted at all until 1985, and then only after
dark, and only at private corporate parties attended by at least five hundred
people. No drink or food purchased outside is allowed into the site, the

consumption of alcohol is now permitted at certain restaurants at Disneyland, Paris, but it has to be actively searched out. The individual is carefully fabricated in the theme park site, led, fed, watered. Visitors may believe themselves to be freely consuming and participating in a spectacle, but they are themselves inscribed as part of that spectacle. Their participation is strictly limited, and subject to all the subtle techniques of surveillance and control, visitors are disciplined to enjoy themselves in proscribed ways.

The theme park and Disneyland do apparently offer a carnivalesque polyphony, an apparently infinite variety of attractions, stories and fantasies. For Bakhtin, however, polyphony allows for (and he's writing here of Dostoevski rather than Disney): "a plurality of independent and unmerged voices and consciousnesses, a genuine polyphony of fully valid voices" (1995: p. 42).

This is precisely what the theme park and Disneyland cannot offer. Though Disney, particularly, may claim an allegiance with the world's favourite stories, nonetheless, the company's concern is to render them palatable to a wide ranging family audience. The 'Disneyfication' of their retelling involves a repression of the conflicts and competitions of languages, in favour of a generalised appeal to everyone.

Fairgrounds, local carnivals and market places can be read as polyphonic, in that they offer a plurality of voices, a variety of small traders, booths, and attractions which derive from different sources. The theme park may offer a representation (a simulacrum) of that — candy floss, small drinks stalls, retail outlets, but these are all licensed from one central corporation. Disney does borrow the vocabulary of the street, sites in the park are named after public spaces such as 'market place' and 'main street', but they are rigorously controlled and private zones. Wherever a theme park may be sited, there is an erasure of local specificity and of particular geographies and histories, The World of Disney can operate in Japan, Paris, Florida and Los Angeles and remain the same familiar multi-national corporation.

The object of surveillance is to ensure 'both the docility and the utility of all the elements of the system'. In theme park terms, that is the maximisation of the 'entertainment presence' of its work force (in the terms of the Thorpe park manager) and also the maximum consumption by visitors.

Carnival is constantly referenced at Disneyland, but the carnivalesque is only there in a form of commodification. Participation is predicated on consumption, and not production: you do not make your own carnival hats or flags, but buy them on site. Theme park Carnival is nothing but spectacle, to be consumed and not produced. The public are positioned entirely as spectators, invited to gaze but firmly discouraged from any other form of participation. Should any child or adult stray into the path of the Disneyland Main Street parade, they are swiftly dispatched. At the end of the parade, the watching crowd is separated from the procession by a rope which is held by members of staff, as the parade troops off, the audience is unable even to dance in the wake of the carnivalesque. The 'free interplay of bodies' of which Bakhtin speaks is markedly absent.

For Foucault, surveillance is intrinsically related to power:

> Our society is one not of spectacle, but of surveillance; under the
> surface of images, one invests bodies in depth; behind the great
> abstraction of exchange, there continues the meticulous, concrete
> training of useful forces; the circuits of communication are the
> supports of an accumulation and a centralisation of knowledge; the
> play of signs defines the anchorages of power; it is not that the
> beautiful totality of the individual is amputated, repressed, altered
> by our social order, it is rather that the individual is carefully fabri-
> cated in it, according to a whole technique of forces and bodies.
> (1979: p. 217)

If carnival is commodified in the theme park, it cannot however be entirely
contained: "the play of signs" is such that the signifiers of pleasure can never
be entirely owned by the Disney Corporation, however sophisticated their
centralization of the powers of control. The tales and the elements of the
carnivalesque on which the theme park depends for its presentation of
'pleasurable' experience are dynamic structures, however 'disciplined' their
pleasures might be.

References

Bakhtin, M. (1995) quoted in: Dentith, S. *Bakhtinian thought: An intro-
ductory reader*. London: Routledge.

———— (1984) *Rabelais and his world* (translated Helene Iswolsky). Bloomington: Indiana University Press.

Eco, U. (1987) *Travels in Hyperreality* (translated William Weaver). London:
Picador.

Foucault, M. (1979) *Discipline and punish: The birth of the prison* (translated
Alan Sheridan). Harmondsworth: Penguin.

McDowell, L. (1995) 'Body work', in D. Bell and G. Valentine (eds) *Mapping
desire: Geographies of sexualities*. London: Routledge, pp. 75-99.

Randell, A. (1997) 'White knuckles' in *Observer Life Magazine*, 8 June: p. 3.

Shurmer-Smith, P. and Hannam, K. (1994) *Worlds of desire, realms of
power: A cultural geography*. London: Edward Arnold.

Zukin, S. (1991) *Landscapes of power: From Detroit to Disney World*.
Berkeley: University of California Press.

Re-defining the Role of Trading in a Museum Service

Gayle McPherson and Malcolm Foley

Glasgow Caledonian University

Alastair Durie

University of Glasgow

Introduction

This paper analyses retailing in five Glasgow Museums during 1997. A growing emphasis on income generation strategies within the context of public expenditure constraints is explored (Walsh, 1992; Harrison, 1993). The paper locates changes in provision for museums and galleries within wider public policies, and evaluates the implications of these in terms of user requirements and managerial preoccupations (Davies, 1994). The apparent move away from a predominately educative role and towards a leisure management orientation based upon contract culture, measurement and assurance of quality, retailing and the adoption of commercial values and structures is at the centre of investigation (Lewis, 1989; Hooper-Greenhill, 1994). Inevitably, these moves conflict with a traditional, 'professional' view of the role of museums and their staff and emphasise a change in policy, direction and culture.

It is these changes in policy and direction which are of most interest and introduce aspects of ideologies of consumerism and consumption (Belk, 1995; Brown, 1995). The paper explores the idea that museums have now become entangled in the postmodern web and argue that what is unfolding is a de-differentiation of the museum and the shop. The concept of the post-modern, whether in the context of museum or elsewhere is highly contentious (Harrison, 1993; Lyon, 1995; Featherstone, 1994) and the authors hope to add to this debate by exploring the view that visitors now consume the museum (in part, at least) through their use of the shop.

Glasgow museums — the current situation

In 1991, the Director of Glasgow Museums asserted that he "would like to achieve one scale (for staff), going right through to the curatorial, technical and conservation staff to give more movement" (quoted in Museums and Galleries Commission, 1991). In 1995, he sought to implement this proposal and a re-structuring document was produced. This included a review of house management and supervision within each museum, as well as the reduction of seventy two museum posts, across all levels. It was anticipated that this would start in February 1996 and it was recognised that it would take some time to implement fully (Glasgow Museums, 1995a). To date the proposals have been implemented in part, although it has taken nearly two years and has been the subject of industrial action by two trade unions representing staff within Glasgow Museums.

Integral to the re-structuring was a review of all retail outlets including their staffing. In 1995 it was argued that the:

> ...performance of shops in Glasgow's Museums could be improved if there were better management controls in place and a stronger emphasis on developing and promoting the mission statement. There is also a need for improved accountability of the Council's resources, both cash and goods. (Glasgow Museums, 1995a: p. 12)

It was concluded that:

> ... the shops should be managed within the Marketing Section of the Department and staffed by dedicated sales staff. The manager of the shop operation should also have responsibility for product develop-ment. Motivation of sales staff would be increased by payment of incentive bonus. (Glasgow Museums, 1995a: p. 12)

In October 1996 this plan was implemented. Twenty three retail assistants and four supervisors were employed in the retail outlets. In reality, these staff were re-deployed from their roles as Museum Assistants and few of them had any retail experience, contrary to the conclusions and recommendations of the review. At the same time, a trading manager was employed to co-ordinate and run the retail outlets under the authority of the marketing manager. The incentive payment scheme for sales assistants, also identified in the re-structuring proposals, has not been implemented. The Head of Corporate Services indicated that the retail outlets have been set a target to increase sales by 14 per cent, in 1996/97. However, Glasgow Museums have also closed one day per week all but one museum, closed a further museum and sold the building; all as an apparent cost saving exercise. It is obvious that if there are reduced hours, then this presents less opportunities for sales.

This has not escaped the interests of the media and the re-structuring of Glasgow Museums has been subject to a great deal of publicity. The changing role and social purpose of the museum service within Glasgow has been questioned in the press recently, as has the Director's vision for the future of Glasgow Museums. For example, McAlpine, writing in the *Sunday Times*, questions the current perceived purpose of museums when she asks: "Do they function principally to conserve objects that the public, who pay the bills, may never see? Or should their prime function be to educate and — horror — entertain visitors? Spalding (Director of Glasgow Museums) and O'Neill (Senior Curator in Glasgow Museums) appear to give more weight to the latter" (McAlpine, 1997). Although Glasgow Museums purport to do both, justification for their activities appears, now, to be based on both commercial and educational arguments, as opposed to educational arguments only.

Glasgow Museums have also been subject to funding cuts of 8 per cent in 1995/6. These have been made under the new unitary authority and this has added pressure to generate income from other sources. An article in the Museums Journal indicates that the legal position of museums remains unaltered under the new authorities, although legislation permits new authorities to act as enablers as well as, or instead of, providing services directly (Page, 1995: pp. 18-19). This has caused concern among museums professionals, although the situation has not changed substantially as the Act only stipulated that "local authorities provide adequate provision for cultural activities in their area" [§14-19, Local Government and Planning (Scotland) Act, 1982]. The Act did not stipulate what amounts to "adequate", and thus some local authorities can choose to provide an outreach service or deem the service provided by the independent sector to be adequate. The main challenge for Glasgow upon re-organisation was to provide the same service with 8 per cent less funding, and also to continue to invest in development of the service.

It is an understanding of the rationale for, and move towards, commercial orientation, the change in the status of retailing and the adoption of post-modern practices within Glasgow Museums that this paper aims to reveal. For example, the recent bid to the Lottery Fund to transform Glasgow's Kelvingrove Museum, opened in 1902, into an interactive museum suitable for the 21st century is one step towards Spalding's belief in creating wider accessibility. A recent article by Arts reporter Duncan MacMillan states:

> [At Kelvingrove] The stress in the new display is to be on storytelling. ... It is a hi-tech labelling system that knows all the answers and leaves no room for awkward questions, reduces museum-going to story-telling soundbites. It proposes that giving the easiest answers to the greatest number of people is the true measure of success in the museum world. It betrays utterly the tradition of inquiry from which our museums come. (Macmillan, 1997: p. 3)

Of course, "from which our museums come" is a modernist interpretation of the museum. Some of the earliest museums were private: for example, Charles Peale Museum, founded in 1820, depended on entertainment and commercial activities to survive. It was only later, when private museums failed, that they were taken over and provided as public institutions, and issues relating to education and purpose were brought into question (Belk, 1995: p. 104).

Postmodernism in museums or museums existing in a postmodern world?

As museums are located by policy-makers both within a leisure services industry and an educational context (Hooper-Greenhill, 1994: p. 114), the debate concerning postmodernity appears to be particularly apposite in the context of this paper. The idea of the "postmodern" is highly contentious and one that is much debated (Featherstone, 1991; Lyon, 1995). This next part of the paper will try to explore the possibility that museums, through their shops, are becoming intimations of the postmodern condition.

Museums are caught in a juxtaposition of modernity and postmodernity. They appear on the one hand, to epitomise the 'entireness' of modernity; power, objects, foundationalism and institutions (Smart, 1994) and on the other, they have transcended this or progressed, depending on viewpoint, to become centres of what has been called "edutainment" (Brown, 1995: p. 112). Museums are controlled by their institutions: the hierarchies and power structures which until recently have kept them safe from external scrutiny. They may have had internal battles, but now that all public services, are called to account for their funding, museums are increasingly expected to justify their value as public institutions. Although, museums have escaped measures such as Compulsory Competitive Tendering, in 1994 the Minister for Heritage emphasised the need for museums to become more financially viable and accountable (McPherson, 1997) and now the new Department of Media, Culture and Sport is undertaking a review of charging in museums — another indicator of museums being placed under financial scrutiny (Hooper-Greenhill, 1994). The paradox of the post museum is evident here, as Duclos (1994: p. 1) highlights: "The post museum museum would ... become the object of its own study, an artefact in itself — one to be analysed and interpreted within its very own exhibition space". No longer is it the latest exhibition or artefact alone that is being debated in the museum world, but efficiency and effectiveness of the museum service and benefits to the user (sometimes "consumer") are also analysed. The language used to describe visitors has changed to accommodate the new focus. Visitors have become users, with spending power (McPherson, 1997: p. 139); further, consumers and museums are now perceived in some quarters as places of consumption. When did this happen? Did museums abandon modernity (or have the change forced on them from above or outside) and become postmodern overnight via a break or rupture consistent with the arguments of Feather-stone (1991) or, as others argue, is this an advanced stage of capitalism, not postmodernism (Harvey, 1989) or, further, has this postmodernity arisen out of an exhaustion of modernity (Lyon, 1995)?

For the purpose of this paper, the authors will investigate the view that the postmodern arises within capitalism and has an element of progression (Featherstone, 1991: p. 6). According to Featherstone, a number of these authors, including Cooke (1988) and Zukin (1988) recognise the spatial effects on society and refer to the rise in the service industry as one of postmodernization. It seems widely accepted that culture is a central theme for postmodernism but there is much debate surrounding cultures of consumption (Belk, 1995). Types of consumption have increased in scale and availability with the expansion of service industries. However, the debate between cultural democracy and democratisation of culture has, arguably, eroded in postmodern societies.

Emergent consumer cultures have heralded a move in emphasis from the production of goods to the consumption of services and with this the rise in museum collecting (Belk, 1995: p. 2) and an increase in the number of museum shops (Belk, 1995: p. 122). Alongside this, Harrison argues that a 'professionalism' developed in museums as service industries gained more respect and importance. She concedes that opinions are divided, with some arguing that professionalism improved what museums do, and others that it further divided the museum sector, thereby allowing some to become specialists and to secure their elite positions of 'knowledge' (Harrison, 1993: p. 165). This hierarchy and control by elites is at the heart of the debate over the future of Glasgow Museums. Management appears to be attempting to bridge that gap between the "front-line" museum assistant and the "remote" museum curator by introducing supervisors, managers and a pool of "flexible" staff who can be 'bought in' to offer advice on areas previously within the realm of the curator.

The museum shop as a postmodern experience

The idea of the postmodern challenges traditional values, order and rationality, yet at times emulates them in the 'nostalgic' representations of the past, through goods for sale in museum shops which appear to be "authentic" replicas. For example, in an article in *Heritage Development* about the opening of the new Thackray Medical Museum, it was asserted that the concept of the museum shop was planned from the outset. It stated that "the museum shop would offer visitors a truly original 'step into the past' shopping experience" (Heritage Development, 1997: p. 10).

Shopping is an experience which can be taken sometimes, but not always, as part of peoples' leisure lives. Department stores are set out in such a way to encourage impulse buying (Belk, 1995: pp. 127-130). Decisions may not be based upon rationality but can be spontaneous and part of the cultural experience of the time (Featherstone, 1991: p. 103). The museum shop is no longer an ancillary service to museums, but has become part of the overall cultural experience of the visitor. It is this role of the shop within the museum which interests the authors.

Museums have traditionally been places of order and security, set out by rational means to allow visitors to map their route around exhibits and to see all of them. The exhibits are either set out chronologically, scientifically or functionally. As Belk (1995) and Featherstone (1991) point out, shops are not set out like this. Initially they may have mirrored museums with their display cabinets and glass cases, but the role of the sales assistants was to engage customers to buy — to let them touch and try goods and to offer help and advice. One approach to the museum of the twentieth century, with traditional displays set in glass cases and 'do not touch signs', is to inform and educate the visitor, but not to encourage tactility. However, the post-modern museum is changing the experience of museum going; with the use of information technology and improved communication systems, such as individual guide tapes, the visitor has become a participant in the experience. Museums are having to compete with other leisure forms and cultural experiences and hence, in the late 1980s, 'blockbuster' exhibitions (cf. Foley, 1985) sought to attract new visitors and for the first time customers (as blockbuster exhibitions charged an entrance fee) to museums which, traditionally, had been free entry. The 1990s are witnessing another change in the museum experience, in that the introduction of integrative technology has added an element of participation and entertainment that was rare in the last century. For example, the Science Museum in London launched an exhibition on sport earlier in 1997, with the opportunity for visitors to compete against a computer in various sporting activities. The Natural History Museum in London has a "creepy crawly" exhibition with real insects on display and most of the exhibition requires participation to reveal information in some way. Linked to this, there are 'replicas' of the insects for sale in one of the three museum shops. Interestingly, gifts for sale in museum shops are mostly described as 'replicas' (not 'fakes') or based on a representation from a display in the museum, and are not described merely as gifts or souvenirs.

This point can be taken a step further to explore the consumption of the museum through the shopping experience. The museum shop is clearly linked to the objects and themes of the museum in most, if not all, cases. However, it can be argued that museum shops can become the museum and that museums can become the shop. Many museum directors would recoil at the suggestion — but, in reality, shops are increasingly being set out like museums (Urry, 1993: p. 131). An attempt is made here to transfer the concept of postmodernity to the museum shop. For example, at Kelvingrove Art Gallery and Museum in Glasgow, the shop sells various gifts, souvenirs and replicas taken from exhibits throughout the city's art collections. Some of the items for sale are jewellery and these are displayed in glass cases. Cards alongside the jewellery give information about the maker and provide details about the specific piece. The jewellery is locked in glass cases, for security purposes, but is this because the items are valuable or because they are original 'art'? It appears at this point that there is a de-differentiation of the museum and the shop. Furthermore, it appears that as much attention is paid to displaying, merchandising and selling items in the shop as there is to museum exhibits. A purchase in the shop is no longer simply a souvenir, but a gift or a replica. The shop appears to have moved beyond being an ancillary service to the museum to become an important part of the overall cultural experience of the visitor and, it is argued here, the visitor is now consuming the museum through purchases in the shop. The blurring of reality and image (Jameson, 1984a and 1984b in Featherstone, 1991: p. 15) has occurred in the purchase, between the gift-object and the museum itself (Greenbatt, 1991: p. 49-50, in White, 1996: p. 38). This relates to the fusion of reality and fiction, a hyperreality to which Baudrillard (1988) refers.

The importance of the shop has grown in the past ten years, especially with increasing emphasis upon self-sufficiency in the public sector by central government. The Museums Association believes that shops are no longer ancillary services and have, in July of this year, published a set of ethical guidelines for trading and commercial activities in museums and galleries (Museums Association, 1997). This publication argues that:

> ... wherever possible, trading and commercial activities should: aim to enhance public access, education and enjoyment, must be consistent with the museum's purpose, enhance the quality of the museum, take account of ethical as well as commercial considerations and should not bring the museum into disrepute or subject the museum's collection to unacceptable risks". It also states that those in commercial and trading activities are "supporting the fundamental role of the museum, and that they advise people involved in other areas of museum work should support their commercial endeavours and respect their expertise. (Museums Association, 1997)

This shift in focus and importance of the shop is placing a higher value on, and changing expectations of, the shop. The Tate Gallery and The British Museum have contracted trading companies to run their shops. For others, the introduction of a trading manager at the retail outlet is the chosen approach. In Glasgow a trading company is not being considered but, in the last year,a trading manager, with experience of the retail industry, and a new Marketing Manager for Glasgow Museum shops have been appointed.

The experience in Glasgow museums

The results of a recent survey of museum shoppers in Glasgow has revealed some interesting findings relating to consumer buying in museums. The paradox of using statistical information is not lost here: adherence to the postmodern condition might disagree over the use of methods that present logical positivism and rational methods of interpretation as evidence of experience. However, although the authors are doing just that, it is not without recognition of the contradictions and controversies inherent in this approach. Nevertheless, a significant criticism of the proponents of the post-modern 'cause' is the absence of any empirical verification of their assertions.

There is no explicit retail strategy or business plan for Glasgow Museums retail outlets. However, within the marketing strategy, two main aims are highlighted. These are: "to provide a service to the public which will enhance the quality of visits made to the gallery and to achieve planned levels of income" (Glasgow Museums, 1992).

Both the new Trading Manager and the Head of Marketing have attempted to change the image of shops in Glasgow Museums over the past

year. Some £8,000 was spent on new lighting for the shop at Kelvingrove Art
Gallery and Museum to make the shop more attractive. The long term aim
for this shop is to re-locate it in a more prominent position. Lack of finance
has been a drawback for the marketing team. Although Glasgow Museums
are trying to increase sales in the shop by 14 per cent, there are limited funds
for investment in capital goods. However, investing in staff has been undertaken specifically to train new assistants in retail sales, merchandising and
display. The Trading Manager and the Head of Marketing have sourced, from
some of the prominent museums in New York, new ideas and products that
could be successfully linked to Glasgow Museums and more widely throughout Scotland. It appears that, even in this relatively short time, and with
limited funding, the investment has achieved some results. On average, shop
sales over the five museum shops within this study have increased by 40 per
cent in the past year. **Table 1** shows the percentage increase in sales at each
museum over the four month period April to end July 1997.

Table 1:   Percentage increase in sales at Glasgow Museums

MUSEUM	Percentage increase or decrease from 1996 to 1997
The Burrell Collection	+39
Gallery of Modern Art	-39*
Kelvingrove Art Gallery and Museum	+66
Museum of Transport	+108
St Mungo Museum	+24
ALL MUSEUMS	+40

* Gallery of Modern Art opened in April of 1996.

It is apparent that this change in the performance of retailing has been recognised within Glasgow Museums service, and with this recognition has come
increased pressure to further increase sales and to introduce managerial
approaches. Yearly sales targets for each museum are now set and investment in an Electronic Point of Sale system is intended to provide up to the
minute stock and sales information for the Marketing Department. This will
highlight exactly what sells well, in what museum, and at what time of year.

The managerial emphasis is now on efficiency and effectiveness and operating the shops in a commercial fashion. This change is consistent with a move to attract more visitors and Glaswegians to the museum — thereby increasing the pool of potential customers. The potential for visitors to spend money through shops and cafes is high, given that entrance to all museums in the city is free. Glasgow Museums are trying to maximise that potential by selling some products unique to their museum shops and, accordingly, selling an association with Glasgow Museums.

In the 1997 survey of retail users, 1,391 users were interviewed in relation to purchases made in the Glasgow Museum shops. Users were asked about their purchasing habits within the museum shops. Some key findings are presented below.

Table 2:   **Whether prepared to visit a museum solely to purchase from the shop according to museum (both winter and summer)**

	Would Visit Solely to Purchase from Shop	
MUSEUM	YES %	NO %
Burrell Collection	39	61
Gallery of Modern Art	49	51
Kelvingrove Art Gallery and Museum	51	49
Museum of Transport	22	78
St. Mungo Museum	36	64
ALL MUSEUMS	40	60

As can be seen from **Table 2**, 40 per cent of those sampled indicated that they would visit one of the city's museums solely to purchase something from the shop. This appears to be significant in examining the changing role and social purpose of the museum service and identifying whether the museum is object or people led (Davies, 1994: p. 20-22). It is inferred from these data that some visitors are now using museums as shops: this the sole reason for their visit. In turn, Glasgow Museums are responding to the needs of such visitors by investing in change and re-structuring the retail outlets to exploit commercial opportunities.

Table 3:   Whether it is first visit to the museum

	First Visit to Museum	
MUSEUM	YES %	NO %
Burrell Collection	53	47
Gallery of Modern Art	65	35
Kelvingrove Art Gallery & Museum	27	73
Museum of Transport	41	59
St. Mungo Museum	78	22
ALL MUSEUMS	48.5	51.5

Source: Survey of Retail Users at Glasgow Museums, 1997

At Kelvingrove Art Gallery and Museum, three quarters of visitors have visited previously (**Table 3**). This is consistent with earlier surveys that indicate 75 per cent of Kelvingrove's visitors are mainly local and repeat visitors (Glasgow Museums Survey, 1995b). It appears that at the Museum of Transport, more than half of visitors have been on previous occasions. This has allowed relationship marketing approaches to be targeted at local visitors and developed in an attempt to ensure that they buy from the shop on a regular basis.

Table 4 isolates those who are regular visitors (once in three months or more regularly) and considers whether or not a purchase was made each time they visited the museum. Just over one quarter of these regular visitors said they purchased something from the shop every time they visited.

Table 5 (based upon all retail purchasers) shows that three-fifths of purchasers indicated that it would have made a difference to their enjoyment if there had not been a shop in the museum. These data suggest that many visitors to Glasgow Museums see the museum shop as a meaningful part of their visit and cultural experience

To take Kelvingrove Art Gallery and Museum as an example of those sampled, half (**Table 1**) said they would visit the museum solely to purchase something from the shop. Three quarters of the Kelvingrove sample (**Table 3**) indicated that they were regular visitors to the museum and of those, one third, said that they buy on every visit (**Table 4**). Kelvingrove Museum receives one million visits per annum and is the most visited museum in the UK outwith London.

Table 4: **Purchased each time visited the shop**

(only asked to those people who visited the museum
once in three months or more regularly)

	Purchased Each Time Visited the Shop	
MUSEUM	YES %	NO %
Burrell Collection	12	6
Gallery of Modern Art	6	20
Kelvingrove	27	22
Museum of Transport	16	10
St. Mungo Museum	8	3
ALL MUSEUMS	16	12

Source: Survey of Retail Users at Glasgow Museums, 1997

Table 5: **Difference to enjoyment if no shop available in the museum**

	Difference to enjoyment if no shop	
MUSEUM	YES %	NO %
Burrell Collection	61	39
Gallery of Modern Art	79	21
Kelvingrove	69	31
Museum of Transport	42	58
St. Mungo Museum	52	48
ALL MUSEUMS	60	40

Source: Survey of Retail Users at Glasgow Museums, 1997

Conclusions

Retailing, it would seem, is part of an important strategy for museum and gallery managers. However, it is not a long term solution to funding deficits, even where Glasgow has demonstrated achievement of the targets set for last year. In a recent interview with the Head of Marketing at Glasgow Museums, it was suggested that similar targets had been set for 1997/98; although they had exceeded targets this year, she believed it would be difficult to achieve these in future years. She went on to add that the introduction of sales targets had only occurred within the last two years and with the investment in new products and staff, this had produced early positive results. She doubted whether continued increases year on year could be achieved. At best, the authors suggest that good retailing practice can act as a short-term measure, whilst other long term solutions are sought to finance the future of museums.

A decision to increase retailing in both scale and importance is not a neutral decision. In Scotland, local authorities underwent re-organisation during 1996, and this has had an impact on services such as museums (Stone, 1997: p. 12). Glasgow Museums attribute the 8 per cent funding cuts imposed last year to the change to unitary authority status. The rest of the UK is only now (1997) undergoing this change, and already there are fears of funding cuts. Both political changes in government and the state of the economy play a part in museums' decisions to introduce more commercial measures to increase independent financial stability. Furthermore, Scotland has different legal requirements relating to free access. In Scotland, the Public Libraries Consolidation Act 1887 stipulates that local authorities are legally bound to allow free entry (Scottish Museums Council, 1997). It appears that, for the foreseeable future (in Scottish local authorities), decisions to generate income have to come from sources other than entry charges.

Viewing retailing as the answer to funding deficits does not take account of the role of the museum as protecting as well as educating and entertaining. There is a tension between displaying, interpreting, educating and entertaining the public with current collections, and predicting or anticipating what should be collected for the future. Museums are struggling with this dual role as trustee for the future and provider for consumers now. There is a danger that museum services will view consumption as being only at the point of sale and as part of an entertaining experience, thereby neglecting educational objectives.

References

Baudrillard, J. (1988) *America.* London: Verso.

Belk, R. W. (1995) *Collecting in a consumer society.* London: Routledge.

Brown, S. (1995) *Postmodern marketing.* London and New York: Routledge.

Cooke, P. (1988) 'Modernity, postmodernity and the city', *Theory, Culture and Society* Vol. 5, No. 2-3: pp. 475-492.

Davies, S. (1994) 'Back to basics: II', *Museums Journal* (September): pp. 20-22.

Duclos, R. (1994) 'Postmodern/Postmuseum: New directions in contemporary museological critique', *Museological Review* Vol. 1, No. 1: pp. 1-13.

Featherstone, M. (1991) *Consumer culture and postmodernism*. London: Sage.

Foley, M. (1985) *Economic impact study of Gold of the Pharaohs*. Edinburgh: Centre for Leisure Research.

Glasgow Museums (1992) *Residents satisfaction survey* (internal document). Glasgow: Glasgow Museums.

—— (1995a) *Marketing strategy for Glasgow Museums* (internal document). Glasgow: Glasgow Museums.

—— (1995b) *Survey of visitors to Glasgow Museums* (internal document). Glasgow: Glasgow Museums.

Harrison, J. D. (1993) 'Ideas of museums in the 1990s', *Museum Management and Curatorship* Vol. 13, No. 2: p. 160-176.

Harvey, D. (1989) *The condition of postmodernity*. London: Blackwell.

Heritage Development (1997) 'Thackray Medical Store: Creating museum retailing', *Heritage Development* Vol. 12: p 10.

Hooper-Greenhill, E. (1994) *Museums and their visitors*. London: Routledge.

Lewis, G. (1989) Preface, in S. Pearce (ed) *Museum studies in material culture*. Leicester University Press.

Lyon, D. (1995) *Postmodernity*. Milton Keynes: Open University Press.

Museums Association (1997) 'Ethical guidelines for trading and commercial activities', in *Museums and Galleries* (July) No. 3.

Museums and Galleries Commission (1991) *Local Authorities and museums: Report by a Working Party*. London: Museums and Galleries Commission.

Macmillan, D. (1997) 'Losers in the gallery numbers game', *The Scotsman*. 29 July.

McAlpine, J (1997) 'Glasgow's jewel is dulled by neglect, *Sunday Times* 2 February: p. 13).

McPherson, G. (1997) 'The changing role of marketing in Local Authority museums', in M. Foley *et al.* (eds.) *Hospitality, tourism and leisure management: Issues in strategy and culture*. London: Cassells, pp. 131-142.

Page, K. (1995) 'The powers that will be', *Museums Journal* (May): p. 18-19.

Scottish Museums Council (1997) 'Local Authorities and museum services', *Museum Issues* (1997): p. 3.

Smart, B. (1994) *Postmodernity.* London and New York: Routledge.

Stone, K. (1997) 'Swingeing cuts for Scotland', *Museums Journal* (March): p. 12.

Urry, J. (1993) *The tourist gaze.* London: Sage.

Walsh, K. (1992) *The representation of the past: Museums and heritage in the post-modern world.* Routledge. London: and New York.

White, K. (1996) 'Material culture meets the consumer: The Pitt Rivers, its shop and the public', *Journal of Museum Ethnography* No. 8: p. 38.
Zukin, S. (1988) 'The postmodern debate over urban form', *Theory, Culture and Society* Vol. 5, No. 2-3: pp. 431-446.

Leisure Consumption and the United Kingdom (UK) Zoo

Philippa Hunter-Jones and Cheryl Hayward

Manchester Metropolitan University

Introduction

The purpose of this paper is to consider the place of the UK zoo within leisure consumption. The paper initially reviews the separate literature on the UK zoo — past and present; the contribution to environmental education; issues of behavioural enrichment; the significance to the day visitor market; the relationship with sustainable development. Subsequent to this, the paper reports the findings of an empirical study carried out to determine consumer attitudes towards the concept of the zoo, information found to be lacking within the literature review. Conclusions are drawn and areas for further research proposed.

Literature review

The zoo — past and present

The concept of the zoo, "a general collection of predominantly wild (not domesticated or endemic) animals, contained in a total area of 110 acres or less, made accessible for human observation" (Pickersgill, 1996: p. 345), or menagerie as they were once called, has existed in one form or another for many thousands of years (Ironmonger, 1992; Worley, 1996). The traditional zoo is often characterized as diverse in terms of size, location, management and marketing expertise, number and varieties of species exhibited (Shackley, 1996). Roles are generally categorized as entertainment, research, education and conservation. In contemporary society, despite contributing to research and development in conservation and special breeding programmes, the zoo finds itself frequently at the forefront of controversy, often fuelled by increasing consumer concern over animal rights. On a more positive footing, however, various researchers attribute the zoo with cultural heritage status — "...today the wild animal is considered to have cultural value; it is regarded as part of our heritage, to which the whole of mankind and in particular future generations has a legitimate claim. Zoological gardens, to which these living items of culture are entrusted, therefore, represent cultural institutions" (Hediger, 1968: p. 8) — and cite the contribution of the zoo to environmental education and behavioural enrichment as justification for their continuing existence.

Contribution to environmental education

Whether zoos are privately or publicly owned, the visitor is the ultimate consumer of the zoo services and provides the financial support for the continued success and viability of the zoo. A compromise needs to be struck, therefore, between the needs of the animal population and that of the consumer. According to the World Zoo Conservation Society there are approximately 1000 zoos world-wide attracting an estimated 600 million visitors each year (Block, 1991). This offers what currently appears an under-utilised opportunity for the development of environmental education. Block (1991) proposes this to be one of the most important responsibilities of the modern zoo. The zoo has a unique and valuable core resource and can inspire the individual to take an active and constructive part in wildlife conservation. According to Robinson (1989) the zoo educationalist can be pro-active in their outlook and embrace conservation in its broadest sense, establishing a link between *in situ* conservation and themselves. Robinson (1989) promotes the idea of *bioparks*, where plants and animals are shown within their ecological system, arguably providing a greater understanding of the species involved. Literature suggests (see for example Kidd and Kidd, 1996) that life-long attitudes and behaviour towards all animals are based on childhood experiences. Long standing positive attitudes towards wildlife and their environments can be instilled in young people by effective education and observation. The zoo has a role to play within this process.

The role of behavioural enrichment

Empirical studies carried out at Edinburgh Zoo (Kidd and Kidd, 1996), demonstrate that the general public, outside the zoo environment, have a number of negative perceptions of zoo animals, for example, animals are bored, sad and indifferent to their surroundings. These negative perceptions are seen to alter to positive attitudes when respondents are questioned within the zoo environment. A greater awareness of environmental and behavioural enrichment is evident suggesting that zoo visitors are influenced by *visual messages they receive as they move around the zoo environment*.

One of the main problems found to create a negative image of the zoo relates to evidence of abnormal behaviour by the animals held 'captive'. Ames (1993) suggests examples of this behaviour to be pacing in big cats, swaying in elephants and large carnivores such as polar bears. In order to eliminate this behaviour, the zoo is looking to enhance the environment of the animals and to try to recreate the wild. Tudge (1991) reviews actions taken at Copenhagen Zoo to achieve this. Such actions include placing live fish into pools used by tigers. This is seen to encourage hunting behaviour and add to the tiger quality of life.

The zoo in the competitive day visitor market

Middleton defines a visitor attraction as "designated permanent resources which are controlled and managed for the enjoyment, amusement, entertainment and education of the visiting public" (Middleton, 1988: p. 227). The British Tourist Authority/English Tourist Board (BTA/ETB) (1996) reports that visits to all visitor attractions in 1995 in the UK rose by 2%, with 53% of all attractions reporting an increase in attendance levels. The last thirty years, however, has seen a decline in zoo attendance — 2% between 1976 and 1994, predominantly of domestic origin, in a period when visits to other attractions rose by 26% (BTA/ETB, 1996). Visits to wildlife attractions fell in 1995 by 1%, despite the hot summer and the fact that outdoor attractions in general fared better than in previous years, for example, country parks +7%, country gardens +5%, historic properties +4%, visitor centres +4%, farms +3% (BTA/ETB, 1996).

From an international perspective, as stated previously, according to the World Zoo Conservation Society, there are approximately 1,000 zoos worldwide, attracting an estimated 600 million visitors each year (Block, 1991). The nature and role of the zoo is generally found to be dependent upon the particular setting it is located within. Common throughout is the significance of the zoo to the domestic tourism market of the destination. Swarbrooke (1995) exemplifies this by reference to Chester Zoo (UK), suggesting that most zoo visitors are drawn from the local area or region.

Literature (see for example Block, 1991; Hutchins and Conway, 1995; Kidd and Kidd, 1996) cites a number of reasons for variable zoo popularity including: demographic changes resulting in an aging population, not traditionally the main audience for a zoo; changes in patterns of leisure consumption with the late twentieth century leisure consumer able to choose from an extensive range of leisure services, both active and passive; poor marketing techniques employed by a zoo; limited recognition of the role of the zoo as a place of learning and expertise; lack of funding; issues of animal welfare. Attitudes of the consumer are seldom considered. Hancocks (1971) argues that local authorities rarely view a zoo as a cultural amenity, in direct contrast to museums and art galleries. However, perhaps the overriding reason for wavering zoo popularity relates to the increasingly competitive leisure environment which the zoo finds itself within. Not only must it compete with other cultural and heritage attractions, but it is also in competition with an increasing number of successful theme parks. Leisure Consultants (1990) suggest that the attractions market is in serious danger of becoming over supplied. Therefore, in order to survive and succeed, the zoo must have the ability to overcome this competition, in part by drawing upon new and repeat visits. Furthermore, it must also respond with positive moves to cope with the opposition from animal welfare concerns.

Literature suggests that the zoo has a profound role to play and not just the perfunctory role of the visitor attraction. The zoo has come to be seen as a modern Noahs Ark, protecting threatened species and endangered wildlife from the encroaching 'flood' of species extinction (Foose *et al.*, 1992). Modern zoological gardens contribute to conservation in many ways, for example, by providing an education to the general public; raising awareness of important issues; through scientific research and the development of new veterinary techniques. The next few decades will be critical for the survival of many species, especially the larger vertebrates. The zoo offers a chance of survival for species that are extinct in the wild, or whose populations have become so fragmented that they are no longer viable without human intervention (Hutchins and Conway, 1995). Given this situation, the question arises as to what should be the ultimate goal of the zoo, captive breeding programmes or field conservation with a view to promoting sustainable development?

Sustainable development and the UK zoo

The zoo is a dynamic institution at a transitional stage in evolution from museum to an invaluable resource centre for future generations. As the core resource of the zoo is its animals, the modern zoo arguably has a key role to play providing a safe haven for rare and endangered species. The World Commission for Environment and Development (WCED) (Brundtland, 1987) argue that there is still time to save species and their ecosystems, a task which should be recognised as indispensable for sustainable development. There can be few people unaware of the threat to survival of many forms of habitat and species on the earth. Species have already been lost and many more will lose their battle against the encroaching demands of man. One would think that this would stimulate and revive public interest in the zoo yet the UK zoo finds itself at a critical stage in its life cycle. There are many contributing factors which have combined to create this effect including changing opinions on animal welfare and direct competition within the wider attractions environment as indicated previously. Yet despite this, this paper argues that the notion of the zoo offers a unique opportunity for the attractions industry to play an active part in the sustainable development debate. It is not the intention of this paper to review this debate. This has been extensively covered elsewhere (see for example Brindley, 1991; Pearce, 1993; Murphy, 1994). Instead the concept is introduced to provide a basis for review of subsequent empirical research findings.

The concept of sustainability is endemic in contemporary literature. The assumption that sustainability is desirable permeates through much of the writings and remains largely unchallenged. The many facets of sustainability are translated into the concept of sustainable development, a generic term, explained by WCED as development that meets the needs of the present without compromising the ability of future generations to meet their own needs (Brundtland, 1987). Sustainable development has been widely studied with research in general addressing: definitions and objectives; reasons; political ideology and approaches; evolution and notably components of sustainable development. Definitions largely represent the viewpoint of economists (see for example Goodland and Ledec, 1986; Repetto, 1986; Pearce *et al.*, 1990). Objectives are defined by Brundtland (1987) as: reviving growth; changing the quality of growth; meeting essential needs for jobs, food, energy, water, sanitation; conserving and enhancing the resource base; reorienting technology and managing risk; merging environmental and economics in decision making. Reasons for sustainable development include the recognition of the world's environmental capacity, the increasing pressures upon the earth's finite resources and issues relating to conservation and stewardship (Murphy, 1994). Political ideology and approaches to sustainable development are classified (see for example, Williams and Gill, 1994) as neo-liberal i.e. the environment is considered to be natural capital to maintain or renew; populist with an emphasis upon local trade and needs; interventionist including international co-operation, treaties and enforcement legislation. The evolution of sustainable development is summarised by Turner (1988), Brindley (1991), and Pearce (1993) into four development decades: 1950s and 1960s; 1970s; 1980s; 1990s. Implicit within these development decades are the economic motives driving policies and practice. So given that the aim of sustainable development is to maintain resources in harmony for present and future generations, what role does the zoo have to play within the debate?

Methodology

To determine this and consumer attitudes towards the zoo, a questionnaire was generated in three stages: stage one, literature searches and semi-structured interviews; stage two, testing of preliminary questions; stage three, modification of original questions and administration of questionnaire. Questions were formatted to determine the pattern of zoo consumption and to consider in particular: why people did not visit a zoo; what, if anything, would encourage them to visit a zoo in the future; public perception of the future role of the zoo. Those who had previously visited a zoo and those who had not were questioned. A questionnaire filtering system was included which enabled responses to be considered in relation to the respondents actual or perceived knowledge of the zoo. The questionnaire was administered to a stratified sample of 240 respondents resident in the UK. It was administered to every tenth person passing the interviewer within two city centre locations: Liverpool and Manchester (selected due to population size). The research was completed obver a four month period. The aim of the questionnaire was to consider the concept of the zoo in general. No reference was made to specific case examples.

Results

Of the 240 respondents, 75% (n=180) had previously visited a zoo, 25% (n=60) had not; 45.8% had visited a zoo more than once. The main age group who had visited a zoo was 35-44 (32.2%). The majority of respondents (56.7%) had visited a zoo within the last two years. **Table 1** (following page) indicates an encouraging level of repeat business during these two years, with no respondent indicating a sole visit during that time.

Table 1: Number of visits to a zoo

Frequency	Percentage
Visited twice	26.8%
Visited three times	41.1%
Visited four times	7.1%
Visited five times or more	25.0%

Not surprisingly, children were an important factor in people choosing to visit a zoo. 82.2% of respondents were accompanied by at least one child spending on average between two and four hours per visit (see Table 2). Large mammals were a popular attraction for people (32.6%) once at a zoo.

Table 2:   Length of stay at a zoo

Length of Stay	Percentage
Less than two hours	5.6%
Two-four hours	63.3%
Four hours or more	31.1%

Table 3 indicates motives behind a zoo visit. Motives differed between age group. What is interesting is that 41.7% of 16-24 year olds associated a zoo with education as did 29.4% of 45-54 year olds. All respondents felt that the zoo presents an educational opportunity not associated with other visitor attractions. Conservation was a popular association for 28.6% of 25-34 year olds, 37.9% of 35-44 year olds, 50.0% of 55-64 year olds and 75% of the 65-74 age range. Such opinions are reflected also in respondents overall perception of the future role of a zoo (see Table 7).

Table 3:   Motives for a zoo visit

Reason for Visit	Percentage
Value for money	18.9%
Treat for the children	31.1%
To see animal conservation	18.9%
Entertainment	10.0%
Education	20.0%
Specific Exhibition	1.1%

When questioned as to what people expected to get out of a zoo visit, opinions were equally divided between simply an enjoyable day out (24.4%), a response most popular with the 25-34 age range (40.9%), and learning about conservation practices (22.2%), a popular response for both age ranges 35-44 and 45-54. What encouraged people to visit a zoo is illustrated by Table 4. Location, previous visits and personal recommendation (through word of mouth) feature as the main influences. The significance of previous visits again confirms the importance of repeat visitors to a zoo.

Table 4:   Factors influencing a visit to a zoo

Factors	Percentage
Personal recommendation	21.1%
Previous visit	24.4%
Influenced by television	8.9%
Location (local)	28.9%
Advert in newspaper	1.1%
Organised trip	14.1%
Treat for children	1.5%

Why people had not visited a zoo formed a major part of the research (see Table 5). This detail was considered important in light of the increasing supply of visitor attractions and the inevitable competition for visitor numbers.

Table 5:   Reason for no previous zoo visit

Reason	Percentage
Concern over animal welfare	41.0%
Problems of access	7.0%
Poor quality of interpretation	38.0%
Alternative attractions	12.0%
Not interested in animals	2.0%

Although constituting only 60 respondents, this response provides a useful insight into factors which may limit zoo popularity in the future. Concern over animal welfare is perhaps to be expected given global concern over such matters, fuelled more recently by horrific scenes portrayed from Europe's worst zoos (Pickersgill, 1996). Problems of interpretation are more surprising, particularly given moves within the leisure industry in general to improve access and understanding. Given the fact that respondents to this question had not previously visited a zoo, the interpretation issue needs to be addressed and improvements marketed widely.

Table 6: Factors influencing a possible future visit

Factor	Percentage
Emphasis upon conservation	56%
Use of new technologies	22%
More 'tourist' facilities	14%
More interpretation material	8%

The responses to this open-ended question indicate the importance of conservation in the future success of the zoo. A clear thread running through the responses offered to this question was the need to maintain resources at the zoo in harmony. What the zoo must do, therefore, to attract those not currently drawn to visit, is capitalise upon the natural environment and seek methods of protecting the animals. Such a stance is encouraging as it reflects closely the aims of sustainable development. This suggests that the zoo is perceived by the consumer as a vehicle for offering a sustainable form of leisure activity.

Table 7: Future role of the zoo (all respondents)

Role	Percentage
Conservation	35.6%
Education	30.0%
Entertainment	15.6%
Scientific Research	18.8%

All respondents were questioned as to their perception of where the zoo should position itself in the future. The question was left open-ended with responses grouped into four categories as indicated in Table 7. Conservation and education (65.6% collectively) were cited as the most important roles for a zoo. In contrast, only 15.6% indicated entertainment would form the main role in the future.

Conclusions

Zoos find themselves within an increasingly competitive market servicing an audience which is becoming more discerning. Because the core resource of a zoo is an animal or plant, they find themselves at the centre of an ethical debate. In terms of the attractions market, the zoo finds itself in a unique situation. Not only does it fulfil a role as a genuine cultural attraction offering a form of entertainment, it also has a role as educator, conservationist and as a scientific resource for the life sciences.

A review of existing literature suggests that there is a lack of research charting the nature, attitudes and motivations behind a visit to the zoo. Furthermore, why people do not visit a zoo is seldom considered. Primary research provides evidence that people visiting a zoo are attaching more importance to watching and learning about the exhibits. The main influences on zoo visits are shown to be location (28.4%), previous visit (23.9%) and recommendation (21.6%) with children an important part of the visitor profile. As 82.2% of all respondents in the study were accompanied by at least one child, spending on average between two and four hours per visit, ample resources should be concentrated upon the under 16 market. Demographics indicate that this age group is shrinking. However, this research demonstrates that most respondents visit the zoo more than once (62.2%), therefore, retaining repeat business and encouraging new business will become a major consideration for marketeers in the future.

Questions establishing the perceived role of the zoo place conservation (35.6%), education (30%), scientific research (18.8%) and entertainment (15.6%) respectively. The significance of education and scientific research suggests that the zoo has a unique role to play within the attractions industry as a leader in education, in addition to any entertainment role it may hold. The significance of conservation suggests it also has a major role to play within the sustainable development debate. As yet there is little evidence within published literature that suggests this has been recognised and appreciated. Further research is needed, particularly given the unique opportunity offered by the zoo to see international animals at first hand. To remain competitive though, zoos must seek a more naturalistic setting for animals so that public perception and appreciation of wildlife, shown by the research findings to be a popular attraction of the zoo, can offer more of a positive response towards captive animals. The need to identify how the leisure consumer can best benefit the interests of the animal whilst promoting conservation, education and research will undoubtedly assume increasing significance.

A potential stumbling block for the future of the zoo highlighted by the research is the perceived lack of interpretative material available. Market researchers must pay more attention to the presentation and interpretation of a zoo with regards also to the environment as a whole rather than just the animals within it. The test for the zoo will be to integrate such opportunities into enhancing visitor experience at the zoo and providing the consumer with a greater insight into the value and purpose of the zoo.

A further problem complicating zoo success is that most of the time the animals are inaccessible. A zoo visit is largely a passive experience lacking in interactive exhibits which inevitably attract a larger audience. As the twenty first century approaches, the need for more interactive exhibits within zoos will be considerable. Through virtual reality — an interactive computer-generated visual display that can offer simulated situations — it will become increasingly possible to create an artificial zoo. Opportunities to make use of this and other technology must play a greater role in future planning. Utilised thoughtfully, the use of such technology could help address concern over animal welfare and increase the educational value of the zoo.

This study was undertaken in part to compensate for a shortfall in published literature about leisure consumption and the UK zoo. To check the validity of the research findings and to further understanding of the subject, additional empirical data is needed. A modified research methodology, including the use of focus groups and semi-structured interviews, would add a specialist perspective to the study. In addition, a re-focusing of the research upon specific case examples could provide further depth for analysis. The results from this study suggest that people are becoming ever more aware of the nature of the environment, the need for maintaining present resources and the welfare of animals. Further research is needed to determine how a positive attitude to a zoo can be established and retained if future success is to be guaranteed.

References

Ames, A. (1993) 'Environment enrichment for polar bears', *Biologist*, Vol. 40, No. 3: pp. 130-131.

Block, R. (1991) 'Conservation education in zoos', *Journal of Museum Education*, Vol. 16: pp. 6-7.

Brindley, B. (1991) 'What is sustainable? Some rules for the development road', *Ceres*, Vol. 128: pp. 35-38.

Brundtland, G. H. (1987) *Our common future. World commission on environment and development.* Oxford: Oxford University Press.

BTA/ETB (British Tourist Authority/English Tourist Board) (1996) *Visits to tourist attractions.* London: BTA/ETB.

Foose, T. J., Flessness, N., Seal, U. S., Deboer, L. M. and Rabb, G. (1992) *Ark into the 21st century.* Apple Valley, MN: IUCN/SSC, Captive Breeding Specialist Group.

Goodland, R. and Ledec, G. (1986) *Neoclassical economics and principles of sustainable development.* London: World Bank.

Hancocks, D. (1971) *Animals and architecture.* London: Hugh Evelyn.

Hediger, H. (1968) *Man and the animal in the zoo.* London: Routledge and Keegan Paul.

Hutchins, M. and Conway, W. (1995) 'Beyond Noah's Ark: The evolving role of modern zoological parks and aquariums in field conservation', *International Zoo Year Book*, Vol. 34: pp. 117-130.

Ironmonger, J. (1992) *The good zoo guide.* London: Harper Collins.

Kidd, A. H. and Kidd, R. M. (1996) 'Development factors leading to positive attitudes towards wildlife and conservation', *Applied Behavioural Science*, Vol. 47: pp. 119-125.

Leisure Consultants (1990) *What's the attraction — success in the market for places to visit*, Vols. 1 and 2. Sudbury: Leisure Consultants.

Middleton, V. T. C. (1988) *Marketing in travel and tourism.* Oxford: Heinemann.

Murphy, P. E. (1994) 'Tourism and sustainable development', in Theobald, W. (ed) *Global tourism. The next decade.* London: Butterworth-Heinemann, pp. 274-290.

Pearce, D. G., Barbier, E. and Markandya, A. (1990) *Sustainable development. Economics and environment in the third world.* London: Earthscan.

Pearce, D. G. (1993) *Managing sustainable development.* London: Earthscan.

Pickersgill, S. (1996) 'Does the traditional zoo have a future in the UK?', in Robinson, M., Evans, N. and Callaghan, P. (eds) (1996) *Culture as the tourist product.* University of Northumbria at Newcastle: Centre for Travel and Tourism, pp. 345-360.

Repetto, R. (1986) *World enough and time.* Yale (USA): Yale University Press.

Robinson, H. (1989) 'The zoo that is not: Education for conservation', *Conservation Biology*, Vol. 3, No. 3: pp. 213-215.

Shackley, M. (1996) *Wildlife tourism.* London: Routledge.

Swarbrooke, J. 91995) *The development and management of visitor attractions.* London: Butterworth-Heinemann.

Tudge, C. (1991) *Last animals at the zoo.* London: Hutchison.

Turner, R. K. (1988) *Sustainable resource management: Principles and practice.* London: Belhaven.

Williams, P. W. and Gill, A. (1994) 'Tourism carrying capacity management issues', in Theobald, W. (ed) *Global tourism. The next decade.* London: Butterworth-Heinemann, pp. 174-187.

Worley, D. (1996) 'Ex-situ conservation', in Spelling, I. F. (ed) (1996) *Conservation biology.* UK: Longman, pp. 186-202.

The Current Growth of Jewish Museums in Europe

David Clark

University of North London

Museums devoted to the culture, history or heritage of a minority group often appeal simultaneously to an internal audience and an external audience, to members of the minority group and to members of the wider society. This paper seeks to clarify and outline some of the driving forces behind the establishment of Jewish museums in Europe, focusing especially on the dynamics between minority and dominant group relationships.

The main contention is that the establishment of a Jewish museum is a dynamic process that entails the formation of various alliances. Such alliances are often quite complex and entail both alliances within the Jewish community and alliances with leading administrators and funding bodies within the wider community. Invariably, such alliances can only come to fruition under a favourable political climate or a set of favourable government or institutional policies.

The precise combination of factors will vary a great deal from place to place, and in a few cases such Jewish museums may even be set up without any initial involvement from members of the Jewish community at all, particularly in areas where such a Jewish population no longer exists.

The formation of Jewish museums at the turn of the century

It is perhaps not surprising to find that the first Jewish museums were established in the late 19th century. By then, museums were coming into vogue all over Europe, with the active participation of central and local governments.

In Britain, an Act of Parliament founded the British Museum in 1753, but it was not till the Museum Act of 1845, which empowered borough councils to levy a halfpenny rate, that the drive towards creating public museums really got under way.

As Tony Bennett notes:

> The nineteenth century transformed museums from semi-private
> institutions restricted largely to the ruling and professional classes
> into major organs of the state dedicated to the instruction and
> edification of the general public. As a consequence of these changes,
> museums were regarded by the end of the century as major vehicles
> for the fulfilment of the state's new educative and moral role in
> relation to the population as a whole. (Bennett, 1988: p. 63)

In this section four factors will be discussed which contributed to the
establishment of Jewish museums at the turn of the century.

Scientific endeavour

Museums all over Europe were themselves caught up in the scientific and
technical enterprise of the time, busy as they were, not only in the collection
of a myriad of objects, but also in the cataloguing and classifying of such
objects into some form of classificatory order. It was precisely this kind of
scholarship which formed the basis for the remarkable endeavour to examine
Jewish history and culture, as well as Jewish texts in a new light, under the
aegis of the Hochschule fur die Wissenschaft des Judentums, founded in
Berlin in 1870.

This new inquisitive mode of examining and re-evaluating Jewish history
and culture led to the formation of Jewish museums in other German-
speaking cities, such as Vienna in 1895, Prague in 1906 and Frankfurt in
1922. But the drive towards establishing Jewish museums goes beyond mere
academic inquisitiveness and scholastic endeavour.

Building bridges

Jewish European society reached an important juncture towards the turn
of the century. As Richard Cohen points out:

> It was not until the second half of the nineteenth century that a
> tendency to assemble Jewish ceremonial objects begins to emerge.
> And only at the end of that century do we witness the first strides
> toward the establishment of Jewish museums ... The turning point,
> then, in the collection and exhibition of Judaica was that juncture
> in the history of European Jewry when the process of leaving the
> "ghetto" was fully matured and the bulk of western and central
> European Jewish society had achieved emancipation. (Cohen, 1992:
> p. 209)

Thus, by 1890, only 20% of the residents in the Jewish ghetto area of Prague
were actually Jewish; the rest of Prague Jews had long since left the ghetto.
A similar pattern could be found in most other western and central European
cities.

Yet the path towards emancipation was by no means smooth. For Jews
in Western Europe it seemed that society, in terms of the host community,

was ready to embrace them and accept them as equals. In Britain, the first Jewish Lord Mayor of London was installed in 1855, the first Jewish MP in 1858, while the professions and the universities gradually opened their doors to Jewish candidates.

Nevertheless, the accommodation that successful Jews had reached with the wider society was still fragile. In the Britain of the 1880s and 1890s, the influx of poorer Jews coming from Eastern Europe threatened to upset the delicate balance that had been established between Jews and Gentiles. Hence, a major reason for establishing Jewish museums was the wish to demonstrate that Jews had made a valuable contribution to European history in all spheres of human endeavour, including the arts.

In Britain, the Anglo-Jewish Exhibition, held at the Albert Hall in 1887 to mark the jubilee of Queen Victoria, displayed letters, mementos and portraits of leading members of the Anglo-Jewish establishment, focusing on their contribution to British society (Kushner, 1992: 80). In Prague, the emphasis was subtly different. The focus was less on eminent Czech Jewish families and their achievements, and more on the long established links between Jewish settlement in the area and the Czech people. Hence, the museum collected items which would be representative of the whole Czech region and cover the entire period of Jewish settlement in the area, dating back to the middle ages.

The loss of the ghetto and nostalgia for a vanishing world

The loss of the "ghetto" has at least two dimensions; the physical loss and destruction, and the emotional loss, leading to a sense of grieving and nostalgia. Many of the larger cities of Europe, and especially the capital cities, were undergoing drastic modernisation at the turn of the century, and in many cases the old Jewish quarters were swept aside to make way for redevelopment. The rescue of Jewish artefacts, as a result of urban renewal and the abandonment of the ghetto, was certainly an important factor in the development of Jewish museums.

But it was more than simply an attempt to rescue objects. The interest of museum curators at the time was not only to rescue and preserve Jewish artefacts, but also, wherever possible, to document the way of life that such objects represented; in other words, it was also meant to be an ethnographic endeavour.

The sense of loss also led certain collectors, such as Isaac Strauss (1806-1888), to collect Jewish artefacts out of a sense of nostalgia for the old ways that were fast disappearing (Cohen, 1992: p. 212). For museum curators, however, the ethnographic concern to document the vanishing world of the ghetto was of greater importance than simple nostalgia.

Alliances within the Jewish community

Jewish museums do not suddenly emerge overnight, but are established as a result of a dynamic process that involves both the formation of alliances and a favourable political climate. As an illustration of this process, it is instructive to examine the establishment of the Jewish Museum in Prague, in 1906.

Three men were principally involved in setting up the museum: Dr. Lieben, a Jewish scientist, Dr. Stein, municipal councillor and president of the Council of Jewish Communities, and Dr. Hahn, lawyer and leading member of the management committee of one of the historic synagogues demolished under the slum clearance scheme. Clearly, the scientist could not have founded the museum without the active support of Dr. Stein, who held a key position within the Jewish establishment in Prague. Both Dr. Lieben and Dr. Hahn were interested in safekeeping the ritual objects from the two synagogues demolished at the time. The slum clearance programme, therefore, provided the necessary impetus for establishing the museum and led to certain alliances within the Jewish community that possibly might not have taken place otherwise (see Clark, 1994, for further discussion on the Prague museum).

The establishment of a Jewish museum often entails alliances involving different interest groups, as this paper will illustrate. Richard Cohen notes that for any Jewish museum to be successfully launched, there needs to be some form of accommodation and incorporation into the local Jewish community structure (Cohen, 1992: p. 232). As we shall see, however, many Jewish museums in the post-war period have been established as a result of the loss of Jewish community, which obviously makes the formation of alliances involving the Jewish community that much more problematic.

Jewish museums after 1945

The move out of the ghetto and the growing emancipation of Jews in the 19th century shaped the development of museums at the turn of the century. The Holocaust, which had such a devastating effect on European Jewry, has shaped much of what has happened in the Jewish museum world since 1945. While the Holocaust overshadows every post-war development in Jewish museums, there are many other agendas that are being played out at the same time. Some of these agendas include: the need to build bridges between Jews and Gentiles; the work of education and reconciliation; scientific documentation; research to focus on art and culture, on architectural heritage, on local history; as well as the need to stimulate tourist development. Not all these factors are present in each case, and each Jewish museum presents a different combination of these diverse agendas. For the sake of simplicity and clarity, five different foci for Jewish museums will be studied in turn.

Commemorating the Holocaust

There are many Holocaust sites in Europe, with either their own memorials or museums. There is now a growing literature on such sites (Hartman, 1994; Milton and Nowinski, 1991; Young, 1993 and 1994). However, attention here will be directed to Jewish museums located away from such sites of mass destruction, located instead in ordinary towns where Jews happened to live, prior to 1939. How such towns represent the history of its Jewish inhabitants varies a great deal, according to the resources available, whether there still is a viable Jewish community in the area, and according to particular local agendas.

Frankfurt has established quite an elaborate Jewish museum, opened poignantly on the 9th of November 1988, 50 years after Kristallnacht, the night hundreds of synagogues and thousands of Jewish shops were burnt and looted. The museum, which is run by the municipality, is housed in the Rothschild palace, acquired by the Rothschilds in 1846, donated to the Jewish community in 1912, and housing the first Jewish museum in Frankfurt in 1922. The museum focuses on the history of Jews in Frankfurt, from 1100 to 1950; including life after the war, the struggle back to normality and the foundation of today's Jewish community in Frankfurt. There is also a documentation centre, photo-archive section and a library on the wider field of German-Jewish relations, helping to put the museum on a sound "scientific" basis. As one of the authors of the special opening brochure for the museum writes:

> The aim of the Jewish Museum in Frankfurt am Main is to provide the knowledge relating to the history, culture and religion of the Jewish people necessary for a dialogue between Jews and non-Jews....
> (Heuberger, 1988: p. 22)

Elsewhere, the Jewish museum in Essen typifies the contradictory responses of smaller towns in post-war Germany and the dilemmas that face them. The first dilemma was what to do with the old buildings, mostly in ruins, that were reminders of a former Jewish community, destroyed or uprooted by the Holocaust.

The "Old Synagogue" in Essen was destroyed by fire on Kristallnacht in 1938. It remained in ruins until 1959. Despite various petitions from the local Jewish residents to turn the building into a community centre and from Israeli sources wishing the building to be turned into a memorial for the victims of the Holocaust, the municipality decided to convert the building for its own use. In the process the municipality managed to obliterate all signs of the building's former use, covering up the mosaics and wall decorations with paint and constructing a low ceiling which hid the soaring cupola. The building was then used to house an exhibition on industrial design. Only after part of the exhibition was destroyed by fire in 1979 did the municipality have a change of heart. On 9th November 1980, the building was dedicated as a memorial site and documentation centre . In 1986, the state of Nordrhein-Westfalen donated funds to reconstruct the building to its former appearance as a synagogue.

Thus, issues of preservation, renovation or reconstruction took a while to be resolved, and the decision to set up a Jewish museum under municipal auspices was by no means straightforward. In addition, there was another dilemma facing such museums. Namely, how to involve the local Jewish community, particularly when most of the city's former Jewish residents had either perished in the Holocaust or had settled elsewhere. As the present curator for the Old Synagogue in Essen states:

> The Alte Synagogue is not a Jewish museum in the narrow sense of the term but a municipal memorial site and a historical and political documentation centre. (Dr. Brocke, letter dated 31 May 1997)

In an effort to collect historical material, photographs and autobiographical records were collected from former Essen Jews now living in other countries. Although there is a small Jewish community now residing in Essen, it does not consist of descendants of the pre-war community. This congregation is not considered of historical relevance to the purposes of the museum and so is not actively involved in the museum.

The Jewish Museum in Rendsburg, however, has adopted a much more positive attitude in seeking closer co-operation with the Jewish community. Their nearest formally constituted Jewish community is in Hamburg, and representatives of the Hamburg Jewish community are on the museum's steering committee. The curator writes:

> Our special aim for the future will be to bridge the divide between the young generation, non-Jewish and Jewish and establish more contacts with the new Jewish population in Schlesswig-Holstein. (Dr. Dettmer, letter dated 12 June 1997)

Indeed the museum has established links with Jews in Rendsburg, Kiel, Lubeck and Hamburg, most of them emigrants from the former USSR. Hence such "Jewish" museums in Germany vary considerably in terms of their emphasis on purely historical events and "memorialising" the past and the extent to which they actively seek to build bridges between Jews and non-Jews in the present. Yet, the Jewish Museum in Rendsburg has many other competing agendas. The first tug of war was between art and history. A historian from Kiel University was keen to stress the historical functions of the museum. However, the director of the state museum for Schlesswig-Holstein was keen for the museum to focus on artistic achievements. The Ministry of Culture for the State of Schlesswig Holstein came down in favour of the arts.

This brief outline of various competing agendas surrounding Jewish museums in Germany is fairly indicative of the manner in which Jewish museums generally evolve through a dynamic process, involving various alliances and depending quite considerably on favourable sets of institutional policies and upon a favourable political climate.

By way of contrast, mention will be made of one other development which is a specifically Jewish response to commemorating the Holocaust, namely the Mechelen Museum of Deportation and the Resistance, in Belgium. The Belgian Association of Jewish Deportees was established in 1956; in the same year the association instituted an annual pilgrimage to the Dossin barracks in Mechelen, the departure point for transportations to Auschwitz-Birkenau.

Maurice Pioro, president of the association, writes:

> In the 1970s a project was set up to alter the initial aspect of the
> barracks and the UDJB (Belgian Association of Jewish Deportees)
> suggested to Mr. Spinoy, then Minister and Mayor of Mechelen, that
> one section of the buildings be set aside to house a museum of
> deportation and resistance. (Mechelen Museum, 1997)

However, further alliances, both within the Jewish community and with other
governmental institutions were necessary for the project to come to fruition.
As Professor Georges Schnek, president of the CICB, the main communal
organisation, writes:

> The CICB responded to the UDJB initiative by approaching the
> Flemish community with a request to set aside a space within the
> former Dossin barracks in Mechelen for the creation of a museum.
> The provincial government authorities at Antwerp and the City of
> Mechelen joined with the Flemish region in financing the acquisition
> of this space, which will be dedicated to the history not only of the
> deportation and extermination of the Jews living in Belgium but also
> the part the Jews played in the various resistance movements and
> Allied armies. The museum space will also depict the role played by
> our non-Jewish fellow citizens in saving numerous Jews. (Mechelen
> Museum, 1997)

It is interesting to note that as institutions outside the Jewish community
are asked to provide further support and assistance, there is a corresponding
widening of the scope of the museum.

While there is much more to be said about the topic of commemorating
the Holocaust, some of the other agendas of Jewish museums will now be
examined in more depth.

Focus on art

I have already mentioned the Jewish Museum in Rendsburg, with its emphasis on cultural achievements. This extends to supporting living artists in their
work. A Czech writer was in residence in 1990, an Estonian painter in 1992,
and an Israeli poet in 1994. In the course of the year various events and
exhibitions take place in the museum. These events include a recital of
Yiddish songs, an exhibition of work by an Israeli artist, sculptures and
paintings by an artist from Schlesswig-Holstein, an exhibition of textile
hangings and various writers reading from their own works, to name a few
of the activities taking place in the museum.

The focus on art as one of the primary objectives of a Jewish museum
is even more emphatic in the Jewish museums in Paris and Vienna. The
director of the Jewish museum in Vienna writes that the museum is particularly keen to ensure that the museum should become an integral part of
the Viennese cultural landscape (Haber, letter dated 9 May 1997). To this end,
the museum has joined in a co-operative venture with the Volkstheater (The

National Theatre) in putting on a play about Theodor Herzl, as part of the outreach work undertaken by the Volkstheater.

Drama workshops were also organised for 12 to 18 year old pupils, in collaboration with the Austrian Cultural Services, on the theme of cabaret song and text from the inter-war period. This was in conjunction with an exhibition on Stella Kadmon, a theatre director who rose to prominence in the Vienna cabaret scene of the thirties. The museum has also put on an exhibition of photographs of contemporary Jewish life in Vienna, an exhibition of leading Israeli artists of Austrian origin, exhibitions of paintings by Emil Orlik (1870-1932) and Tina Blau (1845-1916), both of whom spent some time in Vienna. The clear intention of the museum is to stress the manner in which Jewish cultural life, then and now, blends into the landscape of the Austrian cultural scene. It is worth noting that, here too, alliances and a favourable political climate in the late 1980s also played their part.

The museum is owned and run by the City of Vienna, with some initial funding from central government. Yet the support of the Jewish community was sought from the outset. The Jewish community has three representatives on the Advisory Board of the Museum, which consists of seven people; the three Jewish representatives have the power to veto any of the proposals made by the Advisory Board. The Jewish community also passed on to the museum whatever Judaica and other objects had been saved from the pre-war collection of the original Jewish Museum and lent the museum the community's vast library collection. Nevertheless, the enthusiastic support of the then socialist mayor of Vienna was crucial to the museum; without municipal support the whole venture would have collapsed.

The Museum of Jewish Art in Paris, by contrast, was established in 1948 almost entirely as a result of efforts by the Jewish community, with the specific mission of collecting and displaying Jewish works of art, both religious and secular artistic endeavours. The permanent exhibition is divided into five sections: religious artefacts used for worship in the home or in the synagogue; representations of synagogual architecture, with scale models of synagogues across the world; Jewish sculptural art, including life size reproductions of Jewish tombstones from Prague and Czernovitz; reproductions of synagogual paintings and mosaics; and, finally, a large collection of contemporary art, including paintings, drawings, lithographs and sculptures by Chagall, Mane-Katz, Lipschitz and others. The entire collection of the museum is due to be rehoused in the newly established Museum of Jewish Art and History, to be opened in 1998. The idea of establishing a new museum arose in 1980, when the board of management of the Museum of Jewish Art began looking around for larger premises. Eventually, this initiative received enthusiastic support from Jacques Chirac, then Mayor of Paris, who was able to secure the Hotel of Saint-Aignan on behalf of the new museum. The hotel, a 17th century building, has been entirely renovated and refurbished over the last five years. The Ministry of Culture also lent its support to the venture, and the Jewish representative body, CRIF (Conseil Representatif des Institutions Juives de France), also became involved. A formal steering committee was formed in 1988 with representatives from the Ministry of Culture, the City of Paris, and Jewish representatives.

Once again we can see the need for alliances, the need to involve communal structures, and the importance of a favourable political climate.

Focus on architectural heritage, local history and tourism

These three different foci are treated together in this paper because it is often very difficult to disentangle them from each other. A large number of Jewish museums in Europe are actually located in historic buildings, often in buildings formerly used as synagogues or for other communal purposes. Spain, which expelled its Jews in 1492, has recently had a number of Jewish museums sited in buildings or areas formerly occupied by its Jewish inhabitants.

The Museo Sefardi, in Toledo, was established in 1964 with the aim of documenting and preserving Spanish-Hebraic culture. The museum is now housed in a synagogue, one of only two surviving synagogues dating back to the time before the expulsion. The synagogue was substantially renovated between 1985 and 1994 and is located in the former Jewish quarter, which is now greatly frequented by tourists, as the immediate surroundings contain a large number of historic monuments, of Christian, Muslim and Jewish origin. Indeed, well over 200,000 people annually visit the museum. The director of the museum notes that the main concerns of the central government in funding the museum are architectural heritage, historical and cultural heritage, local history and tourist development (Ana Maria Lopez Alvarez, letter dated 2 June 1997). Clearly there are a number of different agendas involved here.

The renovation of part of the old Jewish quarter, including the synagogue, is part of a strategy to enhance the touristic attraction of the area, in line with Spain's current emphasis on cultural tourism, as opposed to the massive investment in seaside resorts of the 1960s and 1970s.

The year 1992 coincided with the anniversaries of Columbus' trip to America, of the expulsion of Jews from Spain, as well as the Olympics in Barcelona and Expo 92 in Seville. All this helped to galvanise efforts to put Spain on the tourist map in ways which went well beyond its image of sun, sand and sea. Hand-in-hand with an attempt to stimulate cultural tourism through renovating old parts of the city and preserving its architectural heritage, was an attempt to develop serious academic research and to disseminate information concerning the Spanish-Jewish legacy as an essential part of Spanish heritage. In conjunction with the University of Castilla at Toledo, the museum sponsors an annual international conference on the subject of Spanish-Jewish and Sephardic culture, which attracts eminent speakers from across the world.

The municipality of Girona, in Catalonia, is similarly engaged in renovating its old Jewish quarter, the Call, as it is known locally. The City Council of Girona have contributed $1 million toward the expenses of renovating the Call and for creating a museum and institute complex and further funds have been received from central government and from the European Economic

Community. A further $ 3.5 million are still required to complete these projects.

While there is no formally constituted Jewish community in Girona, various Jews are prominently involved on the Board of Directors of the museum and institute. In addition, there are at least five rabbis on the board of advisors and a number of Jewish charitable foundations support the work of the museum. The state of Israel and other Israeli institutions have also collaborated in this venture and there is a "Friends of Girona Museum and Institute" based in New York and a "Friends of the Call in Girona" based in Los Angeles. All this suggests a very active and determined effort to enlist Jewish support and funds in furthering the work of the Museum and Institute.

In Venice the story is slightly different; Jews have been living in Venice virtually without a break since the 10th century. By the 1930s there were 1800 Jews in Venice, of whom some 205 were deported to death camps during the Second World War. Today there are only 600 Jews left in Venice. Venice is the site of the first ghetto to bear such a name, established in 1516. Many of the historic synagogues still standing today date from the 16th century. The Great Spanish Synagogue, still in use today for religious worship, was restored in 1635, probably by Baldassare Longhena, who was responsible for designing a large number of buildings in Venice at the time. In the 1980s new regulations were passed in Venice providing the city with funds to restore some of the city's vast and stunning architectural heritage, and the Great Spanish Synagogue too was restored with city funds in the late 1980s.

The Great German Synagogue is located on the top floor of the building housing the Jewish museum. The synagogue was recently restored with funding received from the Jewish Historical Society of Venice, the Italian Committee of Venice and the Deutscher Koordinierungsrat in Frankfurt (Curiel and Cooperman, 1990: p. 55). The Jewish Museum, located on the first floor of the same building, was opened in 1953, but considerably improved in 1986 when it received a substantial contribution from the Region of Veneto. The museum has displays of ritual objects and Judaica, as well as an important collection of 15th and 16th century manuscripts (Sacerdoti, 1989: p. 77).

The support recently given to the Jewish museum and the restoration of historic synagogues must be seen in the context of wider architectural, environmental and tourist development policies pursued by local government, with the support of both central government, the European Commission and international bodies concerned with architectural heritage.

Focus on education

Virtually all museums see themselves as having an educational role. A few museums place their educational role right at the top of their agenda. One such museum is the Jewish Museum in Stockholm, founded in 1987. The director writes:

Its purpose is to show coming generations the political history of the Swedish Jewish population; to inform about Jewish customs; the Swedish Jews contribution to commerce, industry and culture in the country. (Aron Neuman, letter dated 10 June, 97)

Of the approximately 8,500 annual visitors, more than half are school children and students, and these are the main target audiences, although the general Swedish public and tourists also visit the museum. The museum runs workshops for parties of school children and students, a lecture series, a publication series and a research library. In 1994 it was awarded the Swedish Museum of the Year Award and in recent years has received funding from the municipality of Stockholm and the Swedish Parliament, as well as donations from members of the Jewish community and other charitable foundations. The museum, however, functions quite independently of Jewish communal institutions.

By contrast, the Jewish Museum in London, newly amalgamating the Jewish Museum and the London Museum of Jewish Life, pursues an educational role which is much more specifically geared to the needs of the National Curriculum. While the Jewish Museum in London pursues a number of very diverse goals, including a variety of educational goals, the focus here is on the work of its educational services because it highlights certain important themes. The museum offers specialised teaching of Judaism and Jewish history, in line with national guidelines for Religious Studies and the National Curriculum requirements for History at Key Stages 2, 3 and 4. It has programmes which are designed for students studying A-Level religious Studies and History, GCSE Religious Studies and History (The Jewish Museum: Information Leaflet on its Educational Services). In addition, there is an extensive pack for teachers bringing secondary students on a visit, containing activities and information; there are also activity sheets and programmes on history and religious themes for all ages, for both Jewish and non-Jewish schools. Moreover, the museum now has a specialised Education Gallery, which has as its focus an exhibition on the life of Leon Greenman, a British citizen and Holocaust survivor who was born in London's East End. The accompanying panels set Leon's story in the context of Nazi persecution and show his determination to combat racism and fascism today. This exhibition is suitable for pupils at Key Stage 3 and 4, GCSE and Advanced Level (History and Religious Studies) (The Jewish Museum: Information Leaflet on Holocaust Education).

The point here is the importance of linkages between educational policies of the wider society and the kinds of exhibitions being mounted by museums in general, including Jewish museums. The educational agendas of the wider society do indeed have an important influence on the development of Jewish museums.

Focus on Jewish museums in communist and post-communist countries

The case of Jewish museums in communist and post-communist countries deserves a separate section, as they face quite distinctive issues. Even so, it is difficult to generalise about the various histories of Jewish museums across a number of different countries. In most communist countries, synagogues and Jewish communal properties were taken over by the communist state. Synagogues were often turned to more secular uses, including factories, warehouses, and municipal offices. This was not always the case. In Lancut, in Poland, the municipality restored the old synagogue in the 1950s and then turned it over to the central government, which converted the building into a museum about the former Jewish residents of Lancut. In Prague, the historic synagogues of the Ghetto area survived the war and were managed under the aegis of the Jewish museum, which was taken over by the communist state in 1950. In the former Yugoslavia, The Federation of Jewish Communities of Yugoslavia was able to maintain a certain degree of autonomy, even under the communist regime, and established a Jewish Historical Museum in 1949. The Federation of Jewish Communities received financial help at the time from the American Jewish Joint Distribution Committee.

In 1969 the Jewish Historical Museum in Belgrade opened a permanent exhibition on the history of Yugoslav Jewry. The caption underneath one of the photographs in the exhibition reads:

> Jewish battalion formed in September 1943 in the concentration camp at Isle Rab, later became part of the 7th Banian division. Some 4750 Yugoslav Jews participated in the people's liberation war among which there were about 1320 veterans. (The Jewish Historical Museum in Belgrade, explanatory leaflet accompanying the permanent exhibition)

Clearly, while the Jewish museum maintained its independence and autonomy during the communist period, it was still politic to make explicit reference to the role that Yugoslav Jews had played alongside the Yugoslav people's liberation forces. Yet, the Jewish Museum was equally explicit about the number of Jews who had perished in the Holocaust. The exhibition has a large map showing all the concentration camps in Europe to which Yugoslav Jews had been sent, stating that 67,000 out of a total of 82,000 Yugoslav Jews perished in the Holocaust.

Communist regimes were much more ambivalent about stating precisely how many Jews died in the Holocaust. Thus, in Poland, plaques and explanatory panels at Holocaust sites such as at Auschwitz/Birkenau announced the number of Poles killed at such sites, but not until after the demise of the communist regime was it made clear that many Jews died there as well. An exception to this rule was the decision of the State Jewish Museum in Prague to turn the historic Pinkas Synagogue into a sort of a shrine. To commemorate the memory of the 77,297 Czech Jews who perished in the Holocaust, the names of all of the victims were inscribed on the synagogue walls. But by the 1970s the regime had a change of heart, as a result of the conflict in the Middle East, and the names of the victims were removed from the walls of the synagogue.

Under communist rule, the kind of exhibitions mounted were generally very circumscribed. Since the demise of communism, however, the scope for exhibitions has considerably widened. Jewish museums such as the one in Budapest are able to put on exhibitions comparable in scope and breadth of vision to those mounted in any major Jewish museum. In May 1997 the museum opened an exhibition entitled "Diaspora and Art". Ruth Ellen Gruber writes:

> A major new exhibition at Budapest's Jewish museum has brought together some 500 paintings, sculptures and graphics works to examine the effect of "diaspora identity" on artistic creativity ... Under communism, the museum situated in a building next to the grandiose Dohany Street Synagogue, was little more than just a marginal display of ritual objects. Further explorations of the role of Jewish culture were taboo. (Gruber, 1997: p. 7)

Of course, not all Jewish museums in former communist countries could mount such an elaborate exhibition. The Lancut museum in Poland is still very much in the old mould, struggling with few resources, whilst the museum in Belgrade has been prevented from mounting any ambitious new exhibitions as a result of the recent war. In many cases, the issue of ownership and control of Jewish museums in former communist countries needed to be resolved.

In the case of the Prague Jewish Museum, in 1990 the post-communist regime attempted to sell off part of the museum's treasures, through auction at Christie's. This sparked off quite an outcry from the Jewish community, both locally and internationally, and the plan was abandoned. In 1994, control of the Jewish Museum in Prague was handed back to the Jewish community. Yet the Czech Republic still retains a third share in the ownership of the museum, with the Federation of Czech Jewish Communities retaining another third and the Jewish Community of Prague also owning a third share in the museum.

In Poland, the picture is still quite complex, with negotiations still taking place over the gradual handing over of some Jewish communal property back to the Jewish community. There is however much debate as to whom should be receiving such communal property, with only a very small surviving Jewish community in Poland itself.

Conclusion

Whether Jewish museums are initiated by the members of the Jewish community or by institutions within the wider society, such museums invariably necessitate the formation of various kinds of alliances. There are no hard and fast rules that can be discerned in terms of such alliances. Wherever there is a strong Jewish community present, then the formal Jewish communal organisations are likely to be formally involved in the process, as in the case of the museums in Paris, Prague, Vienna and Venice. Elsewhere, Jewish representatives are likely to be involved on management or advisory committees of such museums, as in Rendsburg and Girona. Yet, in some cases, especially where the Jewish presence is weak or non-existent, as in Essen and in Lancut, Jews are not formally involved in the running of the museum in any way at all.

The necessity for alliances applies to both the Jewish community and to the wider society. Hence, the new museum in Paris required the co-operation of both the management committee of the old museum of Jewish Art and CRIF, the communal representative body for the whole of French Jewry. It also required the collaboration of both the City of Paris and the Ministry of Culture. Similarly, the establishment of the Museum of Resistance in Mechelen required the joint efforts of the Belgian Association of Jewish Deportees and CICB, representing the whole of Belgian Jewry. It also required the support not only of the City of Mechelen but also of the Flemish regional authorities.

Perhaps the inevitable consequence of such alliances is the emergence of a number of different agenda, sometimes complementary to each other, often competing with each other, and sometimes at odds with each other.

The fewer the key players, the easier to maintain a clear-cut agenda, as in the case of the Jewish Museum in Stockholm, founded and initially funded by its director, and independent of Jewish communal organisations. Individual donations from within the Jewish community and funding from the public sector have not diverted the museum from its original objective of focusing on the educational function of the museum, targeted mainly at the younger generation. Similarly, the municipal museum in Essen, dedicated as a memorial site and historical documentation centre, has stuck to a relatively narrow frame of reference. Most Jewish museums, however, are dealing simultaneously with a number of different agendas.

While the Jewish Museum in Vienna is keen to become an integral part of the Viennese cultural landscape, it still has a number of other roles to fulfil. It is an important historical documentation centre, it has a very significant collection of Judaica and Jewish artefacts, it houses a library of Jewish books and manuscripts containing over 30,000 items. In addition, the municipal and central government authorities are concerned that the museum be used for educational purposes, as well as to bridge the divide between Jews and non-Jews, to foster a better image of Austria abroad and to encourage tourism. Indeed, 60% of all visitors to the museum are tourists, mainly Jewish tourists. Similarly, the Jewish Museum in Rendsburg has a cultural mission, but at the same time has a local history agenda and is involved in maintaining architectural heritage. The museums in Toledo and Girona are simultaneously involved in encouraging serious academic research on the history and culture of Spanish Jewry prior to their expulsion in 1492, as well as restoring the architectural heritage and urban landscape of the former Jewish quarters. Both these endeavours are said to benefit cultural tourism.

Usually, the necessity to form alliances will mean that the museums come to reach some form of accommodation and manage to combine a number of different agendas under the same roof, as it were. However, sometimes the various agendas prove incompatible, or personality clashes will suddenly emerge, and the various alliances will unravel themselves, as is currently the case with the Jewish Museum in Berlin (see Avidan, 1997: pp. 42-43). Nevertheless, it is possible that some suitable form of compromise will eventually be reached in Berlin as well, as there is too much at stake to simply drop the whole project.

In conclusion it should be noted that Jewish museums usually not only explore minority-dominant group relations in the past but, by their very constitution and in their day-to-day management, also reflect such group relationships in the present as well.

References

Avidan, I. (1997) 'Berlin's Jewish Problem', *The Jerusalem Report*, 21st August 1997: p. 42-43.

Bennett, T. (1988) 'Museums and the people', in Lumley, R. (ed) *The museum time machine*. London: Routledge: pp. 63-85.

Clark, D. (1994) 'The State Jewish Museum in Prague: The relevance of the concept of Site-Sacralisation', unpublished MA Dissertation in the Sociology and Anthropology of Tourism, University of Surrey.

Cohen, R. (1992) 'Self-image through objects', in Wertheimer, J., *The uses of tradition: Jewish continuity in the modern era*. Cambridge (MA): Harvard University Press, pp. 203-242.

Curiel, R. and Cooperman B. D. (1990) *The Venetian ghetto*. New York: Rizzoli.

Gruber, E. R. (1997) 'Budapest museum examines diaspora identity', *The Jewish Chronicle*, May 23: p. 7.

Hartman, G. H. (Ed) (1994) *Holocaust remembrance — the shapes of memory*. Oxford: Basil Blackwell.

Heuberger, G. (1988) 'A new start in old tradition — the aims and composition of the Jewish Museum in Frankfurt am Main', in the Opening Brochure for the Jewish Museum in Frankfurt.

Kushner, T., (1992) 'The end of the Anglo-Jewish Progress Show: Representations of the Jewish East', in Kushner, T. (ed) *The Jewish heritage in British history*. London: Frank Cass, pp. 78-105.

Mechelen Museum (1997) http:/www.link.be/shoah/init.html (Web home page).

Milton, S. and Nowinski, I. (1991) *In fitting memory — the art and politics of Holocaust memorials*. Detroit: Wayne State University Press.

Sacerdoti, A. (1989) *Guide to Jewish Italy*. New York: Israellowitz Publishing.

Young, J. (1993) *The texture of memory — Holocaust memorials and meanings*. London: Yale University Press.

Young, J. (1994) *The art of memory — Holocaust memorials in history*. Munich: Prestel Verlag.

Consuming the Countryside: Postmodern Hedonism or Responsible Reflexivity?

Jim Butterfield and Jonathan Long

Leeds Metropolitan University

This paper draws on a 'state of the art' review of life-cycle and lifestyle theories that was prepared for Scottish Natural Heritage as one of three studies commissioned to stimulate thinking about future policies, with particular emphasis on the implications for open air recreation (Long and Butterfield, 1996). In identifying issues and trends, we raise questions about whether the present patterns of countryside use will endure into the future: whether walks and picnics in the woods and hills can compete with the new urban attractions and the ever widening choices offered by home entertainment; whether new ecological sensibilities will draw people to green contemplation in their local area; or whether technology will draw us to living increasingly insulated from 'natural' processes. Such questions are framed within a context of changes in work practices, family structures and the globalisation of culture. The new pluralistic individualism will undoubtedly include some groups who enjoy the countryside, but we speculate on how significant they will be and whether their values and practices will be passed on to succeeding generations.

Our review included an assessment of demographic and other trends pertinent to the Scottish scene, which we summarise here to provide a context for the current debate. For example, between 1991 and 2021 there is likely to be a slight reduction in the size of the Scottish population, but we may expect a 31% increase in the number of people over 65 and a 22% increase in those aged between 45 and 64, countered by a 19% decline in those aged 44 or less. Combined with the increased number of early retirals, this may lead to increased demand for countryside recreation, provided the middle aged and elderly retain their incomes and mobility. Many more people will be living alone and by 2021 it is expected that one person households will account for 35% of the total number of households. Some of the increase in such households is attributable to the elderly but 70% of it is expected to be among those between 30 and retirement age. Informal activities have an important social dimension: will those living alone be reluctant countryside users because of their isolation; will they seek more recreation because it offers the opportunity for social interaction; or will they use their social networks to support this kind of recreation?

Furthermore, the need to find land for housing for those wanting to live nearer the countryside may restrict opportunities for recreation in the urban fringe areas. There are similar uncertainties about transport; the trend in recent years has been for journey distances to lengthen and car use to assume ever greater importance, but now we find that persuading people to get out of their cars is on the agenda.

The UK Day Visits Survey, 1994 (Centre for Leisure Research, 1996) highlights the lower involvement of the young, the old, women and those outside the workforce; the higher involvement of the AB social classes and the vital significance of personal mobility. Those in social classes A and B may continue to experience pressures on their time and there may be only marginal shifts in the present pattern of inequality, so that those who are currently excluded may continue to be so.

The idea of the life-cycle has a long history, but was notably introduced to leisure research in this country by Rapoport and Rapoport (1975) and was welcomed by practitioners as a potentially valuable tool for the assessment of leisure needs. According to their thesis, people's lives develop along the three intertwined planes of work, family and leisure, which give rise to predictable shifts in their preoccupations, interests and activities. At the root of this process lies the search for personal identity. Critics such as Clarke and Critcher (1985) recognised that the life-cycle approach represented an advance over the 'stereotypical consumerist family' and dealt with the complexity, ambiguity and uncertainty inherent in leisure provision. More-over, women's experiences were given equal attention to those of men, notwithstanding that for women 'with the birth of children, life becomes not just home-centred but child-centred'. However, they regretted the psycho-biological orientation, pointing out the significance of variables such as social class, housing and education and the influence of stratification, in leading to differences in lifestyles, as opposed to a common pattern of social develop-ment. The incorporation of life-cycle analysis into planning models proved to be highly complex, but its prominence prompted managers of facilities to take account of needs that otherwise might have been overlooked.

We note that the Rapoports completed their studies when there was greater optimism about the power of government to remove inequalities and blur social divisions. Many of their recommendations about closing the generation gaps, education including leisure skills, the tolerance of different lifestyles and the necessity of a 'people-centred approach' stand the test of time. But times *have* changed and we have less confidence in translating an understanding of 'needs' into effective policies, with the concept of need itself subject to differing ideological interpretations (Gough and Doyal, 1991). Until very recently, the dominant policy principle (though not always the practice) was that of rolling back the state and trusting individuals to look after their own interests. Our pluralistic individualism may become less exclusively focused on market freedoms, but a return to paternalistic welfarism seems unlikely. Furthermore, the notion of a standard, predictable life-cycle has been severely questioned by flexible labour markets, major occupational shifts[1], women becoming more prominent in the labour market, growing inequality and a greater diversity in the structure of households. Attitudes too have changed such that wives are less tolerant of the 'Andy Cap' partner who contributes little and makes life more difficult, while some men are prepared to 'trade-in' an older wife for a younger version. Unwillingness to settle for compromises represents a lifestyle choice that undermines the previous life-cycle model.

The leisure revolution predicted in the 1970s has been replaced by the 'time squeeze' (Demos, 1995) and tendencies to social exclusion. If there has been a leisure revolution, then it is in the range of opportunities presented by the leisure industries and the growth of leisure as consumption. The very absence of alternatives that led to family Sunday outings to the countryside becoming so ingrained, is no more. The countryside trip has to compete for attention with visits to IKEA, Sunday sport, all day pub-opening, cinemas and the new urban entertainments. Consequently, we must question whether new generations will necessarily follow the countryside recreations of their parents. Generation X may see the world differently and the inter-genera- tional transmission of values within the family may be assuming much less significance. Thus, family, work and leisure have all changed considerably since the development of the life-cycle concept and so have the ways in which they interact.

Giddens (1991) contends that notions of a life-cycle concept are little more than a hangover from traditional society, and are not compatible with contemporary 'lifestyle':

> The idea of the life cycle makes very little sense once the connections between the individual life and the interchange of the generations have been broken ... [In] high modernity practices are repeated only so far as they are reflexively justifiable. (Giddens, 1991: p. 146)

Reflexivity amounts to a process of subjecting most aspects of 'social activity and material relations with nature' to fundamental revision. Information mediated by experts and rapid cultural transmission across national boun- daries lead to the questioning and abandonment of customary practices. Individuals are obliged to think and act for themselves, choosing their own lifestyles and searching for personal identities in the absence of the certainties passed on through custom and tradition.

Trying to account for difference in the population, various social com- mentators, futurologists and market analysts have approached the problem from different directions. Some of the resultant classificatory models are theory-driven, but most are the product of empiricism or speculation. The work of Savage *et al.* (1992) is one of the few attempts to relate specific leisure behaviour to other lifestyle characteristics, categorising the middle class as *postmodern, ascetic* or *indistinct*. The postmoderns are high income earners, extravagant consumers who may engage in hedonistic, personalised forms of sport, often used to generate business contacts. The ascetic group is drawn from teachers, welfare officers and health service professionals, well endowed with cultural capital but not so well-off financially and looking to the state for many of their leisure opportunities, which may include healthy activities in the countryside. The indistincts include managers and bureaucrats, the former likely to favour 'staid and conventional sports' such as sailing, fishing, golf and shooting. Savage *et al.* group different lifestyles but do not address lower income groups, so their model lacks the general applicability necessary for policy and planning applications.

Market researchers have been quick to make use of lifestyle groups to typify consumer habits on a socio-economic basis. Mintel (1996), for example, identify benefit dependants (9% of the adult population), families on tight budgets (10%), better off families (9%), better off empty nesters (9%) and working women (23%) as being indicative of the sections of the population in a country which is polarising economically.

Classifications based on psycho-demographics relates attitude clusters to socio-economic data. For example, 'Outlook', developed from the Target Group Index, divides the population into *Trendies, Pleasure Seekers, Indifferents, Working Class Puritans, Sociable Spenders* and *Moralists* (Baker and Fletcher, 1987). Taylor Nelson (Ekins, 1986; Kinsman, 1990) divided the UK population according to sustenance values, outer-directedness and inner-directedness, and used the division as a model of social change, which results from changes in values and attitudes. If the model is robust, then monitoring values and attitudes may offer a better guide to the future than statistical forecasting models. Social value groups are a further refinement and we can speculate that different groups will have different demands for outdoor recreation activities, with *self-explorers* looking for solitude in the hills, experimentalists flying microlites, *conspicuous consumers* water-skiing, belongers going to country parks and *survivors* restricted to urban parks.... Equally, we have to accept that in practice, the groups may follow the same activities but with differing motivations and we must acknowledge that we have no empirical basis on which to make such judgements.

We note other attempts to give lifestyle groupings more practical use through geographical systems such as ACORN and MOSAIC, and that market research can link purchasing patterns to consumer profiles; through loyalty cards, for example, the supermarket chains can correlate dimensions such as occupation, residential area and vehicle ownership with product affinities. Unfortunately, the application of such methods to countryside recreation would have doubtful validity, given that data on recreation activities and locations are much less 'hard' than those on recorded purchases.

Veal (1993: p. 248) regrets that much of the work on leisure and lifestyle is largely divorced from theory, and challenges researchers to follow Weber and "to move beyond the simple (sic) identification of lifestyle groups to unravel the processes by which lifestyles are formed and sustained", and the processes by which people choose their lifestyles or have them imposed.

The Brundtland Report (1988) suggested that our current lifestyles are not sustainable:

> Many of us live beyond the earth's ecological means, for instance in patterns of energy use. Perceived needs are socially and culturally determined, and sustainable development requires the promotion of values that encourage consumption standards that are within the bounds of the ecologically possible. (World Commission on Environment and Development, 1988: p. 44)

The close contact with the natural environment that comes through open air recreation may increase people's preparedness to listen to the message. Sustainablity will require changes in government priorities, but will also involve changes in personal lifestyles; and to achieve both of these will need a significant change in public attitudes. However, some writers suggest that the public is already ahead of the politicians in this respect. Conscious decisions to leave a lighter ecological 'footprint' might be examples of Giddens' reflexivity, but would also run counter to most leisure within the culture of consumerism. As Veblen (1899) noted almost one hundred years ago, products may be bought more for their symbolic value than their utility. Shopping merges with leisure so that the act of purchase provides enjoyment and no recreational visit is complete without buying something[2]. Veblen suggested that when faced with the choice, people would prefer extra consumption to more leisure time in what Lasch (1980) characterised as the narcissism and egotism of current lifestyles. Postmodern writers place consumption and self-gratification at centre stage and draw attention to the hedonism of current life styles, which derive their identities from consumption, its signs and symbols, its ephemerality and its product disposability. Within such a framework, developed by the Centre for the Study of Environmental Change (1994), the countryside becomes more and more a commodity to be packaged and marketed, striving for public attention among the kaleidoscope of other leisure opportunities and therefore necessarily having to offer something different from the rest.

Thus, whether we are hedonistic consumers or reflexive environmentalists will have very different implications for policy. Even if we were able to be certain about the orientation of recreationists, we lack the empirical evidence to link them with specific countryside recreation demands. It is doubtful whether we are in a position to identify clear indicators of need (even if full information were available) given that there is no longer a consensus on the role of the state in enabling leisure needs to be met. Moreover, it is doubtful whether it is possible to identify needs for open air recreation in the same sense as we make 'objective' statements about the need for education or health services. However, we point to the long standing view that some form of direct contact with nature should be available as part of an acceptable quality of life, perhaps as part of the strong public culture advocated by Gray (1996) as a way of making individualism less asocial and more convivial.

A further consideration of need takes account of the varying intensity of the recreational experience. Many go to the countryside for relaxation in the company of family and friends — a social occasion in a pleasant environment. Others are more single-minded, dedicated to particular activities and seekers of 'flow' experiences (Csikszentmihalyi and Csikszentmihalyi, 1988), the long distance hill walker or the rock climber, for example, for whom enjoyment of the activity will lead to personal development and perhaps be central to their whole lifestyle. Providers should aim to understand the motivations and needs of the increasing number of 'serious enthusiasts' and we think that there is a good case for research into the sub-cultures of participants in adventure and related activities.

Proponents of the biophilia hypothesis (e.g., Wilson and Kellert, 1992) have attempted to provide some form of scientific justification for the arguments of the Romantic writers in favour of the aesthetic, spiritual and therapeutic values of recreation in the countryside. The suggestion is that affinity with nature has universal expression common, though mediated in different ways, across all cultures — a position supported, but from a different perspective, by Schama (1995) who urges us to explore and identify our landscape traditions. Adams expresses such ideas from a personal viewpoint:

> As an adult I have not lost my senses of the value of places such as this [unspoilt Norfolk beach]. Indeed, I seem to be hard wired to them and to feel concern at the state of their wildlife, landscape and patterns of economic life. Somewhere in my childhood I acquired a kind of instinctive environmentalism with, at its core, a sense of the value and power of nature ... I do not think my feelings are unique ... the turbulence and wildness of nature is a counterpart to human creativity and industry ... we care about the countryside and wild species and habitats, but our very lives and lifestyles threaten them in profound and complex ways. (Adams, 1996: p. 3)

Thus, alongside the view that agencies must adapt to changing needs and values, we have the suggestion that countryside activities may have more enduring qualities. These are not either/or positions — both exist in today's world — hence the potential for conflict. Nor do individuals fall consistently into one category or the other. Research by the Centre for the Study of Environmental Change (1994) and more recently the Countryside Commission (1997) shows that people's responses to attitude surveys will vary according to the context in which questions are asked. For example, support for restricting cars in the countryside stands alongside uncertainty about whether it is legitimate to place restrictions on cars.

There is an assumption that the benefits of countryside recreation include the fostering of deeper understanding of the natural environment and commitments to conservation, but the empirical evidence about such a relationship is mixed. Many features of our current culture — the compression of time and space, insulation and protection from the rhythms of nature, the unbounded possibilities of digital entertainment — point to lifestyles separate from direct contact with nature. This is exemplified in Rojek's (1995) account of the visitor experience in Zion National Park, Utah, where an air-conditioned audio-visual presentation of the park is preferred to the discomfort of the outdoors. By contrast, the work of Schama and that in support of the biophilia hypothesis point to much more continuity in countryside enjoyment — a stable element of otherwise diverse and changing lifestyles whether originating in deep cultural roots or our genes.

Orr (1992) emphasises the importance of childhood experiences as determinants of adult leisure demands and Adams notes the replacement of Mrs Tiggywinkle by Sonic the Hedgehog, questioning whether a relatively secluded childhood in which electronic entertainment is readily available and most journeys are made by car is likely to encourage an enjoyment of open air activities. If we are 'hard wired' as Adams suggests, we may still need to learn to use the hard wiring to realise its potential. Some children will have the benefit of parents who take them to the woods and hills, and adventure and environmental education integrated into the school curriculum, both of which may have consequences for future leisure preferences. Experiences within the family remain important as determinants of future countryside recreation demands but we are unaware of empirical work in this area and are left only with speculative judgements. Hence, we are uncertain whether the many young people who find the countryside dull and unexciting will eventually turn into adults with proclivities for quiet enjoyment.

Conclusion

In conclusion, we note that 'Leisure and the Family Life Cycle' was formulated in a period of greater stability and certainty than the present and when there appeared to be more likelihood of lifestyle convergence. Life-cycle patterns have become less readily discernible, so that lifestyle considerations have come to the fore, although we might usefully retain the insight that leisure interests change over a person's life course. Family structures are much less homogeneous and stable than previously, but perhaps structures may be of less consequence than the quality of experience within the family unit, with large variance between families with similar structures.

Central to our discussion of lifestyles was individualism coupled to the goal of autonomy, but there are competing perspectives between the purposive, reflexivity of Giddens' high modernism and the hedonism and fragmentation of postmodernism. Such differences have great significance for the future of countryside recreation but have to be placed alongside the arguments of Schama and the biophilia supporters who suggest that the enjoyment of natural (or semi-natural) areas may be much more enduring. The challenge for providers will be how to take account of the plurality of lifestyles: how to cater for those whose day out will not be complete without consumer pleasure; and for those who are looking for an escape from commercial pressures; how to reconcile the interests of field sports enthusiasts and those opposed to blood sports; and how to serve the needs of conservationists and those applying the latest in technology to their recreation. In whatever scenario it seems likely that it will remain important for people to have the opportunity to integrate nature into their daily lives and for countryside agencies to promote such opportunities.

Notes

[1] As Castells (1996: p. 268) has observed, in Britain "the traditional form of work, based on full-time employment, clear-cut occupational assignments and a career pattern over the life cycle is being slowly, but surely eroded away".

[2] Glancey (1997) recently bemoaned the commercial trivialisation of artists' work when he observed: "Quite why the British Museum and the Victoria and Albert, for example, feel impelled to have a shop that takes up a vast square footage of valuable gallery space is probably beyond anyone, save perhaps the museum's marketing team and accountants. In the case of the V & A ... the gift shop has grown to supermarket proportions".

References

Adams, W. (1996) *Future nature.* London: Earthscan.

Baker, K & Fletcher, P. (1987) 'Outlook—TGI's new lifestyle system', *Admap*, No. 261, pp. 23-29.

Castells, M. (1996) *The rise of the network society.* Malden (MA.): Blackwell.

Centre for Leisure Research (1996) *UK Day Visits Survey 1994.* Cardiff: Countryside Recreation Network.

Centre for the Study of Environmental Change (1994) *Leisure landscapes. Leisure, culture and the English countryside: Challenges and conflicts.* London: Council for the Protection of Rural England.

Clarke, J. & Critcher, C. (1985) *The devil makes work.* Basingstoke: Macmillan.

Countryside Commission (1997) *Public attitudes to the countryside.* Cheltenham: Countryside Commission.

Csikszentmihalyi, M. and I. S. Csikszentmihalyi (1988) *Optimal experiences: Psychological studies of flow in consciousness.* Cambridge: Cambridge University Press.

Demos (1995) *The time squeeze.* Issue 5. London: Demos.

Elkins, P. (1986) *The living economy.* London: Routledge.

Giddens, A. (1991) *Modernity and self identity.* Cambridge: Polity Press.

Glancey, J. (1997) 'My friends went to the Tate and all they got me was this lousy pair of gloves', *The Guardian Week Supplement*, 19 July: p. 6.

Gough, I. and Doyal, L. (1991) *A theory of human need*. London: Macmillan.

Gray, J. (1996) *After social democracy*. London: Demos.

Kinsman, F. (1990) *Millennium*. London: Penguin.

Lasch, C. (1980) *Culture of narcissism*. London: Sphere.

Mintel (1996) *Sporting activity in the "Great Outdoors"*. London: Mintel.

Orr, D. (1992) 'Love it or lose it: The coming biophilia revolution', in Wilson, E. O. & Kellert, S. (eds) (1992) *The biophilia hypothesis*. Washington: Island Press, pp. 415-440.

Rapoport, R. & Rapoport, R. N. (1975) *Leisure and the family life-cycle*. London: Routledge and Kegan Paul.

Rojek, C. (1995) 'Leisure and the dreamworld of modernity', in I. Henry (ed) *Leisure: Modernity, postmodernity and lifestyles* (LSA Publication No. 48). Eastbourne: Leisure Studies Association, pp. 3-12.

Savage, M., Barlow, J., Dickens, P. and Fielding, T. (1992) *Property, bureaucracy and culture*. London: Routledge.

Schama, S. (1995) *Landscape and memory*. London: Harper Collins.

Veal, A. J. (1993) 'The concept of lifestyle: a review', *Leisure Studies* Vol. 12, No. 4: pp. 233-252.

Veblen, T. (1899) *The theory of the leisure class*. New York, Macmillan.

Wilson, E. O. and Kellert, S. (eds) (1992) *The biophilia hypothesis*. Washington: Island Press.

World Commission on Environment and Development (1988) *Our common future* (Brundtland Report). Oxford: Oxford University Press.

Rural Recreation: Perspectives on Landholder Attitudes and Public Access to Private Lands

John Jenkins

Centre for Tourism and Leisure Policy Research,
University of Canberra

Introduction

Rural areas have become increasingly important locations and backdrops for tourism and recreational activities. Whereas much of the focus of recreational and tourism activity — and related research and public policy making — in rural areas has been on public lands, attention to the potential and roles of private lands in the provision recreational opportunities is relatively lacking, particularly in such countries as Australia and Canada.

The amount of private land available in any area for recreation is largely dependent on the goals and attitudes of landholders (Coppock and Duffield, 1975; Cullington, 1981; Pigram, 1981; 1983; Sanderson, 1982; Butler, 1984). Much research concerning public access to private lands for recreation has been conducted in Canada, North America and the United Kingdom (UK) (e.g., see Ironside, 1971; Conservation Council of Ontario, 1975; Troughton, 1975; Bull and Wibberley, 1976; Cullington, 1981; Middleton, 1982; Swinnerton, 1982; Patmore, 1983; Butler, 1984; Butler and Troughton, 1985; Centre for Leisure Research, 1986; Countryside Commission, 1996; Perdue, *et al.*, 1987; Wall, 1989; Glyptis, 1991; Watkins, 1996). Such research indicates that landholder attitudes are determined by: landholder values and personal beliefs; legal, economic, social and ecological concerns; national, local and family traditions; government incentives; the type and volume of recreational activities; and past encounters with recreationists (Cullington, 1981) (see **Table 1 and Figure 1**, following pages). However, research findings in particular localities may be site or regional specific and therefore have little application outside their context because of different institutional arrangements, legal situations, historical development processes, land use intensities and, in all likelihood, the different attitudes to land of landholders.

Table 1a: Negative impacts of recreational activities

NEGATIVE IMPACTS

ENVIRONMENTAL

— erosion of trails, campsites, picnic sites, and water-side areas

— loss of vegetation and disturbance of livestock

— pollution of streams from farm land effluent

— dumping of garbage

ECONOMIC

— damage to property (crop damage, livestock loss, vandalism and theft)

— littering, gates left open

— fire risk, illegal shooting

— cost of providing and maintaining recreational facilities e.g. picnic sites, roads, trails

— legal (liability) and accountancy fees, fire insurance, policing and other costs stemming from recreational provisions

— changes to farming practices or other such requirements

LEGAL

— occupier liability

— limiting access and trespass

— compensation for property damage and related civil

SOCIAL

— differing attitudes between recreationists and residents

— increased stress, crowding, traffic congestion

— lack of/or reduction of privacy

— change in lifestyle and quality of life on a seasonal or permanent basis

— non-permitted activities (e.g. indiscriminate use of firearms, trail bikes, fire lighting)

OTHER

— change in the status quo

— gradual urbanisation of rural areas

— increasing loss of control over rural areas by rural residents (this could relate to all the above concerns).

Figure 1 about here

Rural Recreation 137

Table 1b: Positive impacts of recreational activities

POSITIVE IMPACTS

ENVIRONMENTAL
— increased environmental awareness and education
— greater support for financial support for the environment

ECONOMIC
— sale of goods and services to recreationists
— leasing land to groups or government agencies
— sale or lease of land for recreational development
— income for recreational ventures

LEGAL
— legislation of access is cheaper then land acquisitioned avoids problems associated with land severance
— secures desirable public rights
— compensation to farmers for maintenance, including conservation activities

SOCIAL
— political change resulting from increased representation of seasonal or temporary urban residents
— urban rural interaction
— escape for city dwellers
— altruism

OTHER
— wider (e.g. political) recognition of importance of recreation and the need for strategic recreational planning and development strategies educational programmes

Source: Adapted from Cullington, 1981; Pigram, 1981; Sanderson, 1982; Butler, 1984

Figure 1:   Factors influencing the availability of private land for recreation

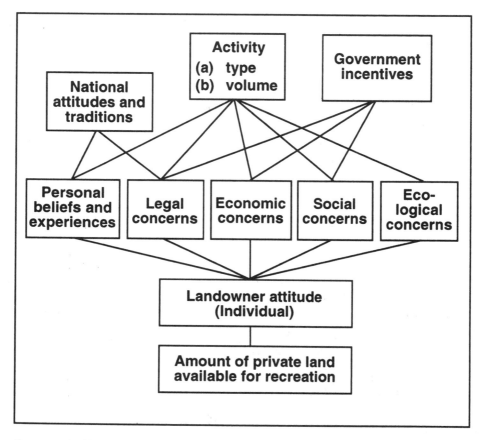

Source: Cullington, 1981

In Australia, despite the increasing use of the countryside for recreation and tourism, and the attention given to the potential for these activities to contribute to rural regional development and more specifically farm incomes, information concerning landholder attitudes to recreational access to private rural lands is scant. Therefore, the aims of this paper are:

- to outline recent research and developments concerning recreational access to private rural lands in Australia; and

- to examine landholder attitudes to recreational access to private lands in a case study of central western New South Wales (NSW), Australia.

Attitudes and approaches to providing recreational access to public and private lands vary around the globe. These variations relate to different

historical developments (landscape images; public policy; private development), land ownership rights and attitudes (the latter perhaps reflecting
historical trends and issues), government initiatives or lack thereof, and past
and present legislative provisions (which may reflect past public policy
experience and practice). In Australia, there is no parallel system to the rights
of way network which gives people access to much of the countryside in
England and Wales. Conflict in the use of private rural lands for public
recreation is common, but has yet to attract much attention from planners
and policy makers.

Context and settings

Rural recreation is just one competitor for the use of non-urban/metropolitan
land and water (Green, 1977). Other uses include primary production (e.g.,
agricultural, aquatic, horticultural, pastoral and timber production), conservation or preservation of the natural and built environment (e.g., national
parks, wilderness areas), and transport and communication networks.

The relationships between rural tourism and recreation and other land
and water uses are largely influenced by landholder attitudes. Landholders
include individuals (e.g., farmers), businesses (e.g., agribusiness; tourist
resort) and groups (e.g., recreation clubs) with private ownership rights,
leaseholders (whose land use may be regulated by public agencies), and
resource management agencies (e.g., national parks, forestry, nature/wildlife
reserves, public owned recreational facilities, water reservoirs). In short, there
is a wide variety of individuals and agencies with different value sets and
interests with respect to the rural and environment, and with different rights
as landholders according to land tenure and other institutional, legislative
or contractual arrangements.

The complexity of institutional and ownership arrangements and the
multi-functional character of rural areas has led to conflict between competing uses, and between land managers. Land ownership and the exercise
of landownership rights are thus critical elements in the supply of tourism
and recreation opportunities because access to land and water in this context
is generally contingent upon legislation, public policy interpretations, and
landholder/management attitudes (Pigram, 1981; Corfield, 1987).

Agreements and compromise between recreationists, responsible
agencies and landholders are often difficult to achieve. On the one hand, as
farmers seek to improve productivity (e.g., through more intensive land use
practices, including the development of cattle feed lots), 'aesthetic and
functional' changes to the landscape occur and impact on recreational supply
and visitor experiences and satisfaction. On the other hand, rural recreation
activities can become more contentious as their environmental impacts
increase (e.g., large numbers of people visit sensitive sites; the use of such
recent and potentially destructive recreational technologies as four wheel
drive vehicles and snowmobiles). Recreational activities such as hiking,
camping, fishing and nature observation may be passive and have less

inherent and actual potential to cause conflict between participants and land managers. However, landholder attitudes, perceptions and experiences may be influenced by small numbers of people who fail to consider the relationship between the type and intensity of their activities and the resulting impacts on the environment, including other people. Indeed, there are those whose intentions and activities are deliberately environmentally destructive and criminal (e.g., indiscriminate shooting of stock, and stealing). Clearly, an understanding of land use involves both an understanding of the values of the physical, biological, productive, spatial, and visual/aesthetic attributes of land, and "an awareness of the different standpoints from which land use may be considered" (Mather, 1991: p. 6).

Australia: A case study of Central Western New South Wales

Participation in rural recreation in Australia has grown rapidly since World War Two, and particularly since the 1960s (Pigram, 1983). The rates of recreational participation have been affected by such factors as greater available leisure time; higher disposable incomes; increased mobility of people (by way of the development of private motor vehicles and other forms of transportation); the influence of commercial interests; the promotion of high-risk recreational activities; emphasis on health and fitness programs; increasing environmental awareness; and a growing focus on human services (Pigram, 1983; Parker and Paddick, 1991).

Several writers have drawn attention to the lack of research and substantive results in rural recreation and tourism studies, and especially the absence of sound theoretical frameworks in Australia (Pigram and Jenkins, 1994) and overseas (see Butler and Clark, 1992). In Australia, research in rural recreation and tourism has attracted only spasmodic interest (Pigram and Jenkins, 1994). The attitudes of landholders to public recreational access is one aspect of rural recreation which requires much more research attention. According to Pigram (1981: p. 111), in Australia:

> ... the concept of inviolate rights of property is widespread and generally accepted... Landowners generally regard access to private land for sport and recreation as a privilege, not a birthright, which may be earned by good behaviour and responsibility. The landholder's attitude is typified by this statement made by the Graziers' Association of New South Wales: 'This Association will not consent to accept the entry upon private land, without the permission of owners or occupiers, of any persons who are not performing a statutory function, as other than trespass'.

As part of its submission to the NSW State Government Committee of Enquiry into the fishing industry, the Graziers' Association of New South Wales (1975) conducted a survey of its members in order to obtain factual evidence to substantiate objections to easing entry on private lands. Permission to enter private lands was granted by less than 50 per cent of rural landholders, and these cases were dependent on specific conditions being met. According to the study, graziers were concerned about guns, dogs, litter, gates, unattended fires, and disturbance to stock. Further enquiries indicated that the farmers' reservations concerning public access were justified as "evidence gathered

Table 2: Trespass damage in New South Wales

Damage category	Number reporting (n=83)
Gate problems	30
Fire hazard	34
Litter	34
Shooting	35
Stock disturbance	28
Violence/vandalism	23
Theft	19
Other problems	28

Source : Graziers' Association of New South Wales 1975 in Pigram (1981: 118).

covered a wide range of damaging incidents and potentially dangerous situations" (Graziers' Association of New South Wales, 1975, in Pigram, 1981: p. 117-118) which are summarised in **Table 2**.

Following this report the Committee of Enquiry supported the view that "it would be a major and serious departure to in any way interfere with the rights of property owners ... by allowing free public access for whatever purpose" (Pigram, 1981: p. 118).

A 1987 study of landholder attitudes toward public recreation access to private rural land in North-Western NSW reported on the substantial reluctance of landowners to permit such access. Only 20 per cent of respondents were willing to allow access to the wider public (i.e.. excluding friends and relatives), while only 21.6 per cent showed any willingness to even consider possible government measures to improve the access situation (Corfield, 1987).

In late 1995, the author undertook surveys of rural landholders in the Shires of Blayney and Cabonne, central western NSW . The following section outlines the study aims, research method and some of the findings of that study.

Study aims

The aim of the study was to examine rural landholder attitudes to recreational access to private lands in NSW (see map below). It was designed to assist in the identification of barriers to recreational access to private lands, the reconciliation of conflicts in the recreational use of private lands, and to enhance the spectrum of recreational opportunities in the countryside.

Given these broad aims, the specific objectives of the study were:

- to identify rural landholder attitudes to recreational access;

- to identify the underlying dimensions which explain those attitudes, and therefore to determine whether attitudes differ because of ownership, land tenure, government incentives, income and other arrangements;

- to review the systems of incentives and disincentives under which landholders are operating; and

- to identify means of ameliorating rural land use conflict by way of incentives and removal of disincentives identified by landholders.

The study is significant because it is one of few studies (and statistically the largest), to address the subject of rural landholder attitudes to public access to private lands for recreation in Australia (also see Pigram, 1981; Corfield, 1987).

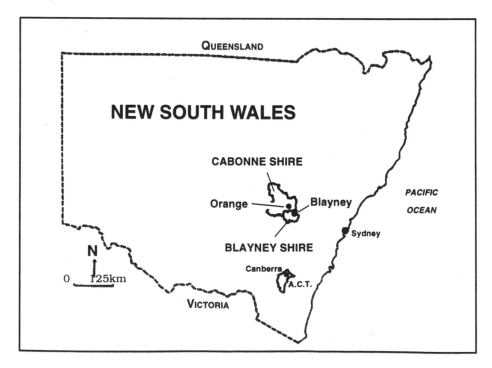

Study methodology

A systematic random sample of 200 landholders in Blayney Shire (response rate 51 per cent) and 500 landholders in Cabonne Shire (response rate 54 per cent) were selected from lists of landholders whose properties were designated 'farmland'. Lists of landholders were provided by the Blayney and Cabonne Shire Councils. Only landholders whose properties were designated 'farmland' were included in the sample. A mail out pilot study of 20 respondents in Blayney and 50 in Cabonne (response rate with one mail out — 38 per cent) was undertaken in October, 1995. Subsequent, minor, alterations were made to survey content and presentation.

Section 493 of the *Local Government Act*, 1993, requires that NSW local councils categorise land into one of four categories — 'farmland', 'residential', 'business' or 'mining'. The definition for each category is contained in that Act. Section 515(1) of the LGA sets out the prerequisites for occupied land to be categorised as 'farmland'. Section 519 facilitates the categorisation of vacant land and it should be noted that scope exists for vacant land to be categorised as 'farmland' in certain circumstances via those provisions.

For land to be categorised as 'farmland' in terms of section 515 it must be a parcel of rateable land, valued as one assessment, the dominant use of which is for farming (that is, the business or industry of grazing, animal feedlots, dairying, pig-farming, poultry farming, viticulture, orcharding, beekeeping, horticulture, vegetable growing, the growing of crops of any kind, forestry, or aquaculture within the meaning of the *Fisheries Management Act*, 1994, or any combination of those businesses or industries) which has a significant and substantial commercial purpose or character, and which is engaged in for the purpose of profit on a continuous or repetitive basis (whether or not a profit is actually made).

Study findings and discussion

Respondents were predominantly males (Blayney — 70.5 per cent; Cabonne — 78.9 per cent), which in itself raises questions of gender distributions in land ownership and attitudes with respect to access; and 40 years of age or more (Blayney — 89.6 per cent, over a third of whom were 60 years of age or more; Cabonne — 82.4 per cent, of whom nearly 30 per cent were 60 years of age or more).

Respondents' membership of leisure or sporting organisations, occupation, and levels of education attained are shown in **Tables 3**, **4** and **5**, respectively (following page).

Table 3:   Membership of leisure and sporting organisations

Element	Cabonne Results	Blayney Results
Yes	37.14	38.04
No	62.86	61.96
Total	100.00%	100.00%

Table 4:   Main occupation

Occupation	Cabonne Results	Blayney Results
Farmer	67.360	61.957
Retired	3.720	3.261
Professional	14.050	17.391
Trade	2.479	2.174
Clerical	2.066	3.261
Home duties	3.306	7.609
Unemployed	0.000	0.000
Social Services	0.000	0.000
Student	0.413	0.000
Other	6.612	4.348
Total	100.00%	100.00%

Table 5:   Highest level of education attained

Level	Cabonne Results	Blayney Results
Primary School	2.834	11.828
High School	37.247	46.237
TAFE/College certificate	21.457	17.204
TAFE/College diploma	8.502	2.151
University diploma	8.907	2.151
University degree	12.955	11.828
University post-graduate degree	4.858	6.452
Other	3.239	2.151
Total	100.00%	100.00%

In response to the question "Do you or would you allow any members of the public to use your land for recreational purposes?", 73 per cent of respondents from Blayney and 63 per cent of respondents from Cabonne replied "No". The most popular reasons cited for denying access were:

- damage to crops;
- disturbance of stock;
- failure to shut gates;
- littering and associated problems;
- vandalism to property; and
- indiscriminate shooting.

The problem of access is also manifested in people using property without landholder permission. In response to the question "Have you ever had any members of the public use your land for recreational purposes without your permission?", 61 per cent of respondents from Blayney and 60 per cent of respondents from Cabonne replied "Yes".

Perhaps unsurprisingly, and reflecting, in part, the findings of earlier studies, landholders in Blayney and Cabonne expressed little or no interest in entering into incentives or agreements for recreational access to their property with the following:

- the then Labor Federal government (86.8 per cent in Blayney and 81.4 per cent in Cabonne respectively) (in March, 1996, the conservative Liberal/National Party coalition ascended to power);
- the then NSW Department of Land and Water Conservation (86.8 per cent and 78.9 per cent);
- the NSW National Parks and Wildlife Service (80.4 per cent and 80.2 per cent);
- Local government (81.1 per cent and 76.3 per cent); and
- private recreation organisations (81.3 per cent and 76.5 per cent).

Contrastingly, a number of conditions hold some promise as means of encouraging recreational access to private land. Positive ("Yes") responses to the question "Would any of the following conditions encourage you to allow or increase public access to your land for recreational purposes" were as follows:

- only certain types of recreational activities be allowed (25.8 per cent in Blayney and 33.3 per cent in Cabonne respectively);
- that activities be confined to a particular area of your property (26.1 per and 30.6 per cent);
- that activities be limited to set times of the day (19.8 per cent and 21.6 per cent);
- that activities be limited to certain seasons (24.1 per cent and 24.3 per cent);

- that people arrange times with you (30.3 per cent and 35.8 per cent);

- that you can prevent people from undertaking recreational activities if the conditions you agreed to are not being kept (42.7 per cent and 46.1 per cent);

- that legal liability not rest with the landholder (40.7 per cent and 45.8 per cent); and

- that people pay for using your property for recreational purposes (20.7 per cent and 25.2 per cent).

Clearly, the ability of landholders to regulate recreational activities and the absence of legal liability of farmers for people who use lands for recreational activities appear to be aspects which (1) warrant further research, and (2) present potential public policy avenues for increasing recreational access to private lands.

    This study indicates that there is much resistance, if not direct opposition, to the use of private rural lands for public recreation in the Blayney and Cabonne shires (**Table 6**, opposite, provides examples of comments that were far from supportive). Earlier studies (Graziers' Association of New South Wales 1975; Pigram, 1981; Corfield, 1987) indicate similar findings in other areas of NSW. Nevertheless, there are avenues for increasing recreational access to private rural lands. In short, the results of the surveys in the Blayney and Cabonne Shires largely support the findings of Corfield (1987) and reflect some of the concerns raised in Canadian studies. The views of respondents largely reflect those views expressed almost twenty years earlier in the Submission of the Grazier's Association of NSW.

Conclusion

Leisure has become a vital part of the lives of all Australians; in an increasingly complex society, the task of creating and enhancing leisure environments will call for many fresh initiatives. At the same time, participation in outdoor recreation is very much a function of available opportunities. The challenge of rural accessibility planning is to expand the supply of opportunities by enlarging the space-time prisms available for outdoor recreation. Perhaps access to countryside is a good place to begin (Pigram, 1981: pp. 122-123).

    Whatever one's stance on the issue of public access to private lands, and there are diverse opinions with respect to landholders' rights, more empirical research on this issue is needed in Australia, particularly with respect to how and why landholder attitudes vary spatially and even with respect to land tenure. Unfortunately, however, with the increasing emphasis on economic returns on public sector investment, and with well established rural land ownership rights and ethics, particularly in Australia, much rural recreation research and planning is likely to remain conservative and unimaginative, lacking in sound theoretical frameworks, and tied mainly to tangible initiatives.

Table 6 **Respondent comments on use of private rural lands for public recreation in the Blayney and Cabonne shires**

- Government should provide the land for public recreational activities, for example, State forests... the farmers and landholders have a big enough responsibility just surviving.

- A lot of people have no idea about farming. If they come onto your place they are just as likely to drive over new crops etc and do damage or get bogged and then you have to pull them out. Irresponsibility with fire is our major fear, dog control also worries us.

- Most people that visit the property are honest and attempt to do the right thing. We are concerned about the small number of less civic minded souls who do on occasion turn up. They ruin the property, owner's confidence and trust and make one wary of strangers in general.

- We feel that private property should be just that. Access on invitation only.

- Once access is given its very hard to stop people - they think that they have an inalienable right to your place.

- Would you like people camping in your garden without permission

- Surely there is enough land controlled by crown lands to satisfy the bush walkers etc without the farmers of Australia having to put up with yet another intrusion into their privacy.

- Having been burgled... to the extent of $15 000, I am now very reluctant to draw any attention to our remoteness, as we are not in residence permanently.

- I am entitled to have quiet enjoyment of my own land. This is given by the Law of the Land and must be retained unless I choose to give up those rights.

- Would you like the general public camping and walking around your front yard?... we like our privacy as much as city dwellers.

Although policy-making and planning with respect to recreational access to private rural lands are likely to remain somewhat neglected issues, we should raise several critical questions. Is the concept of inviolable rights attaching to land ownership appropriate to lands in private ownership? Should policy-makers take care "that land is used to satisfy the needs of the majority and not of the few with some special interest [because] it is no more legitimate to advocate closing the countryside to the population to avoid pollution or the loss of native flora and fauna than it is to close the roads to motorists as a means of preventing car accidents" (Davidson, 1972: p. 212)? Are landholders merely stewards or custodians of 'their' property, holding and using it on trust for later generations?

Who does 'own' the land? Who does have a right to access? These questions are being raised not just in limited circles with respect to recreational and tourist access to private lands, but very much more widely with respect to indigenous land rights, mining and other issues, such as heritage management. Interestingly, in Australia, there is strong opposition from landholders to Aboriginal land rights which have been upheld by the High Court of Australia and supported, to different degrees in legislative, institutional and policy developments, among the Australian States. In attempting to reach solutions to these and other similar complex problems, Lowenthal's ideas are worth recounting:

> To be effective...planning and design should be grounded on intimate knowledge of the ways people think and feel about the environment; this calls for a substantial familiarity with social and intellectual history, with psychology and philosophy, with art and anthropology. All these fields contribute to our knowledge of how we see the world we live in, how vision and value affect action, and how action alters institutions. (Lowenthal, 1968, in Mitchell, 1989: p. 144)

Interestingly, studying tourism, an often disputed or underrated discipline (Hall and Jenkins, 1995), and recreation issues offers a very useful position to contribute to our understanding of the ways people think and feel about their environment because the study of tourism and recreation is fluid and transcends disciplinary boundaries. Surely indigenous peoples want rights or access to 'their' land for recreational activities as much as other aspects of their lives which seem to receive greater attention. The study of rural tourism issues, including research on landholder attitudes to public recreational access, then, can make a much wider contribution to our understanding of society than perhaps first appears.

References

Bull, C. and Wibberley, G. (1976) *Farm-based recreation in South-East England*. Studies in Rural Land Use No. 12. Countryside Planning Unit, School of Rural Economics and Related Studies, Wye College.

Butler, R. W. (1984) 'The impact of informal recreation on rural Canada', in M. F. Bunce and M. J. Troughton (eds) *The pressure of change in rural Canada*. Downsview, York University, Ontario: Geographical Monograph 14.

Butler, R. W. and Clarke, G. (1992) 'Tourism in rural areas: Canada and the United Kingdom'., in I. R. Bowler, C. R. Bryant and M. D. Nellis (eds) *Contemporary rural systems in transition: Economy and society*. Wallingford: CAB International.

Butler, R. W. and Troughton, M. J. (1985) *Public use of private land*. Ontario, London: University of Western.

Centre for Leisure Research. (1986) *Access to the countryside for recreation and sport: Report to the Countryside Commission and the Sports Council by the Centre for Leisure Research.* Cheltenham: Countryside Commission.

Conservation Council of Ontario. (1975) *Private land, public recreation and the law.* Toronto: Conservation Council of Ontario.

Coppock, J. T. and Duffield, B. S. (1975) *Recreation in the countryside: A spatial analysis.* London: Macmillan Press.

Corfield, R. (1987) *Recreational access to private rural land.* University of New England, Armidale: Unpublished Bachelor of Arts with Honours thesis.

Countryside Commission. (1986) *Access to the countryside for recreation and sport: Report to the Countryside Commission and the Sports Council by the Centre for Leisure Research.* Cheltenham: Countryside Commission.

Cullington, J. M. (1981) *The public use of private land for recreation.* Department of Geography, University of Waterloo, Waterloo, Ontario: Unpublished Master of Arts thesis.

Davidson, B. R. (1972) 'Agriculture and rural land use', in A. Rapoport (ed) *Australia as human setting: Approaches to the designed environment.* Sydney: Angus and Robertson.

Glyptis, S. (1991) *Countryside recreation.* Harlow: Longman.

Graziers' Association of New South Wales. (1975) *Submission to select committee of the Legislative Assembly upon the fishing industry.* Sydney: Graziers' Centre.

Green, B. (1977) 'Countryside planning: compromise or conflict?', *The Planner* Vol. 63: pp. 67-69

Hall, C. M. and Jenkins, J. (1995) *Tourism and public policy.* London: Routledge.

Ironside, R. G. (1971) 'Agriculture and recreation land use in Canada — potential for conflict or benefit?', *Canadian Journal of Agricultural Economics,* Vol. 19 No. 2: pp. 1-12

Mather, A. (1991) *Land use.* Harlow: Longman Scientific and Technical.

Middleton, V. Y. C. (1982) 'Tourism in rural areas', *Tourism Management,* Vol. 3: pp. 52-8.

Mitchell, B. (1989) *Geography and resource analysis,* 2nd. ed. Harlow: Longman Scientific and Technical.

Parker, S. and Paddick, R. (1991) *Leisure in Australia: Themes and issues.* Melbourne: Longman.

Patmore, J. A. (1983) *Recreation and resources: leisure patterns and leisure places*. Oxford: Basil Blackwell.

Perdue, R. R., Long, P. T. and Allen, L. (1987) 'Rural resident tourism perceptions and attitudes', *Annals of Tourism Research* Vol. 14: pp. 420-9

Pigram, J. J. (1981) 'Outdoor recreation and access to the countryside: Focus on the Australian experience', *Natural Resources Journal*: pp. 107-123

———— (1983) *Outdoor recreation and resource management*, London: Croom Helm.

Pigram, J. P. and Jenkins J. M. (1994) 'The role of the public sector in the supply of rural recreation opportunities', in D. Mercer (ed) *New viewpoints in outdoor recreation research in Australia*. Williamstown: Hepper Marriott and Associates.

Sanderson, K. (1982) *Recreation on agricultural land in Alberta: Summary*. Edmonton: Environment Council of Alberta,

Shoard, M. (1996) 'Robbers v. revolutionaries: what the battle for access is really all about', in C. Watkins (ed) *Rights of way: Policy, culture and management*. London: Pinter.

Swinnerton, G. S. (1982) *Recreation on agricultural lands in Alberta*. Edmonton: Environment Council of Alberta.

Troughton, M. J. (1975) 'Agriculture and the countryside', in M. J. Troughton, J. G. Nelson and S. Brown (eds) *The countryside in Ontario*. London: University of Western Ontario.

Wall, G. (1989) *Outdoor recreation in Canada*. New York: Wiley.

Watkins, C. (ed) (1996) *Rights of way: Policy, culture and management*. London: Pinter.

III

REPRESENTATION

Coastal Tourism as Comparative Consumption of Cultural Landscapes

Daniel O'Hare

Queensland University of Technology

Introduction

There is a worldwide concern that tourism can erode the special qualities that attract tourists to particular destinations, ranging from historic cities to coastal regions (Hough, 1990; HRH the Prince of Wales, 1996). At the same time, the resource value of place distinctiveness is receiving the attention of urban authorities and the tourism industry (Ashworth and Goodall, 1990).

This paper is drawn from a larger research project investigating the integration of tourism in small coastal settlements using a multi-method research strategy for interpreting cultural landscapes of tourism (O'Hare, forthcoming). The case study of Noosa, a well known resort area on the east coast of Australia, combines data from tourist guides and brochures with focused conversational interviews and the more 'formal' sources of documentary research, published literature and field survey. The combined methods interpret the tourism landscape through achieving an interplay between individual experiences, the formal, documented story of the place (including maps and 'rules'), popular and marketing images, and 'thick description' of the four dimensional place, in which the fourth dimension, time, is important. Recurrent themes and patterns, and similarities and differences emerging from the five method components, are of particular interest because they indicate convergences and divergences between narrative and physical landscape patterns.

The Queensland resort of Noosa has been selected for case study for a number of reasons. It has a history of vigorous public debate over the influence of tourism on the special qualities that attract tourism. Its development for tourism has received widespread publicity throughout Australia for nearly three decades. This publicity has resulted from formal and informal promotion of Noosa's natural and cultural qualities, and from national coverage of several conservation battles. Noosa continues to be promoted, and widely accepted,as an 'unspoilt' resort, despite periodic publicity claiming that particular development proposals would spoil it. In addition, Noosa has moved in a relatively short time through several definable stages of tourism development to its current state of maturity as a tourist resort (cf. Butler, 1980, and Smith, 1991).

Despite the depiction of Noosa as a 'distinctive' small coastal settlement, aspects of its continuing development and transformation are in many ways 'typical' of other coastal tourism transformations. This enables findings from the case study to be generalised to theory, in this case expanding cultural landscape and tourism theory through analytic generalisation (Yin, 1994). By exploring the dialogue between several themes (after Shields, 1991), the case study is used to address broader questions of the transformation of small coastal settlements by tourism. In particular, the case study contributes to a theoretical reexamination of the widely held proposition that tourism 'spoils' 'unspoilt' places (see O'Hare, forthcoming).

Cultural landscapes, tourism landscapes

The cultural landscape is the environment as modified, classified, and interpreted by humankind. This morphological concept portrays places, at all scales, as consisting of a cultural overlay on the natural landscape (O'Hare, 1991: p. 33), so that the identity of any one place derives from the historical interactions between the natural and cultural components of the landscape. The concept is not just a way of viewing special or unique places, but extends to cover the everyday places where people live, work or travel (Jackson, 1984; Meinig, 1979). This paper focuses, however, on the cultural landscapes of distinctive small coastal settlements that attract tourists, in the context of comparative regional, national and global landscapes.

A tourism landscape is a cultural landscape in which tourism is an element. Several kinds of cultural landscape may exist in a place. A city might be simultaneously an industrial landscape and a tourism landscape; a rural area might be simultaneously a farming landscape, an Area of Outstanding Natural Beauty, and a tourism landscape. There are potentially as many tourism landscapes as there are cultural landscapes. Tourism is both an agent of landscape change, and a component of certain cultural landscapes. Distinctive cultural landscapes are attractive to tourists, and are subsequently changed by tourism, physically and perceptually.

Tourism landscapes as consumption landscapes

Tourism landscapes are landscapes of consumption (Mullins, 1992). The tourism landscape as consumption landscape is at its zenith in shopping malls that serve as tourist destinations, as at Canada's West Edmonton Mall (Sorkin, 1993). The creation of a tourism landscape may even transform a landscape of production into a landscape of consumption, as in recycled factories and waterfront warehouses (Shields, 1991). Cultural landscapes of religious significance may be converted into tourism landscapes, as at Angkor Wat or Lourdes. It could be argued that sites of pilgrimage tourism have always been associated with consumerism, as indicated by medieval sales of relics and indulgences, and the sale of religious ornaments in more recent times. The extension of that consumerism beyond religious consumption is evidenced by the tourist running through Notre Dame cathedral yelling "Wait, I'm out of film!".[1]

Tourism as comparative consumption of tourism landscapes

Waikiki, the Riviera, Acapulco, Carmel, Malibu — give me Noosa any day. (Groom, 1993)

The spontaneous tendency to compare tourist destinations, as demonstrated in Noosa tourist brochures, planning documents, published sources and case study interviews, supports two themes in recent scholarly writing on tourism. Firstly, there is evidence that tourists are 'looking for differences' (Hough, 1990) — primarily from their places of origin (Krippendorf, 1987; Rojek, 1993). Secondly, tourism has similarities to other forms of consumption and consumerism, particularly the activity that retail marketers and land use planners call 'comparison shopping'. This second theme relates to the fact that, in a global market, tourism destinations are competing with other similar 'products'. Comparison shopping for a coastal tourist *resort* is assisted by the international brochures published by transnational tourism operators such as Club Med, and by sun, sand and surf travel wholesalers such as Thomsons in the UK.

Towner (1996: p. 215) notes that coastal resort marketers have deliber-ately constructed associations between English seaside resorts and overseas model resorts since at least the early twentieth century. These comparisons range from the associative labelling of resort areas to share in the prestige of famed resorts (as in the 'Cornish Riviera' and even the 'Scottish Riviera'), to visual re-imaging, as in early twentieth century railway posters portraying Weston Super-Mare with a beach, townscape and light more like the Cote d'Azur than Somerset (Towner, 1996: pp. 215-216). In similar vein, a 1925 advertisement extols Byron Bay as "the Honolulu of New South Wales".

Both tourists and locals compare particular destinations with other 'known products'. Comparisons and contrasts motivate holiday decisions and tourism design and development decisions. This process of comparison operates at both formal and informal levels. The formal level includes the many positive references to the Mediterranean and the negative references to Hawaii and the Queensland Gold Coast, published in Cato's *Noosa Story* (1979, 1989) and the 'lifestyle magazine', *Noosa Blue*. The informal level includes the spontaneous comparisons most of the interviewees for this research made to other places. Somewhere between the formal and informal levels lie the eclectic design references (Mediterranean-French provincial-

London-Paris-California!) of expensive luxury apartments built on the Noosa beachfront in 1996 (Cooper, 1996), and the naming of approximately fifteen per cent of advertised individual tourist accommodation after exotic locations such as Bermuda or Bali, or with generic Mediterranean names such as "Maison La Plage". The comparative process helps to 'label' a particular resort, to define its level of prestige and reputation. The process draws on the proven and tested labels of other coastal resorts and other places having qualities that Noosa seeks to emulate.

Paul Theroux (1995), in his grand tour of the Mediterranean, notes the application of tried and proven labels to newer beach resorts: "... the muddiest beach at Ieratpetra [Crete] was called Waikiki" (1995: p. 335); Carmel Beach, Israel, as "the Riviera of Israel" (p, 386); and the Tunisian village of Sidi Bou-Said as "the St Tropez of Tunis" (p. 484). These are simply later versions of Noosa's 1880s escape value as "the Brighton of Gympie", a comparison that has been updated in the past two decades to capture the Mediterranean. Theroux suggests that:

> The dream of the Mediterranean ... is the dream of [the French] Riviera as a brilliant lotophagous land — the comer of the Mediterranean from the outskirts of Toulon eastward to Monte Carlo, a hundred-odd miles of Frenchness — food, wine, style, heat, rich old farts, gamblers and bare-breasted bimbos. All that and art too. (Theroux, 1995: p. 101)

'Mediterranean' is therefore a reliable label for increasing the prestige of a resort. Noosa's claimed Mediterranean qualities extend beyond the character of the light, air and natural setting (Cato, 1979: p. 1; Mainwaring, 1996) to also include food, wine, Noosa style, heat, art, and the 'laidback' lifestyle shared by the wealthy and the beautiful people, and idiosyncratic 'characters' (interviews, numerous tourist brochures).

The case study interviews and literature contain constant comparisons between Noosa and other places, including the cities where so many of Noosa's tourists and residents originate. **Table 1** and **Table 2** summarise the way in which descriptions and perceptions of Noosa are articulated by means of comparison and contrast with other resorts in Australia and overseas. The tables show that the resort comparison dialogue tends to emphasise the positive aspects of Noosa, through both comparison and contrast with other tourism landscapes: Noosa is generally likened to 'unspoilt' places, and contrasted to 'spoilt' places. The process of comparison and contrast with other Australian places results in a picture of Noosa as a small town integrated with a beautiful natural setting. A warm subtropical climate and good accessibility enable visitors to enjoy the sheltered north facing beach, good surfing, and attractive waterways. The low-key, low-rise urban form is subservient to the natural environment. Community involvement is held to have created a non-urban ambiance, marked by an absence of traffic lights, four lane roads and high-rise buildings. In contrast with some of the other resorts cited, Noosa is described as being uncrowded and combining prestige

Table 1:   Comparisons/contrasts between Noosa and other Australian tourist resorts

Noosa is like:	because Noosa is/has...	Noosa is not like:	because Noosa is/has...
	Positive		*Positive*
Byron Bay	Natural setting + north facing surf beaches + warm climate + Environmentally oriented planning and design	Byron Bay	Friendly + uncrowded + river
Brunswick Heads	Small town in natural setting + holiday atmosphere	Cities	No traffic lights, 4-lane roads or high-rise
Manly (Sydney)	Town right on beach	Surfers Paradise / Gold Coast	low-rise development in natural setting
Agnes Water - 1770	Good surfing	So.Sunshine Coast (Caloundra, Maroochy)	Low-rise + natural + not overdeveloped
Victorian beach resorts	Natural, prestigious	Coffs Harbour, Port Douglas	Tasteful + natural + not overdeveloped
Caloundra	Still waters + surf	Agnes Water - 1770	Less remote
NSW central coast villages	Natural setting	Victorian beach resorts	Year round climate makes good facilities viable
Port Macquarie, Port Stephens	Natural setting + good surf + waterways + water activity	North Queensland beach towns	Good surf beach
North Stradbrole Island	Similar integration of fishing villages in similar natural setting	Mission Beach	Subtropical climate
Port Douglas	Tropical tourist goldmine + laid-back lifestyle		
	Negative		*Negative*
Surfers Paradise, Manly	Expensive + no longer nature based	Byron Bay	Too touristy + less remote + no alternative lifestyle
Begara, Mon Repose	Beauty and peace spoilt by tourism	Caloundra	No longer family oriented
Melbourne	Suburban sprawl	Victorian beach resorts	No sense of history
Whitsunday Islands	Nature spoilt by overdevelopment	Woodgate	No longer nature based

(Sources: Case study interviews, ephemeral tourist literature, published tourist guides, popular and formal literature on Noosa.)

Table 2:   Comparison/contrasts between Noosa and international tourist resorts

Noosa is like:	because Noosa is/has...	Noosa is not like:	because Noosa is/has...
	Positive		*Positive*
Honolulu	Sidewalk cafes, stylish people, exotic ambience	Waikiki/Hawaii	Low-rise development in natural setting
Carmel	Nature myth + low key development + elegant people interested in environment	Spanish Mediterranean	As above
Noumia + Bali	Sunny beach + quality accommodation	French Mediterranean	Public beaches open to all
Teneriffe	Generic: small + cute	Monte Carlo + Sorrento	Low-rise and laid-back
NZ beach towns	Beautiful	NZ beach towns	Warm climate
Greek islands	Unspoilt + casual + good coffee at beach		
Mediterranean beaches	Relaxed + informal		
Monte Carlo + Sorrento	Beauty of natural setting + upmarket tourists		
French Mediterranean	Low-rise village atmosphere (Hastings Street)		
Mexican resorts	Mediterranean lifestyle		
Paris streets	Hastings Street stylish atmosphere		
Marbella + nearby town	Natural beauty and stylish shops and cafes		
Phuket + Pattaya	Beach + climate + relaxed		
	Negative		*Negative*
San Francisco and 'international' cities	Expensive galleries, shops and 'city coffee'	Marbella	Wasted opportunity for riverfront promenade
St Tropez	Promenade of expensive shops	Puerto Banus (Marbella	No marina
Banff	Touristy, crowded	Banff	Crowded, gimmick and touristy shops

(Sources: Case study interviews, ephemeral tourist literature, published tourist guides, popular and formal literature on Noosa.)

with a friendly holiday atmosphere. The international comparisons perpetuate Noosa's nature myth and overlay the casual, relaxed, laid back atmosphere with an emphasis on elegance and stylish people. The beachfront tourism business district of Hastings Street is the focus of comparisons with stylish European resorts and cities. Where more negative comparisons and contrasts are made, Noosa is described as too "expensive", too "crowded", too "touristy", and "spoilt by overdevelopment" and "commercialism". In comparisons with international resorts, there is an evident bias towards "stylish" European resorts rather than less "tasteful" American resorts. Noosa tourist brochures and key local interviewees suggest that the presence of international oper-ators is an important component of the "upmarket" image (for example Tourism Noosa, 1992: p. 24).

A more official example of the tendency to compare Noosa with inter-national resorts regarded as stylish and tasteful, rather than with other Australian resorts, was the first *Noosa Shire Design Manual* prepared in the mid-1980s by the Noosa Shire Council (NSC), with community input (NSC, 1986: p. i). Under the subheading, "aesthetic aspects", support is expressed for "a unified resort feeling" (NSC, 1986: p. 15) and well known international resorts are cited: "Examples of continuity in design providing popular memories of resort areas include Bermuda, the Greek Islands and ... the Mediterranean" (NSC, 1986: p. 15). This section of the *Design Manual* focuses on the creation of "continuity of character" at the eastern end of Hastings Street through the use of similar roofing materials (NSC, 1986: p. 15), and can be seen as a direct prelude to more recent descriptions of this area as 'the Paris end of Hastings Street' (see below).

Despite the frequency of international comparison, Queensland's Gold Coast receives the most comparative mention. The Gold Coast is frequently cited as significantly different from Noosa due to the presence of high-rise development, urban sprawl tendencies, and a greater modification of the natural environment.

The Gold Coast as an archetypal coastal tourism resort: from exemplar to anathema

The attractiveness and distinctiveness of Noosa has come to be defined, in part, in terms of what it is not. In the conversational interviews and other data sources, Noosa is consistently spoken of as being markedly different from the Queensland Gold Coast, and from Surfers Paradise, the centre of the Gold Coast (**Table 3**). The descriptions of these differences are frequently used as ways of articulating Noosa's own cultural landscape characteristics.

Surfers Paradise, or 'Surfers', as it is usually called by Australians, is Australia's most highly urbanised and best-known coastal resort (Smith, 1991). Surfers is the main resort on the Gold Coast, a forty kilometre stretch of urbanised coastline that stretches from seventy kilometres south of the Queensland capital, Brisbane, to the New South Wales state border. The Gold Coast and its urbanised hinterland, with a combined population of over

300,000, is one of the most rapidly growing regions in Australia. The long,
flat, coastal and estuarine strip is backed by a lush green hinterland and
rainforest covered volcanic mountains. The coastal strip is characterised by
an almost continuous band of high-rise apartment buildings, many of which
shade the beaches in the afternoons. For much of the twentieth century and
particularly the third quarter of the century, the Gold Coast, and Surfers
Paradise in particular, was acclaimed in Australia as the epitome of what a
good coastal resort should be. In 1950s references to Noosa, the Gold Coast
is depicted as a benchmark of desirable tourism development (Anon., 1955).

Table 3   Noosa Heads vs Surfers Paradise and Gold Coast

NOOSA HEADS	SURFERS PARADISE / GOLD COAST
Unique	International
European	American
Low-rise	High-rise, skyscrapers
Natural	Commercial
Tasteful	Distasteful
Style, elegance	Disneylandish, touristy, trendy
Relaxing, laid back	Busy, razzle-dazzle, rat race
Low key	Glitzy, ritzy
Village atmosphere	Fast and furious atmosphere
Small	Big
Like Southern France	Like eastern Spain, Hawaii
Manly, Mediterranean	Las Vegas, America
Environmentally responsive	Environmentally damaging
Quiet, intimate	Hectic. overcrowded
Beautiful	Ugly, vulgar, a mistake
Outdoor oriented	Indoor oriented
Country town, in the bush	City
Parking/traffic problems	Parking/traffic solutions
Good	Bad
Developers controlled	Developers dominant
Things to do	Things to visit/see
Vulnerable	Resilient
Product of motor car era	Established in railway era

(Descriptions from interviews and formal and informal literature.)

Not the Gold Coast means...

> [Noosa] is very different from the Gold Coast. There is none of the glitzy, ritzy, fast and furious atmosphere here. The ambience is quieter, softer, more in tune with nature.... [T]here is strong resistance by locals to 'another Gold Coast' and development has been kept low-key and low-rise. (Bowen, 1992: p. 138)

The contrasts between Noosa and the Gold Coast revealed in the research data contribute significantly to a broader narrative of Noosa as a low-rise 'village' in a natural setting, yet with an aura of style and sophistication. These two reported characteristics of Noosa are outlined below.

(i) No high-rise: Noosa as a village in the trees

Tourist brochures and published guides are quick to point out that there are no high-rise buildings at Noosa. Some brochures attribute the lack of high-rise buildings to an "edict that no building shall be higher than the trees" (for example Sunshine Coast Tourism Promotions, 1994: p. 101). This point was also mentioned consistently by those interviewed in this research. Although the ban on high-rise has been formalised in local planning controls, the move was led by community activism, and helped in fortuitous ways by the combination of the severe storms of the early 1970s and the economic slump which followed the boom of the late 1960s and early 1970s. The simplistic claim that "residents have prevented any development higher than the tree line" (Tourism Noosa, 1995) is therefore only a partial explanation. A court case brought by local residents, though legally unsuccessful, signalled to Noosa Shire Council, developers and investors that development proposals would be closely scrutinised by an articulate and well organised community. The catchcry of "no buildings taller than the trees" became a firm element of the Noosa narrative.

The Noosa Parks Association, a highly effective community organisation formed in 1962 to lobby for the expansion of Noosa's National Parks, has been a strong opponent of high-rise development. The Association's concern about potential impact on the natural environmental was accompanied by sometimes sensationalist concern at potential social problems such as crime and the isolation of elderly residents (Noosa Parks Association, 1981: p. 9). In voicing these concerns, the Association drew on media reports of high-rise living in Surfers Paradise and Honolulu. The constant reiteration of the anti-high-rise theme over the past three decades is matched by a physical tourism landscape in which the natural environment has remained prominent despite extensive tourism and residential development.

Noosa's 'not the Gold Coast' theme is the narrative of a village atmosphere rather than an urban character. Noosa Shire Council identifies as part of its tourist attractiveness a "lifestyle factor relating to Noosa's low key development and slower pace, as compared to cities and other tourist resorts" (NSC, 1991). Because this aspect of Noosa's lifestyle is recognised as significant to the Shire's economy, 'city symbols' such as traffic lights and four lane roads are explicitly discouraged by Council policy.

Through the visual media, several tourist interviewees had a strong image of Surfers Paradise as high-rise, overdeveloped and less 'aesthetically pleasing' than Noosa Heads. Some likened Surfers Paradise to "the Las Vegas Hawaii sort of feel", describing it as "Disneylandish" and "distasteful" in contrast to Noosa. A young Canadian woman had found Surfers to be "very, very, very touristy". A young Gold Coast couple, holidaying at Noosa Heads, said "It's nice to get away from [Surfers] and have the bush. It's all high-rises everywhere.... We like looking out to the National Park, rather than at high-rises casting shadows over the beach". They disliked the crowded beaches and parking difficulties of Surfers Paradise, and didn't perceive Noosa as having these problems. It could be inferred that such problems are less irritating in a more natural physical setting. Another informant preferred Noosa as more "laid back" and less "trendy" than Surfers Paradise.

While talking about Noosa's height limits, a retired operator of holiday units said "I've had a lot of [holiday tenants] remark: they like [Noosa]; it's more natural and smaller, not like the Gold Coast.... [W]e've had people come to the units from the Gold Coast, to have a holiday away from the rat race, and how it was down there". A Californian backpacker also spoke of the Gold Coast as being more like a city. An elderly couple who first came to Noosa from Melbourne for winter holidays in the mid-1960s, had switched from the Gold Coast because "it was getting nearly as bad as it is now. We don't like that razzle dazzle hassle thing about the Gold Coast, and Noosa didn't have any of that. It was quiet, [a] beautiful little country spot". Having made Noosa their retirement home in the early 1970s, they felt that the Noosa community-led opposition to high-rise development had prevented developers from "taking over" Noosa, as they had the Gold Coast.

(ii) Style and sophistication

Over the past two decades, the attraction of Noosa's natural beauty has been supplemented by an increasing emphasis on style and sophistication. Two key elements of these supplementary myths[2] in the Noosa narrative are expressed as 'the Paris end of Hastings Street' and 'the Noosa style'.

'The Paris end of Hastings Street'

In recent years, the eastern end of Hastings Street has come to be referred to as "the Paris end of Hastings Street" (Mainwaring, 1993: pers. comm.; Tourism Noosa, 1992, 1995). This grand description conflates two aspects of Noosa: Noosa as a place with connections to Melbourne, and Noosa as a place with pretensions to European style and sophistication. Since the late nineteenth century, part of Melbourne's most fashionable city street has been popularly known as 'the Paris end of Collins Street'. The attachment of a similar label to part of Noosa's most fashionable street is an indication of the influence that Melburnians and ex-Melburnians have had on the construction of Noosa's image.

'The Paris end of Collins Street' in Melbourne is an allusion to an elegant tree-lined boulevard edged by boom-style Victorian buildings, a place for stylish people to promenade and be seen. In a less formal way, "famous Hastings Street" (in ephemeral references too numerous to list) has been constructed physically and perceptually as a stylish street for elegant people to promenade, to sip coffee at sidewalk cafes, to shop at expensive boutiques, to see and be seen. The declaration of a 'Paris end of Hastings Street', and its formalisation in the developer-named French Quarter resort, successfully translates cultural capital into real estate capital.

The emergence of the 'Paris end' of Hastings Street can be tracked in the locally produced tourist brochures of the 1990s. The term appears in adver-tisements for individual resorts in 1992, when both the Hotel Laguna, at the western end, and Saks, at the opposite (eastern) end of the street, are described as being at the Paris end of Hastings Street (Tourism Noosa, 1992, pp. 7, 12). By 1995, with the opening of The French Quarter resort, the "Paris end" becomes firmly located at the eastern end of the street, in the advertisements for Saks and the Ocean Breeze resort (Tourism Noosa, 1995, p. 11). By 1996, the long-established Netanya beachfront resort also describes itself as being at the Paris end of Hastings Street (Queensland Tourist and Travel Corporation [QTTC] *et al.*, 1996: p. 5), and the term is in use in some brochures' general descriptions of the eastern end of Hastings Street. The invention of the Paris end of Hastings Street represents a broadening of the projected appeal of Noosa: the focus on the beach and National Park is supplemented by an equal focus on Hastings Street as a place of style and sophistication.

'The Noosa style': a dialogue between Mediterranean and vernacular influences

The idea of a 'Noosa style' of design appears frequently in the research interviews, ephemeral and popular literature, and in Council documents. The term covers a wide range of design, including fine arts, commercial design, interior design, architecture and urban design. The currency of the term by the mid-1990s can be seen in the title of a major exhibition of local applied arts held in June 1995: *Noosa: the style* (Noosa Regional Gallery Society, 1995). A key interviewee involved in leadership of both the local arts commu-nity and the influential Noosa Parks Association, outlines the contributions of the Queensland vernacular response to the local materials and climate, the creativity brought by new interstate and overseas residents in the 1960s and 1970s economic booms, and the resort style of the 1980s and '90s. The latter, composed of "vast expanses of pastel, concrete — instant palm landscapes [is] very Noosa — but just like every other tourist trap" (Moroney, in Noosa Regional Gallery Society, 1995: p. 1). For Moroney, a "Noosa style" can only be developed out of the community demand for "preserving its natural environment, and encouraging a built environment that is in sym-pathy with the nature of Noosa" (*ibid.*). Thus the idea of a Noosa style is closely related to the themes of nature and of community involvement.

Early articulation of a Noosa style of architecture and urban design appears in the study accompanying the Hastings Street Development Control Plan (DCP) (NSC, 1983: Part B), which includes a brief evaluation of the built form of Noosa Heads in the early 1980s. The term 'Noosa style' is yet to appear, but this planning and urban design study provides clues to its origins and components. The study observes that "the recent Mediterranean style of architecture appears to be satisfactory for the seaside tourist context" (NSC, 1983: p. B35). The acceptability of the Mediterranean design approach is based on "the climate, the strength of the sunlight, the colour of the sea and the resort atmosphere" (NSC, 1983: p. B49). The " 1970-1980s Mediterranean style apartment buildings with bagged brickwork painted in warm colours ... with concrete or terra-cotta roof tiles ... although having nothing in common with the [vernacular] ... perhaps point the way towards an attractive and cohesive future" (NSC, 1983: p. B29).

In architecture and urban design, the evolution of a Noosa Style has been attributed to three nationally known local architects — Gabriel Poole, Lindsay Clare and John Mainwaring — and to two local property developers (Poole, in Jarratt, 1993: pp. 15, 16). Gabriel Poole describes the Noosa Style as "creating architecture which has been thought out for this climate, architecture that actually works", rather than the problem of "people coming up from down south and building without thinking" (in Jarratt, 1993: p. 15). Poole states that he and Mainwaring created the Noosa Style, "a concept that came from the ideas of [two developers] who liked the *Mediterranean influence* that I found attractive at the time. My other great influence was the Mexican architect [Louis Barragan]" (cited in Jarratt, 1993: p. 16, emphasis added).

John Mainwaring has helped to define the Noosa Style through articles in Noosa Blue and through his role as co-editor of the regional design magazine, *Casa*. The philosophy of the magazine is articulated in terms of the nature myth that permeates all five sources of case study data: "[W]e are for anything that preserves or complements the *natural environment*, against anything that threatens it or detracts from it" (Anon., 1993: p. 1, emphasis added). Mainwaring states that Noosa resisted the American high-rise influence, and backdates the emergence of the Noosa Style to Gabriel Poole's 1960s Tingirana motel and holiday units on the beachfront in Hastings Street. The Tingirana, "the connoisseur's favourite '60s building in Noosa", is a simple structure with Mediterranean-style single skin blockwork walls (Mainwaring, 1992a: p. 24). The only constraint in the brief was "the preservation of the large eucalypt which had become a Hastings Street focal point" (Mainwaring, 1992a: p. 24). This Moreton Bay Ash continues to dominate Hastings Street. The Tingirana Arcade responds to the subtropical climatic by being kinked "to keep out the savage nor'easters" (Mainwaring, 1992a: pp. 24, 26). Mainwaring suggests that the canvas roof on the popular restaurant at the beach end of Tingirana Arcade was an unconscious prototype of Poole's internationally known tent house at Eumundi in the Noosa hinterland (Mainwaring, 1992a: p. 27).

A move towards lighter-weight "timber and tin" construction is part of a current diversification in the Noosa style, encouraged by the Council. The Council is, however, only one participant in a broader community debate. This new stream of 'the Noosa style' is inspired by the few remaining examples of the early twentieth century Queenslander style of resort architecture, by simple vernacular "weekenders", and by the holiday homes and retirement cottages designed by fashionable Brisbane architects Froud and Job in Noosa Heads in the 1960s. Mainwaring (1991, 1992a, 1992b) argues that these buildings should be used as a guide for designing in harmony with the local environment, climate and contemporary way of life.

Alan Starkey, a local architect-developer of over twenty holiday apartment buildings, is not mentioned in the "official" narrative on the emergence of a Noosa style. In an interview, Starkey (1996: pers. comm.) spontaneously mentions the Noosa style in reference to Council encouragement for a distinctive Noosa design approach. Starkey describes the elements of the Noosa style in terms of "... the Mediterranean influence. It's not truly Mediterranean but it's got that influence, with the plastered walls and the tiled roofs and draped pergolas". He acknowledges Gabriel Poole's work in Hastings Street, and adds several of his own post-1980 designs for holiday apartments as examples of the style. The aspects which he says exhibit the Noosa style are the freedom and looseness of the architecture, "the simple feeling of the Mediterranean", simple pitched roofs, orangey-red roof tiles, curved polycarbonate awnings over the Hastings Street footpaths, and "a sort of timelessness" that endures while the environment changes around the building. A "curvy feeling" is now used in the design of Starkey's buildings near the sea. A "sub-tropical feel" is important in Starkey's definition of the Noosa style. Because Noosa is "a place of shade"[3], Starkey believes it is "nice to see trees rather than heavy buildings imposing themselves". Like several other interviewees, Starkey stressed the central importance of having "the built and natural environment working in harmony".

The idea of a 'Noosa style' of architecture is a powerful myth whose full dimensions could only be judged with a more detailed investigation, which is beyond the scope of this paper. It is never made clear whether the Mediterranean influence is derived from contemporary Mediterranean resort designs or from the Mediterranean vernacular, or whether there is such a thing as a generic Mediterranean style. References in the case study data to Mediterranean design influences always focus on Noosa applications rather than on Mediterranean origins. Investigation of the latter issue is unlikely to shed much light on 'the Noosa style'.

Council documents contain veiled references to the Gold Coast as an undesirable model. The Council's *Design Manual* (NSC, 1986, p. 25). makes it clear that architecturally " [attractive shops and well designed themes are a better investment" than "[flashy treatment of building exteriors and dull landscaping". In other words, Noosa is tasteful and discreet, in contrast to other, flashy, coastal resorts.

Conclusion

In Noosa, a distinctive built form has evolved in parallel with the narrative of the place as a relaxed but stylish resort village dominated by nature. Both the narrative and physical landscape have been shaped by a local process of constant comparison and contrast with well known Australian and international coastal resorts. Tourism is an area in which tourists make place comparisons in order to choose from a range of potential holiday destinations. Comparison shopping between places is assisted by published tour guides, ephemeral tourist brochures, and the place images and reputations built up in the general media. These comparisons are reinforced by travel writers. As tourism is a form of escape, tourists may also seek contrasts to their home environments.

Tourist destinations also use a form of comparison of their town with others that provide similar or competing tourist products, The operation of this process helps to identify what is valued in the cultural landscape, as well as helping to articulate the built form and atmosphere of the place. These values and characteristics, and the associated landscape preferences, can be identified by the methods developed in the case study. In this way, comparison can be used constructively in the urban design process.

The "not the Gold Coast" myth that motivates Noosa and several other small coastal settlements on the Australian east coast appears to have international parallels in other coastal tourism areas, in themes that might be labelled "not Waikiki" and "not Torremolinos/Benidorm". These myths are manifestations of a preference for nature, smallness and lack of high-rise buildings.

Notes

1. I was all but knocked over by this person.

2. The term 'myth' is used here in the sense of "an intellectual construction which embodies beliefs, values and information, and which can influence events, behaviour and perception" (Short, 1990, p. xvi).

3. The name "Noosa" is believed to have the meaning of "a place of shade" (Cato, 1979). This meaning is reinforced in the Noosa narrative, while an alternative translation, "place of spirits or ghosts" (Cato 1979; Steele 1984), is ignored.

References

Anon. (1955) 'The Noosa narrative, *Gympie Times*, (undated clipping from Mrs Olive Donaldson's scrapbook).

Anon. (1993) Editorial, *Casa* Vol. 1, No. 1: p. 1.

Ashworth, G.J., and Goodall, B. (eds) (1990) *Marketing tourism places*. London and New York: Routledge.

Bowen, J. (1992) *The Queensland experience: A comprehensive guide to enjoying the Sunshine State.* Sydney: Simon and Schuster.

Butler, R.W. (1980) 'The concept of a tourist area cycle of evolution', *Canadian Geographer,* Vol. XXIV(I): pp. 5-12.

Cato, N. (1979) *The Noosa story: A study in unplanned development.* 1st edition, Milton, Brisbane: Jacaranda Press.

Cato, N. (1989) *The Noosa story: A study in unplanned development.* 3rd edition, Milton, Brisbane: Jacaranda Wylie.

Cooper, J. (1996) 'Luxury for landmark hotel site', *Courier Mail,* 23 March: p. W19.

Groom, T. (1993) Letter to the editor, *Noosa Blue,* No. 11: p. 4.

Hough, M. (1990) *Out of place? Restoring identity to the regional landscape.* New Haven: Yale University Press.

HRH the Prince of Wales (1996) 'Work to stop tourism from spoiling the world's finest sites', *International Herald Tribune,* 13 September: p. 6.

Jackson, J.B. (1984) *Discovering the vernacular landscape.* New Haven: Yale University Press.

Jarratt, P. (1993) 'The Casa interview: Gabriel Poole', *Casa: Sunshine Coast houses and gardens,* Vol. 1, No. 1: pp. 13-18.

Krippendorf, J. (1987) *The holiday makers: Understanding the impact of leisure and travel.* London: Heinemann.

Mainwaring, J. (1991) 'Queenslanders: old and new', *Noosa Blue* No.3: pp. 30-35.

——— (1992a) 'A case for tribal diversity', *Noosa Blue* No. 6: pp. 40-41.

——— (1992b) 'From penthouse to tent house', *Noosa Blue* No. 6: pp. 24-27.

——— (1993) interview at the architect's office.

——— (1996) 'Noosa green acre meets urban resort', *Oueensland Architect* Number 1 of 1996, pp. 14-16.

Meinig, D.W. (ed) (1979) *The Interpretation of Ordinary Landscapes.* New York: Oxford University Press.

Mullins, P. (1992) 'Cities for pleasure: The emergence of tourism urbanization in Australia', *Built Environment* Vol. 18, No. 3: pp. 187-198.

Noosa Parks Association (1981) Unpublished submission to the Senate Standing Committee on Science and Environment Inquiry into the Need for a Coordinated Approach to Major Land Use Problems in Australia.

Noosa Regional Gallery Society (1995) *Noosa the style: Applied art, craft, design.* Exhibition catalogue, sponsored by Noosa Enterprise Group, Noosa.

NSC (1983) *Hastings Street development control plan.* Noosa: Noosa Shire Council.

——— (1986) *Noosa Shire design manual.* Tewantin: Noosa Shire Council.

——— (1988) *Shire of Noosa strategic plan.* Tewantin: Noosa Shire Council.

——— (1991) Local Planning Policy No. 19: Traffic lights, adopted 3 October. Noosa: Noosa Shire Council.

O'Hare, D. J. (1991) Reconciling tourism and local identity in Prague. Unpublished MA dissertation. Joint Centre for Urban Design, Oxford Brookes University.

——— (forthcoming) Tourism and small coastal settlements: A cultural landscape approach for urban design. Draft doctoral thesis, Joint Centre for Urban Design, Oxford Brookes University.

QTTC, Tourism Sunshine Coast and Tourism Industry Partners (1996) *Take your time on Queensland's Sunshine Coast.* Brisbane: Queensland Tourist and Travel Corporation.

Rojek, C. (1993) *Ways of escape: Modern transformations in leisure and travel.* Basingstoke: MacMillan Press.

Shields, R. (1991) *Places on the margin: alternative geographies of modernity.* London and New York: Routledge.

Short, J.R. (1991) *Imagined country: Environment, society and culture.* London: Routledge.

Smith, R. (1991) 'Beach resorts: a model of development evolution', *Landscape and Urban Planning,* 21: pp. 189-210.

Sorkin, M. (ed) (1992) *Variations on a theme park: The new American city and the end of public space.* New York: Oxford University Press.

Starkey, A. (1996) interview.

Steele, J. G. (1984) *Aboriginal pathways of Southeast Queensland and the Richmond River.* Brisbane: University of Queensland Press.

Sunshine Coast Tourism Promotions (1994) *Discover Queensland's Sunshine Coast,* Maroochydore: Sunshine Coast Tourism Promotions.

Theroux, P. (1995) *The Pillars of Hercules: A grand tour of the Mediterranean.* London: Hamish Hamilton.

Tourism Noosa (1992) *Noosa the guide.* Ist edition, Noosa Heads: Benefactum Informative Publishing.

——— (1995) *Noosa the guide.* 4th edition, Noosa Heads: Wordsworth Publishing.

Towner, J. (1996) *An historical geography of recreation and tourism in the western world, 1540-1940.* Chichester: Wiley,

Yin, R.K. (1994) *Case study research: Design and methods.* Thousand Oaks, California: Sage.

From 'Gayety and Diversion' to 'Developer's Lorry' — Representations of Bath since 1760

Judith E. Brown

Cheltenham and Gloucester College of Higher Education

Introduction

The aim of this paper is to discuss and evaluate a range of texts about Bath, both fictional and non fictional, in the three periods: 1760–1810, 1880–1930 and 1970–1997. This discussion and evaluation will be carried out within a framework of what are perceived as the three main reasons for visiting Bath: historical, medical and social (Kerr, 1888). These three reasons can be used to summarise the information in most of the texts relating to Bath. The paper attempts to show how changes in the relative importance of medical, social and historical reasons for visiting Bath are represented in the texts.

The methodology involved a textual analysis of guidebooks to the town. A guide from every 10 years was analysed, from 1762 onwards. In the last period discussed, there was a wider variety of guidebooks: either very general texts; or related to a specific group such as families, young people or those with a certain historical interest. A range of these was studied. Relevant leaflets and information from the Internet were also analysed. Contemporary documents were also studied such as the local and national newspapers, printed Census reports and journals. Also considered were treatises on the waters of Bath and the work of John Wood (the architect of much of the town). In the last period under scrutiny, the work of various authors critical of the building work going on in Bath in the early 1970s was also considered. Where they were available, contemporary fictional works were studied, in particular the work of Christopher Anstey, and authors Tobias Smollett and Jane Austen. Although Jane Austen's novels, *Northanger Abbey* and *Persuasion* were published after her death in 1817, she was familiar with Bath from 1801, when she lived there with her family. The work of John Betjeman was also considered.

1760 — 1810

Social

From the middle of the seventeenth century to the early eighteenth century Bath was considered to be one of the most important spas in England (Hembry, 1990: p. 113). The period from 1760 -1810 is the time when most of the building of what is now regarded as Georgian Bath was completed and the town was well established as a resort (Wood, 1969: p. 50). In England as a whole there was a growing middle and upper class, who were wealthy and had leisure time to spend travelling (Briggs, 1983: p. 207). These people came to take the waters in Bath rather than the other spa towns of England because of its reputation for respectability (Hembry 1990: p. 134).

Between the years 1760 and 1810, the guidebooks of Bath promoted it as a town suitable for the "sound for their pleasure" and for "the sick for their health" (Anon, 1762: p. 2). However, it is clearly recognised by the writers of the guides that most of the visitors to the town came for pleasure (Anon., 1762: p. 2). Jane Austen (1994a: p. 7) describes in *Northanger Abbey* the pleasurable aspects of a visit, describing her heroine's arrival in Bath: "Catherine was all eager delight, her eyes were here there and everywhere, She was come to be happy, and she felt happy already".

The use of the baths and the waters was a legitimate excuse for a visit, and most people did use them, usually not for medical reasons but for social ones. Anstey (1980: p. 25) describes the visits of one of his young female characters to the Pump rooms:

> There Hygeia, goddess, pours
> Blessing from her various stores
> Let me to her altars haste
> Tho' I ne'er the waters taste
> Near the pump I take my stand
> With a nosegay in my hand

The guides to Bath did not admit to this social use of the Pump Rooms until around 1810. The pump rooms are described as "a numerous assemblage of ladies and gentlemen, walking up and down in social concourse during the performance, present(ing) a lively and animated spectacle" (Anon. 1810: p. 10).

Jane Austen (in *Northanger Abbey* 1994a: p. 48) also refers to the Pump Rooms as a social centre; "In the Pump Room one so newly arrived in Bath must be met with; and that building she had already found so favourable for the discovery of female excellence".

Bath's importance as a social centre has been seen as partly due to its strict code of conduct (Hembry 1990: p. 144). Eleven Articles (rules) for 'people of fashion' were drawn up in 1742 (Wood, 1969: p. 443) (**Figure 1**) and these were still in force in 1810 (Anon. 1810: p. 10).

Figure 1

Articles of Bath (to be obeyed by people of rank and Fashion)

1. *That a visit of ceremony at coming to Bath, and another at going away is all that is expected or desired by ladies of quality and fashion — except impertinents*

2. *That ladies coming to a ball appoint a time for their footmen coming to wait on them home, to prevent disturbances and inconveniences to themselves and others.*

3. *That gentlemen of fashion never appear in a morning before the ladies in gowns and caps, show breeding and respect.*

4. *That no person take it ill that any one goes to another's play or break-fast and not to theirs — except captious by nature*

5. *That no gentleman gives his tickets for balls to any but gentlewomen — NB unless he have none of his acquaintance*

6. *That gentlemen crowding before the ladies at the ball, show ill manners; and that none do so for the future; — except such as respect nobody but themselves.*

7. *That no gentleman or lady take it ill that another dances before them; — except such as have no pretence to dance at all.*

8. *That the elder ladies and children be contented with a second bench at the ball, as being past, or not yet come to perfection.*

9. *That the younger ladies take notice how many eyes observe them — NB this don't extend to the have at alls*

10 *That all Whisperers of lies and scandal be taken for their authors*

11. *That all repeaters of such lies and scandal be shunned by all the company except such as have been guilty of the same crime*

Source: Wood (1969)

These Articles were posted around Bath and also listed in the guidebooks. There were also well publicised rules to be adhered to when dancing, regarding the ladies' dress and the sequence of people, the ladies of highest rank being at the top of the sets (Wood, 1969: p. 446). This aspect of Bath life meant that it seemed a safe and respectable place for people, especially the young, to visit and, indeed, young people were often encouraged to use the opportunity to find a partner (Hembry, 1990: p. 135).

According to many texts, young people enjoyed the visits to Bath because of the freedom from the confines of normal life, as well as the opportunities to meet people. Anstey (1980: p. 40) describes Bath in one of his young narrators words:

> O the charming parties made
> Some to walk the south Parade
> Some to Lincomb's shady groves,
> Or to Simpson's proud alcoves ...

Smollett (1985: p. 68) also describes Bath from the point of view of a young woman: "Bath is to me a new world — all is gayety, good humour and diversion".

A very public lifestyle was conducted in Bath. A set routine was followed and most visitors did the same things at the same time each day, such as taking the water and attending the assemblies (Hembry, 1990: p. 147). The guides supported this by giving the best times to attend the Pump Room, bathe and so on (Anon, 1762: p. 29; Wood, 1969: p. 437, 443). This meant that most people were aware that they were being watched by other visitors. Anstey (1980: p. 44) makes clear the importance and consciousness amongst the visitors of the public life style of Bath when one of his characters says:

> My spirits flag, my life and fires
> Are mortified au desespoir
> When Sim, unfashionable ninny
> In public calls me cousin Jenny.

It seems that gossip caused concern for the Council of Bath since two of the eleven articles concern the spreading of malicious gossip (Wood, 1969: p. 443). However, it appears that the publicising of rules concerning gossip did not stop it from being spread. Many of the writers about Bath refer to it directly or indirectly. Smollett (1985: p. 62, 69) refers to one of his characters visiting coffee shops "where he picks up continual food for ridicule and satire", and the ladies' coffee shops where the conversation consists of "politics, scandal, and philosophy". Jane Austen (1994b: p. 151) also refers in *Persuasion* to the gossip when one of her characters hears about an event "through the shortcut of a laundress and a waiter".

As indicated by the Articles of Bath (Wood, 1969: p. 443), social status was very important, particularly as it was an important attraction to Bath to be mixing with the right sort of people, in many cases with a view to marriage. In *The Improved Bath Guide* (Anon., 1810: p. 11), for example, there is a long list of royal visitors to Bath. Jane Austen (1994b: p. 146) satirises this awareness of status in some detail when some of the characters make an inelegant attempt to show off their aristocratic relations, "our cousins the Dalrymples". Despite rules regarding who could attend various functions within the town, many people who frequented Bath were not considered respectable, or of the correct sort. Anstey (1980: p. 154) refers to the type of people visiting Bath:

> If a broker or statesman, gamester or peer
> An nat'ralis'd Jew or a bishop comes here
> Or an eminent trader in cheese should retire.

Shopkeepers and others of that social class were not allowed to attend the balls (Wood, 1969: p. 443) but Smollett (1985: p. 66) comments that "a very inconsiderable proportion of genteel people are lost in the mob of impudent plebeians".

Medical

Opinions differed regarding the value of bathing or drinking the waters at Bath. As well as a writer of fiction, Smollett was a medical doctor and, as such, questioned the efficacy of the waters, indicating that it was the cleanliness and freshness of the water that gave its healing properties rather than the salts dissolved in it (Smollett, 1752). This view was contradicted, however, by various other contemporary doctors. Their views are later described by Kerr (1888: p. 18), who stated that the waters had healing properties for gout, rheumatism, skin diseases and debility, amongst other diseases. The New Bath Guide (Anon., 1762: p. 10) and later the Improved Bath Guide (Anon., 1810: p. 47) were cautious in their recommendations for the use of the waters. They both suggested that the waters be drunk between 6 am and 10 am to give them a chance to work through the system (1762: p. 10). The later guides stated that medical advice should be sought before using the waters (Anon., 1810: p. 17). The Improved Bath Guide (Anon., 1810: p. 16) also stated that it may have been imprudent to drink too much of the water and that it was important to "keep good hours, a light regimen" and take "due exercise" It was also suggested that "the neglect of these means the efficacy is lost" (Anon., 1762: p. 9). The New Bath Guide (Anon., 1762: p. 9) cautiously says that the waters are beneficial in almost all chemical distempers and "can hurt no-one except in haemorrhages, inflammations or bad lungs" or, if "too high or too low a regimen be joined with the other". It seems then that waters did little harm, even if they did little good.

Smollett (1985: p. 75) expresses his characters' worries that infection might spread through the waters, and while Anstey (1980: p. 50) recognises that some doctors who recommended the waters did not use them themselves. Smollett (1985: p. 57) also questions the reality of some of the visitors' illnesses. It appears, then, that the curative properties of the waters may have been exaggerated in the guide books. However, the image created by Smollett (1752, 1985) and Anstey (1985) of hypochondriacs bathing in dirty water with a number of other people, thus risking worse illness, can also be questioned.

Historical

Guide books about Bath express a sense of pride in the town's history. They devote quite large portions to the history of the town, particularly its classical and Saxon connections. By 1810 there had been considerable excavation of the Roman remains and these are more widely discussed than in the earlier Guides (Anon. 1810: p. 13). Wood, whose designs for many of the new buildings in the town are of classical style, and who wanted Bath to echo the style and layout of a Roman town, goes to great lengths to compare the town with the great cities of ancient Greece and the Roman Empire (Wood, 1969:

p. 7). He even describes Bladud, the Saxon king, as a classical figure. These classical and Saxon connections are given considerably more space in the guide books of the town than is Bath's controversial involvement in the Interregnum and the Jacobite Rebellions. By 1810 the Improved Bath Guide gives a more complete history of these events.

1880 — 1930

Social

The late Victorian and Edwardian periods were a time of expansion and renewed of interest in the spa facilities of Bath. A number of hotels were built, including the Empire and the Grand Pump Room Hotel, to accommodate both short and long term visitors to the spa facilities. This renewal of interest in the spa was partly due to the opening up of the Roman Baths, and partly to the interest in the new cures imported from Continental spas. During the first years of the 20th century, there was a renewal of the fashion for healthy living amongst the middle and upper classes, meaning that people increasingly visited the spas or the seaside (Haddon, 1973: p. 176).

The Original Bath Guide of this period (Anon., 1891: p. 2) gives a very different picture of the town to that of similar guides in previous years, saying that "The charms of Bath are for quiet enjoyment". Hudson describes Bath in similar terms, as "a quiet drifting back" with "a sense of harmony and repose", and emphasises the name of Quiet Street (Hudson, 1909: p. 154). This is no longer the Bath of "gayety and diversion" as described by Smollett.

The consciousness of social status was still very important to those writing about Bath. At this time, guidebooks still liked to make much of Bath's royal connections and the fact that it attracted people of the middle and upper classes. Kerr (1888: p. 96) describes the visitors book (held at the Pump Rooms) by saying "The well-known social standing of the writers is best proof of their genuine characters", and describes the York House Hotel as "the posting establishment" which "still maintains its connections with the best county families" Kerr (1888: p. 15). The Court Circular of *The Times* of 5 April 1920 gives details of the titled people visiting Bath, including the Countess of Radnor and Sir Frederick MacMillan, who stayed at the Empire and the York House Hotels respectively. The following day's circular has information about the balls to be held in Bath over the Easter period. The Original Bath Guide (Anon., 1891: p. 14) listed "the royal visits in modern times" : about fifteen minor members of the royal family visited Bath during the years 1738–1889. Princess Victoria is mentioned despite anecdotal evidence, often repeated by tour guides, that she hated the town and never returned. The Book of Bath in 1928 continued this tradition of pride in the royal connections by including a short, but very flattering introduction written by the Prince of Wales (Hutton, 1928, intr.). Writers of these guides clearly intended to impress visitors through these links with the upper classes, so encouraging them to visit the town.

During this period the writers of the Bath guidebooks were becoming increasingly aware of the importance of the links the town had, not just with the aristocracy, but also with other famous people. The Pictorial and Descriptive Guide to Bath (Anon., 1916: p. 9) describes "the poets, novelists and historians who have enshrined the praises of Bath in enduring literature". Many anthologies of quotations about Bath were compiled at this time and the guidebooks reproduced what certain well-known people such as Anstey, Austen, Pepys, Chesterton had said about Bath; Arthur Waugh described "a city of the eighteenth century, bland and beautiful, dreaming with her grey stone eyes of the glories of an unforgettable past" (Anon., 1916: p. 49). These quotes are always complimentary and act as endorsements for the town. As well as listing the famous residents, the Original Bath Guide (Anon., 1919: p. 3) contains a map indicating where they lived. Various locations are described in terms of how they relate to famous writers. For example, the Assembly Rooms are described in the Pictorial and Descriptive Guide to Bath (Anon., 1916: p. 15) as "immortalised by Austen and Dickens".

Medical

During the late nineteenth and early twentieth centuries, the spa facilities were widely promoted. New facilities were developed with the opening of the Grand Pump Hotel and the acquisition of new treatments from Continental spas. Detailed descriptions of these facilities and of the older ones, such as those provided by Kerr (1888), are given in very serious language, in order to educate the reader in the treatments and how they work. Kerr (1888: p. 40) describes the use of massage and its physiological effects, as well treatments such as 'Aix les Bains douches'. Instructions are even given on how to enter the baths: "the bath should be entered slowly, one step at a time, the water being laved over the body before it is immersed" (Kerr, 1888: p. 51). These texts indicate that the people using the baths should take the business of bathing a lot more seriously than in the late eighteenth century.

The early guides of this period describe the waters in much the same terms as the guides of one hundred years previously. Those of the early twentieth century were more cautious in their affirmation of the use of the waters, although still encouraging people to use them. The Original Bath Guide (Anon., 1906: p. 31) stated that the waters were "unserviceable in the acute stage of any disease, but constantly promote recovery when all other helps have failed".

Later, the Original Bath Guide (Anon., 1919: p. 28) describes the treatises on the waters as "alike curious and instructive to the student", indicating that they should be read for interest and amusement rather than for their judgement of the waters. However the same book also quotes the Lancet: "Not every patient will benefit, but the majority will"; that Bath "may be better than other English and Continental Spas"; and that "Bath can successfully hold its own against any medical resort in Europe" (p. 28).

Historical

In the early twentieth century, the story of Bladud was still included in the various guide books, but he is no longer described as a classical or historical figure. In this period such stories were treated as legend rather than as fact and, as such, are separated from the rest of the history of Bath, unlike the earlier guides (Anon., 1919: p. 4).

The texts of this period not only discuss the old buildings of the town in an extraordinary amount of depth, but also show a great deal of pride in the modern buildings and engineering structures. Photographs are included in the guidebooks of new bridges, railway lines and the Bath Oliver factory, proving that Bath may have been an historical centre, but also had a lot of new technology to be admired (Anon., 1916; 1929). The electric light and hydraulic lift at the York House Hotel are described in the Original Bath Guide (Anon., 1906: p. 15), as well as the cleanliness and cheapness of the town's water supply in the Original Bath Guide (Anon.,1891: p. 15).

1970 — 1997

Social

Bath now has a large tourist industry based around the Roman Baths, the Georgian architecture and links with Jane Austen. The form in which information is presented to the visitor has changed: guidebooks are either general or specific to groups such as students, families or people with particular interest in architecture, history, Jane Austen or other historical figures. The once 'official' guides, the New Bath Guide and the Original Bath Guide, are no longer published. There are a now a number of guides to Bath on the Internet, aimed primarily at the young reader (Ainsley. 1996; Anon., 1996). Many local proprietors produce leaflets and booklets to promote their establishments; these vary from a small free leaflet, giving an outline of the attraction and a map (leaflets about the Guildhall market, for example), to a fairly sophisticated glossy publication with a substantial amount of text and numerous photographs, which usually incurs a charge (for example, the Guide to No. 1 Royal Crescent).

The guidebooks generally give the impression that Bath is a visitor friendly place, through the 'tone' of the text and the provision of maps. The guide to the Abbey starts by saying "Welcome to Bath Abbey", continues "please find a seat and read this" and ends "We hope you enjoy your visit". At least one book about the city includes photographs of various residents. The *Dream of Bath* has pictures of residents of the past but also has pictures of a contemporary traffic warden, a nurse and a curate, all smiling a welcome to the reader (Winsor, 1980: pp. 58-73).

Writers on Bath still like to proclaim its links with royalty and the famous, but the people discussed are usually historical figures. The Guide to No. 1 Royal Crescent mentions previous residents, including the Duke of

York (who stayed there in 1796) and the Princesse de Lamballe (1787), while the Family Guide to Bath lists the famous people associated with Bath, none of whom are royal (Simpson, 1985: p. 65). Some guidebooks have been written solely about the famous people who have visited Bath. Like many of the contemporary texts about the town, these contain a number of anecdotes about the visitors (Lowndes, 1982). The Knowhere Guide (Anon., 1996) has a section entitled the 'Cringing Cult of Celebrity' and lists contemporary famous people who have been spotted in Bath including Hugh Grant, Paula Yates, Rolf Harris and most of the England rugby team. The importance of famous figures in the attraction of people to Bath is still realised by those writing about the town.

Perhaps the figure currently most commonly associated with Bath is Jane Austen and there are many books relating to her stays in the town. This use of Jane Austen as a major feature of the town's past has grown since the 1970s (perhaps associated with the 1970s television series of *Pride and Prejudice*). Books such as *In the Steps of Jane Austen* (Edwards, 1979) and *Bath in the Life and Times of Jane Austen* (Lane, 1988) have been produced to promote the connection. The Bath Tourism Bureau has also made use of the link with Austen, by sponsoring a document on the Internet entitled *Jane Austen's Bath* (Bath Tourism Bureau, 1996). This document associates many of Bath's notable buildings with Jane Austen, through statements such as "The majority of Bath's squares and crescents had been built when Jane Austen first arrived" (Bath Tourism Bureau, 1996). However, the same document states that "today many of the activities remain identical to those she and her contemporaries would have enjoyed", which would seem to indicate either a lack of knowledge of the period in which Austen lived, or a very romantic view of contemporary Bath (Bath Tourism Bureau, 1996). The examples given of these activities are concerts at the assembly rooms and social gatherings at the pump rooms, neither of which currently bear much resemblance to those of the early nineteenth century.

Medical

As the last of the spa facilities closed in 1976, Bath can no longer claim to be a medical centre. However, a leaflet is produced describing the water, its geological source, mineral content and curative properties. This leaflet also states that "today it is fashionable to be sceptical about the curative properties of spa water, although spas in Europe remain popular". There are now plans to re-open the spa facilities, with controversy already arising out of the suggested use of a modernist architect.

Historical

There has been a distinct trend, particularly during the early 1970s, towards guidebooks which are sharply critical of the demolition and rebuilding work being carried out in the town. Prior to the addition of Bath to UNESCO's list of World Heritage sites, much was written about the demolition of old buildings in Bath and their replacement with unimaginative new structures (Ison, 1969; Gadd, 1971; Coard and Coard, 1973). This protest, which took place largely in the 1970s, led eventually to the preservation of many old buildings in the town. Betjeman compares the "follies and fashions" of Anstey's time with "the follies and fashions since then", and describes the old buildings as being "carted off by developer's lorry" (Betjeman, 1993: p. 303). Ferguson and Mowl (1973: p. 59) bemoan the fact that in the fifteen years up to 1973 Bath had been "terribly defaced". They claim that eighteenth century Bath had virtually no decay, and that the artisan housing that remained until the early 1970s was "as perfect and graceful and harmonious as the Bath of the middle and upper classes" (Ferguson and Mowl, 1973: p. 11). The photographs of Bath, taken in the early twentieth century, of housing of this type show that, on the contrary, the conditions of the people living in these houses were fairly awful. This was made worse by the fact that at least some of the artisan housing in the town was liable to flooding (Hunt, 1983: p. 50).

Conclusions

In the eighteenth century Bath was presented as a well regulated social centre particularly for the young and fashionable. This changed in the nineteenth and early twentieth centuries, when Bath was described in the various texts as a centre for the retired and sick: Hudson's place of "quiet drifting, harmony and repose" (Hudson, 1909: p. 154). By the late twentieth century Bath was promoted, through Internet articles and books targeted at the young, as a place for the young and fashionable to meet. Bath is also represented as a place for people with a range of leisure interests. These changes reflect the changing political and economic status of the country. In the early nineteenth century, Britain had a growing wealthy middle and upper class (Briggs, 1983: p. 207) who had time to take an interest in the fashions of the time and take holidays in Bath. In the late nineteenth and early twentieth century there was a strong Victorian sense of morally correct, private behaviour (Briggs, 1983: p. 226) which seems to have been reflected in the quiet repose of Bath. In the late twentieth century, Bath seems to have followed trends of improved leisure provision for a variety of people.

The guides encouraged people visiting Bath in the late eighteenth and early nineteenth centuries to spend a lot of time watching other people, as they participated in the experience of Bath's social life. This can be related to the concept of the choraster — the person who derives 'social value' from the tourist experience (Wearing and Wearing, 1996: p. 231). In the early twentieth century, later editions of similar guides encouraged the transfer of this 'gaze' to buildings, not because of their inherent beauty, but because of who lived in them. The visitor could also observe institutions associated with the people of the upper classes, rather than socialise with them. In the late twentieth century, the tradition of relating the buildings to the historic figures of Bath continues, but the guides also encourage the visitor to look at the buildings for their own sake.

This would indicate that the guides intend the reader purely to look — to take the role of the flaneur, the non participant viewer of tourist sites (Wearing and Wearing, 1996: p. 231). However, the guidebooks of the late twentieth century expect the visitor to participate in a version of history, by visiting a house of the Georgian period, or by following in the steps of Jane Austen. The guides also encourage an interest in the personal aspects of social history, so the visitor is informed about the way in which people lived, as well as where they lived. This type of participation does not, however, require the tourist's direct involvement.

The texts related to Bath show the changing social structure of the periods in which they were written. In the earliest period, the class structure is overtly indicated by the guidebooks. It is made quite clear what is acceptable behaviour in all the guides to Bath of the late eighteenth century. However, there is indication that this system was challenged in fiction, in Jane Austen's (194b) case, by introducing a character in *Persuasion* who is outside the social caste. In Anstey and Smollett there are some allusions to the ways in which the less socially acceptable people gained entrance to the social functions. That the guide books are supportive of the social system indicates to a certain extent how profitable this support was to the town. Links with prominent contemporary and historical figures are mentioned throughout the texts. In 1760 these famous people were usually members of the royal family who had visited the town. By the beginning of the twentieth century, as well as royalty, the guides had broadened their scope to include other historical figures, such as Pope, Gainsborough and Smollett. In the late twentieth century, guidebooks often indicate places in the town where fictional characters are supposed to have visited, as well as real ones, and are consistent from 1760 in using even the most tenuous links with a famous person as a marketing ploy.

The earliest period of growing wealth and leisure time is suggested in the information on leisure activities in the guides to Bath. In the late nineteenth century, the guidebooks suggest Victorian pride in engineering and technological progress, as well as stressing the importance of quiet and privacy. The present day representations show the importance of catering to a wide variety of people, who are expected to have differing interests. From being described in the eighteenth century as primarily a social centre, Bath became a medical resort in the late nineteenth and early twentieth centuries. In the present day the things that made Bath a popular modern resort in the eighteenth century have become its most important attractions, but as historical aspects of the town.

References

Anon. (1762) *New Bath Guide or Useful Pocket Companion.* Bath: Pope.

Anon. (1810) *Improved Bath Guide or Picture of Bath and its Environs.* Bath: Wood and Cunningham.

Anon. (1891) *Original Bath Guide.* Bath: Wm. Lewis and Son.

Anon. (1906) *Original Bath Guide.* Bath: Wm. Lewis and Son

Anon. (1916) *Pictorial and descriptive guide to Bath.* London: Ward Lock.

Anon. (1919) *Original Bath guide.* Bath: Wm. Lewis and Son

Anon. (1929) *Pictorial and descriptive guide to Bath.* London: Ward Lock.

Anon. (1996) *Bath according to the Knowhere Guide.*
http://www.state51.co.uk/knowhere/1.html

Ainsley, R. (1996) *Rob's best of Bath.*
http://www.futurenet.co.uk.People/RobAinsley/bathbest.html

Anstey, C. (1980) *The new Bath guide* (reprinted edition). London: Broadcast Books.

Austen, J. (1994a) *Northanger Abbey.* Harmondsworth: Penguin.

———— (1994b) *Persuasion.* Harmondsworth, Penguin.

Bath Tourism Bureau (1996) *Jane Austen's Bath.*
http://www.openworld.co.uk/austen/austen1.html.

Betjeman, J. (1993) *Collected poems.* London: John Murray.

Briggs, A. (1983) *A social history of England.* London: Weidenfeld and Nicholson.

Coard. P. and Coard, R. E. (1973) *Vanishing Bath.* Bath: Kingsmead Press.

Edwards, A. (1972) *In the steps of Jane Austen* (2nd edition). Southampton: Arcady Books.

Ferguson, A. and Mowl, T. (1973) *The sack of Bath and after.* Bath: Michael Russell, repr. 1989.

Gadd, D. (1971) *Georgian summer, Bath in 18th Century.* Bath: Adams and Dart.

Haddon, J. (1973) *Bath.* London: Batsford.

Hembry, P. (1990) *The English Spa 1560–1815, a social history.* London: Athlone.

Hudson, W. H. (1909) *Afoot in England.* London: Oxford University Press, repr.1982.

Hunt, S. (1983) *A Bath camera 1850–1950.* Bath: Dovecote Press.

Hutton, J. (1928) *The book of Bath, The Premier Spa Resort of the Empire.* Bristol: Van Dyke.

Ison, W. (1969) *The Georgian buildings of Bath 1700–1830*. Bath: Kingsmead Reprints.

Kerr, J.G. (1888) *Popular Guide to the use of the Bath Waters*. Bath: Bath Herald.

Lane M. (1988) *Bath in the life and times of Jane Austen*. London: Millstream.

Lowndes, W. (1982) *They came to Bath*. Bristol: Redcliffe.

Simpson, J. (1985) *Family guide to Bath*. Bristol: Redcliffe.

Smollett, T. (1752) 'An Essay on the External Use of Water', *Bulletin of the Institute of the History of Medicine* Vol. iii, No. 1.

————— (1985) *Humphrey Clinker*. Harmondsworth: Penguin.

Wearing, B. and Wearing, S. (1996) 'Refocusing the tourist experience: The flaneur and the choraster', *Leisure Studies* Vol. 15, No. 4: pp. 239-243.

Winsor, D. (1980) *The dream of Bath*. Bath: Trade and Travel Publications.

Wood, J. (1969) *A description of Bath 1969*. Bath: Kingsmead Reprints.

History as Leisure: Business and Pleasure at Beamish

Jennifer Iles

Roehampton Institute London

Introduction

In the United Kingdom, heritage is big business. Over the past twenty years there has been a tremendous increase in concern about the preservation of the past. Out of this concern has grown a massive enterprise and what has been dubbed 'the heritage industry' is now seen as one of the growth industries of the past decade. Today there are at least forty-one heritage centres in Britain and well over 2,000 museums. With the help of the tourist trade these places attract enormous numbers of people. According to the Department of National Heritage (1994), the main purpose of a quarter of the 983 million day trips made within Britain in 1991–92 was connected with the heritage sector, and 81 per cent of overseas visitors gave heritage as an important factor in their decision to visit Britain. The past and cultural heritage have indeed become a lucrative economic enterprise.

Obviously these museums and heritage centres give pleasure. They also generate jobs and investments. Yet, despite its popularity, heritage has had a very bad press. It has been accused of making history a selling point, of trading on nostalgia, of sentimentalising the past and wanting to turn it into tourist kitsch. In the world of tourism where reality and fantasy are interwoven, the main challenge to heritage has been posed by tourism's search for different ways to sell itself. As Neil Cossons, Director of the Science Museum, wryly observed, "numbers through the door are the measures of its success" (Cossons, 1989). The marketing of certain aspects of history considered suitable for tourists has led to claims that through the pursuit of profitability, the portrayal of the past has been compromised (see Gathercole and Lowenthal, 1994; Walsh 1992).

The debate about heritage representations of history was initially aired by Robert Hewison (1987) in *The Heritage Industry*, where the author comments that against a background of perceived national distress and actual

economic decline, Britain was now producing heritage in place of manufacturing goods. Hewison condemns the way in which the heritage tradition
has romanticised and glamorised Britain's industrial past by a rose-tinted,
nostalgic selection of history. Heritage history is, "for all its seductive delights,
bogus history" which has been produced and imposed on the public by
marketing managers from above. In Patrick Wright's book, *On Living in an
Old Country* (1985), heritage is also perceived as "part of the self-fulfilling
culture of national decline". Like Hewison, Wright suggests that heritage
history tends to portray a pastoral myth of the British past by concentrating
on the charms of stately homes.

Other critics concerned with heritage representations include Tony
Bennett, who, in his incisive essay, 'Museums and "the people"', examines
and disapproves of the way in which heritage representations of the past
appear to be divorced from the economic and political relations in which they
were located in their time (Bennett, 1988). Kevin Walsh's (1992) contribution
to the debate views the whole process of heritage development as one which
has commercialised history and placed emphasis on a consideration of super-
ficialities, rather than a concern to consider the past and its contingency
upon the present.

Not everyone, however, has levelled their guns at the heritage industry.
May, in his paper on heritage tourism (1993), concedes that although the
term 'heritage' has become overworked, there is little doubt that some
important historical sites must be preserved and that tourism, by interpreting
and marketing the nostalgic, provides a source of much-needed finance to
preserve key sites. In a similar vein, Gareth Shaw's (1992) study of the
Ironbridge Gorge Museum shows that economic and environmental benefits
can be obtained from heritage tourism, even though it may be at the expense
of commodifying the past. Adrian Mellor (1991), in his case study of the
renovated Albert Dock in Liverpool, claims that many of the attempts to
understand the heritage industry have invoked the wrong explanatory
framework and as a result, a variety of institutions has been conflated into
a single category.

Most important of all, the historian Raphael Samuel, the founding figure
in the History Workshop movement, makes a remarkable defence of heritage
in his book, *Theatres of Memory* (1994). Samuel takes issue with the heritage
baiters and suggests that envy may play some part in their hostility. He points
out that in contrast to the historian's captive audiences in the lecture hall,
which can sometimes be counted on the fingers of one hand, heritage enjoys
a large following from a historically-minded public who care passionately
about it. Samuel also reminds us that the transformation of heritage from
an enthusiasm to an industry was not due to the endeavours of country
house owners or the National Trust, as suggested by Hewison and Wright,
but rather to the efforts of local authorities (many of them Labour), museum
curators and enviornmentalist campaigns. He advises that instead of joining
in the chorus of complaint against heritage, historians should speculate on
the sources of its energies and strength.

So, are the heritage baiters right? Has the heritage industry compromised history? Or is heritage a good thing? Heritage, however, does not break down into the simple politics of Left or Right. In this article I intend to bring some critical perspectives on the portrayal of history at one of the most celebrated examples of the recent spread of heritage centres, namely Beamish, the North of England Open Air Museum in County Durham. In examining its representations of the past, I am not measuring Beamish against an 'ideal' museum, but evaluating the cultural and p olitical effects generated by its particular kind of heritage interpretation from within the context of the current heritage industry debate.

Beamish Open Air Museum

Every year, half a million people visit the Open Air Museum at Beamish, now the largest tourist attraction in Northumbria. Beamish is an industrial heritage museum set in 300 acres of pleasant, rolling countryside within the grounds of Beamish Hall, the home of a former coalmine owner. Although the buildings and artefacts in the museum are real, most of the settlement is not. Apart from a drift mine, Home Farm and Pockerley Manor which were already in existence, it is an artificial place, made up of an assembly of buildings and artefacts which have been brought in from all over the north east region and rebuilt with, as far as possible, the original materials. By gathering together everything that reflects industrial, urban and rural ways of life in the North East in two historical areas, one showing life in the early nineteenth century and the other in the period shortly before the First World War, Beamish aims to be an embodiment of the region's social and industrial history.

Now let's take a closer look at the Beamish site. The museum consists of a series of linked sites, each of which are complete 'areas of operation'. One of the main sites is the Town, officially opened in 1985, which has been furnished as a North-Eastern street at around the 1913 period. The location is made up of a terrace of middle-class houses brought from Gateshead; a reconstructed co-operative store, brought to the site from the nearby town of Annfield Plain; the Dainty Dinah Tea Room; a garage; a reconstructed Victorian bandstand and a municipal park. The terrace houses a solicitor's office, a music teacher's house, a dentist's surgery and a family home. There is also a print shop and stationers; a sweet shop; a Victorian pub, originally from Bishop Auckland; and lastly a brewery yard and stables. The stables house the dray horses of Newcastle Breweries, which operates the pub as a going concern.

Next to the Town is a railway station from Rowley, near Consett, and adjoining it a complete railway yard has been constructed, together with a signal box and goods shed. A Gateshead-built locomotive of 1889 and other locomotives are on display and occasionally in steam.

Another cluster of buildings is in the colliery area of the site, which recreates a typical pit in the early 1900s. The colliery yard contains the drift mine, a reconstructed pit heap, a colliery winding engine and a winding engine house. The drift mine, now partially re-opened for visitors, was worked from the 1850s to 1958. Nearby is a row of pit cottages and their gardens, which were brought to the museum from Hetton-le-Hole near Sunderland. These cottages used to form part of a row of twenty-seven houses built by Hetton Coal Company in the 1860s and were lived in by pitmen's families until 1976. Their interiors are shown as they would have appeared just before the First World War. Next to the pit cottages are a nineteenth century Wesleyan Chapel from the village of Beamish and a school dismantled from East Stanley.

The history of farming in the north east of England is also portrayed at the formerly derelict Home Farm. Now fully restored to an approximation of its mid-nineteenth century operating conditions, it houses Durham Short-horn cattle, Saddleback pigs, ducks, geese and hens. In the dairy, traditional semi-hard cheeses of the northern dales are made and in other farm build-ings, a large collection of agricultural implements and machinery is on display.

The latest acquisition is the recently-opened and renovated Pockerley Manor, set in the 1820s at the start of the Industrial Revolution. Pockerley Farm is currently being developed as part of the Beamish farm operation. Although the present director, Peter Lewis, admits that the development of two historical areas will "make life a little more difficult for ourselves" (Lewis, nd), he believes these are important dates as they mark the beginning of the region's traditional industries and the point at which they started to decline.

The idea of using an 'open air' museum format was conceived by Beam-ish's founding director, Frank Atkinson, who wanted to encourage both passing visitors and residents of the north east to "look with a fresh eye" at the region's heritage (Atkinson, 1987). He was frustrated with the approach of traditional museums because he considered their techniques to be un-imaginative and restrictiveas they usually only displayed narrow inventories of great men and their deeds. Instead, Atkinson wanted to set up a new kind of museum which would combine elements of the European folk-museum tradition with an emphasis on urban and industrial life. Above all, he wanted to create a "living museum" that would illustrate the history of the ordinary people of the north of England and envisaged the collections at Beamish to be essentially "of the people, by the people and for the people".

The beginnings of Beamish go back to 1958, when Atkinson was appointed Director of the Bowes Museum at Barnard Castle in County Durham. Atkinson was concerned that a traditional way of life was being rapidly destroyed by far-reaching changes taking place in Britain's economic and social life. He became convinced of the urgent need to build up collections of industrial materials before they disappeared forever in the midst of the dramatic process of de-industrialisation which affected the North East region particularly deeply.

Twelve years were to elapse before Atkinson's conception was to become a reality. Finally, in 1970 the social history and industrial collections were moved from the Bowes Museum to Beamish and Atkinson took up his duties as Director.

The impact of Beamish Open Air Museum

From its inception Beamish has always enjoyed a high public profile. Atkinson's adoption of a controversial, wide ranging policy of collecting anything and everything he came across, attracted the widespread attention and support of newspapers, magazines and television. Over the years the museum has won several major awards, including the British Museum of the Year in 1986, the Heritage Section of the UK Tourism Marketing Awards for the Town Street in the same year, and the European Museum of the Year award in 1987. In addition, the museum was recognised in Kenneth Hudson's (1987) review of the worldwide museum scene, *Museums of Influence*, as being one of thirty-seven museums which had "broken new ground in such an original or striking way that other museums have felt disposed or compelled to follow their example". More recently, Beamish has been awarded designated status for the preeminence of its collections — a 'gold star' that will make it more attractive to funding organisations.

Yet, in spite of all these accolades the museum has also attracted a fair amount of criticism from museum professionals, academics and local residents alike. Of particular concern has been the way in which the museum has interpreted the area's regional history. Beamish, it might be argued, has been caught fast in the potent spell of a sentimental nostalgia for a just-vanished age. With many of the buildings and objects on display still extant, and the hard sell of publicity slogans such as "acres of nostalgia", the whole place seems to be geared for nostalgia and selective memory. The realities of time appear to be denied; death and decay do not exist. "Time to return!" beckons one of its publicity pamphlets. "Turn of the century (just off the A1)", "travelling back to the turn of the century is easy", it informs the visitor. Its guide books and pamphlets are replete with pictures of men, women and children — and there is nothing inappropriate about that as Beamish is, after all, a museum about ordinary people. What is disquieting is the way in which photographs of the costumed interpreters have been placed next to old photographs of bar tenders, miners' families and church congregations, as if to suggest that the people of the pre-First World War era and the people of today are one and the same. As Sorensen observes, "we have but to don a mobcap or a nylon wig and the centuries roll away" (Sorensen, 1989: p. 65).

Peter Lewis, the present director, has taken exception to "unproductive mockery" of the "heritage industry jibes" directed at the museum, asserting that although nostalgia "implies a wish to look back" it does so "with a sense of pain" (Lewis, 1991). Yet the idyllic surroundings of Beamish show nothing of the real squalour which existed in the regions within close proximity to the coalfields. One of the most marked features of the restored structures is the complete absence of any disrepair. The Sun Inn, removed from Bishop Auckland and re-erected at Beamish in 1985, was remembered by a former local resident as "a shabby pub at the top of the hill". It was hardly recognisable as being the same place when he visited the museum a few years later.

The row of pit cottages in the colliery area of the site are nestled in a leafy, rural haven and look rustic and pristine. No coal dust dirties the windows, no roof tiles have slipped, there is no evidence of chipped or peeling paint, no mud dirties the back yard, no smell emanates from the privvies. The houses are probably in a better condition now than they were at any time since they were initially constructed. Their present day physical appearance and surroundings are in stark contrast to a description written in 1942 of the same cottages when they were in their original location at Hetton-le-hole:

> ... the discomfort and inconvenience of the dwellings ... a lack of adequate water supply, an outside tap shared between several house-holders, communal ash bins close to the cottage doors, bad roads with a dreary outlook — for pit heaps dotted here and there, with their monotonous regularity of outline and colour, cannot be said to have other than a depressing effect on the landscape. (Redmayne, 1942, quoted in Church, 1986: p. 620)

Although the interior furnishings of the cottages reflect the taste for contemporary creature comforts possessed by miners and their wives, no mention is made of the limited choice of housing opportunities available to them nor how they had to endure low standards of sanitary and social facilities.

With female costumed interpreters dressed in clean ironed clothes, baking bread next to the roaring fire of the spotless kitchen range, Beamish gives the impression that the lot of colliery women was one of comfort and domestic harmony. Tastefully overlooked is the drudgery and slavery experienced by most pitmen's wives, where the preparation of meals and the back-breaking labour of the washing and mending of pit clothes were almost continuous processes. At Beamish, the idyllic family is the norm. But there were widows, widowers, old people, illegitimate children, the chronically-ill, the married and the unmarried, crowded into many of these cottages. There was petty crime too, which, particularly in coalmining districts, was rife. Around the collieries the "picking" of coal from pit heads and slag heaps was so deeply ingrained that it formed part of the daily domestic routine for many children who were expected to salvage coal both before and after school. The museum's static and sanitised tableaux cannot represent the experience of people of the time, and their weariness, insecurity and ill-health.

The reconstructed colliery, with its fresh paint and clean bricks, neat and tidy surrounds, also presents the same peaceful, sanitised and harmonious vista. But mining conditions were "dirty, filthy and rotten", which is not the impression given when visitors see the clean, well-fed, costumed interpreters, dressed in "pit hoggers" and colourful neckerchiefs. Many pitheads, including the one which used to be in the nearby town of Stanley, were right in the town centre, belching out smoke and steam, not discretely nestled on the side of hill. Visitors to the site who have worked in mines will no doubt remember the less appealing aspects of industrial life — the danger, unemployment, illness, and the fact that their village or town probably was not situated in idyllic countryside. But what about the effect this type of museum might have on those people who have never lived near a mine or are too young to remember? What images of the industrialised past are they taking home with them?

Where other museums have labels and glass, Beamish has costumed interpreters who give a "special and personal insight" into the region's history. In an article for *Friends of Beamish Newsletter*, Lewis wholeheartedly supports the use of first-person interpretation, and comments that most curators rely too heavily on labels, or "books on walls":

> They (the curators) presume that all museum visitors are scholarly literate. Museum labels can be very intricate. One London museum actually displays an enlarged label at its entrance in order to instruct visitors how to read labels — so much for communication. (1985: p. 14)

Lewis believes that the true purpose of museum interpretation is to provoke thought and stimulate discussion, which he considers the more conventional museums fail to do:

> The German museum director who complained that we over-influence our visitors, "infecting them with fever", received no apologies from me. Better a fever I insisted than the "athletes foot" school of museum interpretation, the kind that is mildly interesting but which doesn't stimulate you to do anything about it. (Lewis, 1995: p. 20)

Although any interpretation has to be selective and thus incomplete, the museum's promotion of a personal, 'empathetic' approach has drawn a few brickbats. Hewison (1991: p. 15) has suggested that the use of 'empathetic' representation paints a picture of the past as though it was the present, "only dressed in funny clothes"; museums should be "neutral, mere facilities for the presentation of individual acts of creation". Walsh (1992: p. 104) goes as far as arguing that this "is one of the most dangerous and anti-critical modes of representation available". He maintains that this approach exploits pasts purely for their surfaces and allows heritage marketeers to avoid the more radical and investigative debates that have taken place in recent years. If used at all, it should be employed as one technique among many.

Apart from the dangers of presenting a bland and sanitised image of the past, there is the very real hazard of relying solely on people to convey accurate information about exhibits. Lewis is aware of the hazards of empathetic interpretation but believes that the risks are worth taking:

> There is ... a great temptation to embroider facts, to tell the visitor what they expect to hear, extravagant stories of want and deprivation. We need to eavesdrop on interpretation and correct the over-elabor-

ate. Stottie cakes were not invented, as once heard, by the wife of a Methodist Minister in the early 1920s. Their origins are far older and far more interesting. Theatre directors always return to see plays in performance, to provide notes for the actors. The longer the run, the greater chance of errors. (Lewis, 1995: pp. 18-19)

But eavesdropping on hapless interpreters aside, errors and misinformation are an unfortunate reality. Opportunities abound on all the sites for costumed interpreters to tell visitors what they like. For instance, the guide book states that the shops in the Co-op are stocked with goods available in a typical store of 1913, and that the drapery department sells "everything from pit hoggers ... to liberty bodices and corsets" (Beamish Museum, n.d.). Being once a proud owner of a liberty bodice myself, I asked where they were kept, but the interpreter replied that there were none on display as they were not made until the early 1920s. This may be a small point, but such inaccuracies or conflicting pieces of information are puzzling.

Despite the claims made by Lewis that the use of personal interpretation is thought-provoking and the best way to "get the message across", my experience is that the information conveyed is either partial at best, or non-existent at worst. The visitor is encouraged to make use of the interpreters, yet due to the pressure of visitor numbers, at times it is impossible even to get near one. Many people just have a glance at the reconstructed rooms and then walk away, none the wiser about anything.

Even greater interpretive challenges are being confronted at the newly-opened Pockerley Manor area of the site, where the time slot is set to the early 1820s. As Lewis frankly acknowledges, "the further back you go in history the more difficult it is to empathise with those who lived then" (Lewis, 1995: p. 20). At this part of the site, the costumed interpreters are not stationed behind counter tops but are moving around among the visitors. The day I visited Pockerley the weather was hot, yet in the pursuit of authenticity, costumed interpreters were stationed in front of blazing fires which were roaring away in two areas of the manor. Their role is different at Pockerley. Here they perform as actors, assuming specific roles and identities. Yet, how does anyone know today how the original inhabitants of the place actually felt and behaved? What dialect did they speak? With the main thrust of interpretation appearing to focus on baking techniques, the impression created is one of congenial contentment. Were 'the people' always so cheerful, industrious and good natured?

Officially, Beamish claims that it exists to tell history from the bottom upwards. Yet, although the extension of the social range promoted by the museum is to be welcomed, its ideological function remains curiously the same as the traditional museums, but evoked in a different and less obvious manner. According to Bennett, the past has again been politically weighted in favour of ruling class culture but, by working on the grounds of invoking popular memory, Beamish has created a familiar rather than intimidatory historical narrative (Bennett, 1988: p. 73). The special insight into the past which is offered as part of 'the Beamish experience' appears to focus mainly on the traditions of quilting, cheese-making and bread-making. The traditions of politics, labour and trade-unions are conspicuously absent. Little is said of industrial relations in the mining industry, the 'them and us' mentality which existed between management and colliery workers. There are no accounts of the pitched battles fought between protestants and catholics; no references are made to strikes, lockouts, unemployment or evictions, while mining disasters are scarcely mentioned. As a local historian remarked, "the important parts of history have been kept in closed cupboards" (Little, 1995).

A former resident of the nearby village of Tantobie stated that Beamish was "too commercialised" and did not reflect the area's local history. He remarked that the very location of Beamish in a pocket of affluence had deterred many locals from visiting. Their children might have seen Beamish through school visits, but many parents did not bother to go. The recon-struction of a town street which contains middle-class houses originally built for fairly well-to-do tradesmen and professional people, may fool visitors into believing that it is representative of a typical north-eastern town, but the local people know better:

> Garages were few and far between then, and you wouldn't find a dentist in the main street — a visit to the dentist was a fight down at the pub. Beamish is representative of a middle class idea of what life used to be like. It's designed to be seen by the affluent about the poor. It's a specific viewpoint of what someone wants it to be like. They lifted whole buildings from our community, then they have nothing to do with us. (Gibson, 1995)

Atkinson's initial vision saw Beamish as belonging to the region's people, and in the early years admission prices remained low to ensure that they had easy access. Now however, with the reduction in financial support from the public sector, Beamish receives two-thirds of its revenue budget from visitor income and admission charges have risen significantly. According to a local authority employee in Stanley, the local people stay way from the museum because they can't afford the admission charges. At £7.99 for adults and £4.99 for senior citizens and children in the high season (July–September 1997), most locals "resent having to pay so much for what they see as very little". In addition, Beamish is seen by the locals as very much a separate entity:

> People come to Beamish — Beamish doesn't come to the people. Beamish doesn't play any role in the community. It has no link with the district. It is run more like a business than a community facility. (Anon, 1995)

A further source of local disappointment has been generated by Atkinson's adoption of a controversial and unselective collecting policy. Atkinson's plea to the locals, "you offer it to us and we'll collect it!", attracted over a million donations of all shapes and sizes, from hats and hearses to shops and spectacles. Atkinson believed that it was better to collect and hold material, even if not in ideal museum conditions, than it to be lost forever. Such an open-ended policy, however, inevitably led to problems of physical capacity and an alternative store, a disused bakery known as "Kelly's", was acquired in 1971 to house the vast collection of artefacts. To the dismay of many of those people who had been encouraged by Atkinson to donate their possessions, thousands of items have remained locked up in Kelly's Bakery, never to be seen again.

But it is not only the locals who have felt alienated by Beamish. The Durham National Union of Miners (NUM) are presently locked in a legal battle in an attempt to retrieve forty Miners' Lodge banners which were loaned to Beamish in 1984 by the Durham Miners' Association. A year after the banners were lent to Beamish, the NUM Committee at Redhills discovered the existence of a legal document which had apparently been signed "behind the backs of the Committee", giving Beamish entire custody of the banners for a period of 99 years. The collection of historic banners was originally loaned to Beamish on the understanding that they would be restored, paraded and hung so that they could be seen by the people of the region. None of these conditions have been honoured. According to an NUM official, the banners can be found unrestored, wrapped up in clingfilm and kept on top of a cupboard.

Conclusions

Frank Atkinson's determination to save and record local customs and traditions during a time of rapid change in the North East has been a remarkable achievement. Through his policy of unselective collecting, an outstanding range of social history material has been assembled which is unsurpassed in Britain, in terms of both its scope and its size. In addition, there is no doubt that Beamish offers an entertaining day out for all the family, with plenty to see, plenty to do, plenty to enjoy. There are tram rides, ice cream and cakes to eat in the Dainty Dinah Tea Room, wonderful sweets and chocolates for sale in the Jubilee Confectionery Shop, a pint to drink in the Sun Inn and music to listen to at the bandstand. In an area of relatively high unemployment, the museum has generated jobs for the local region. It has also brought many thousands of visitors to a part of Britain which is relatively under-represented in terms of tourism activity.

At the same time, however, Beamish's problems are real. The museum's alienation of the local people, together with its misrepresentation of the past, are not just issues of interest to pedantic historians. They have direct political implications for the people of the North East. Given the North East's history of depression and unemployment, a sense of regional identity takes on a particular importance. An air-brushed, nostalgic presentation of a past without mention of politics is not seen by the locals as a celebration of their social history. Ironically, in the 1995 Guide Book Lewis writes that he believes "there has never been a greater need for real history". Yet curiously, on the cover of one of its latest publicity pamphlets are illustrated caricatures of

Rhett Butler and Scarlett O'Hara, locked in an embrace. The pamphlet announces: *"Beamish. The Epic Story of the North East and its People. Share the hopes, the fears. The pain, the pleasure"*. Read the book. See the film. Visit the theme park.

Of the former iron and steel works at Consett, there is no mention at all. With its site now landscaped and grassed over, all evidence of Consett's industrial past has been erased, leaving only "700 acres of emptiness" (Moore, 1992). The entrepreneurial initiatives and achievements of the Consett Iron Company, one of the largest coal owners in the north of England and arguably the biggest enterprise in the local area to fall under the hammer of industrial and economic progress, are excluded from the museum's portrayal of the industrial history of the region.

Beamish is not alone in the promotion of a rose-tinted and idealised past. Along with other heritage museums it has generated ways of not seeing by confining history to the provision of entertainment and nostalgia. As Wallace (1986) has argued, people are clearly interested in the past, but heritage museums do little to foster a critical awareness of history. If the present director really intends the museum to be thought-provoking, then the story of the North East should be told in all its dimensions. By covering up exploitation, class struggle, sexism and the existence of broad-based oppositional traditions, the museum has blunted the sharp edges of reality. A politically uncensored representation of the uncomfortable events of the past would give visitors to Beamish a fuller and more informed appreciation of the region's distinctive cultural history.

Note

An earlier version of this article was published in *Northern Review*, Vol. 5, Summer, 1997.

References

Anon. (1995) Confidential interview, 24th July, 1995.

Atkinson F. (1987) 'The Beamish Open Air Museum', *Museum*, Vol. 155: pp. 132-138.

Beamish Museum (nd) *Beamish: The North of England Open Air Museum. A brief guide*. Beamish: Beamish Museum.

Bennett, T. (1988) 'Museums and "the people"', in Lumley R. (ed) *The museum time machine*. London: Routledge, pp. 63-85.

Church, R. (1986) *The history of the British coal industry, Vol. 3, Victorian Pre-eminence*. Oxford: Clarendon Press.

Cossons, N. (1989) 'Plural funding and the heritage', in Uzzell, D. (ed) *Heritage interpretation* Vol. 2. London: Belhaven Press, pp. 16-22.

Department of National Heritage (1994) *Preserving the past, shaping the future*. London: Department of National Heritage.

Gathercole, P. and Lowenthal, D. (1994) *The politics of the past*. London: Routledge.

Givson, J. (1995). Personal communication, 3 August, 1995.

Hewison, R. (1987) *The heritage industry. Britain in a climate of decline*. London: Methuen.

—— (1991) quoted in Lewis, P. (1995) 'Getting the message', *Friends of Beamish Newsletter*, No. 99 (Spring): pp. 14-20.

Hudson, K. (1987) *Museums of influence*. Cambridge: Cambridge University Press.

Lewis, P. (nd) 'Past, present and future,' in *Welcome to Beamish*, guidebook.

—— (1991) 'Making or mocking?', *Museums Journal*, July: pp. 33-35.

—— (1995) 'Getting the message', *Friends of Beamish Newsletter*, No. 99 (Spring): pp. 14-20.

Little, D. (1995) Personal communication, 20 July, 1995.

May, V. (1993) 'Heritage tourism: Marketing fashion or sustainability in action?' (editorial), *Tourism Recreation Research*, Vol. xix, No. 2.

Mellor, A. (1991) 'Enterprise and heritage in the dock', in Corner, J. and Harvey, S. (eds) *Enterprise and heritage. Crosscurrents of national culture*. London: Routledge, pp. 93–115.

Moore, T. (1992) *Consett. A town in the making*. Durham: County Durham Books.

Samuel, R. (1994) *Theatres of memory. Vol. 1: Past and present in contemporary culture*. London: Verso.

Shaw, G. (1992) 'Culture and tourism: The economics of nostalgia', *World Futures*, Vol 33: pp. 199-212.

Sorensen, C. (1989) 'Theme parks and time machines', in P. Vergo (ed) *The new museology*. London: Reaktion Books, pp. 60-73.

Wallace, M. (1986) 'Visiting the past: History museums in the United States', in S. P. Benson, S. Brier and R. Rosenweig (eds) *Presenting the past: Essays on history and the public*. Philadelphia: Temple University Press.

Walsh. K. (1992) *The representation of the past, museums and heritage in the post-modern world*. London: Routledge.

Wright P. (1985) *On living in an old country. The national past in contemporary Britain*. London: Verso.

Index